# ARCHITECTURAL HISTORY RETOLD

How much do you know about Greek architecture? Roman? Gothic? Renaissance? Modernist? Perhaps more important, do you know how these are connected or how one style evolved to become another? Or what happened historically during each of these periods?

*Architectural History Retold* is your road map for your journey through architectural history. Offering a fresh take on what the author calls the 'Great Enlightenment project', it traces the grand narrative of Western architecture in one concise, accessible volume. Starting in Ancient Greece and leading up to the present day, Paul Davies's narrative, written in an unconventional, engaging style, brings the past back to life, helping you to think beyond separate components and styles to recognise 'the bigger picture'.

The author is an academic and journalist with three decades of experience in introducing students to architectural history. The book is based on his successful entry-level course, which has used the same unstuffy approach to break down barriers to understanding and engagement and inspire generations of students.

**Paul Davies** was born on Mersea Island in 1961 and studied at Bristol University and the Polytechnic of Central London. He has taught across Britain's schools of architecture, including the Architectural Association, for more than twenty-five years. A regular contributor to the *Architectural Review*, he is widely published and is a senior lecturer teaching history and theory of architecture at London South Bank University.

"We're going to buy everybody in the office a copy!"
—Clive Sall, *Clive Sall Architecture, London, UK*

"Paul Davies' erudite and (sometimes) misanthropic insights into architectural culture have entertained me for 25 years. His thinking was a key influence on my own as it has been for countless students who have enjoyed his unique take on the subject. His scholarship, critical insight, and the ability to place architectural history into a relevant cultural context are all beautifully captured here. Davies shows why architectural history matters. It is a brilliant introduction to the subject."
—Sean Griffiths, *Founding Director of FAT and Professor of Architecture, University of Westminster, London, UK*

# ARCHITECTURAL HISTORY RETOLD

*Paul Davies*

*Illustrated by Emily Forgot*

LONDON AND NEW YORK

First published 2016
by Routledge
2 Park Square, Milton Park, Abingdon, Oxon OX14 4RN

and by Routledge
711 Third Avenue, New York, NY 10017

*Routledge is an imprint of the Taylor & Francis Group, an informa business*

© 2016 Paul Davies

The right of Paul Davies to be identified as author of this work has been asserted by him in accordance with sections 77 and 78 of the Copyright, Designs and Patents Act 1988.

All rights reserved. No part of this book may be reprinted or reproduced or utilised in any form or by any electronic, mechanical, or other means, now known or hereafter invented, including photocopying and recording, or in any information storage or retrieval system, without permission in writing from the publishers.

*Trademark notice*: Product or corporate names may be trademarks or registered trademarks, and are used only for identification and explanation without intent to infringe.

*British Library Cataloguing in Publication Data*
A catalogue record for this book is available from the British Library

*Library of Congress Cataloging-in-Publication Data*
Davies, Paul, 1961–
  Architectural history retold / Paul Davies.
    pages cm
  Includes bibliographical references and index.
  1. Architecture—History.  2. Architecture and society—History.  I. Title.
    NA200.D36 2015
    720.9—dc23
    2015011529

ISBN: 978-1-138-79946-2 (hbk)
ISBN: 978-1-138-79948-6 (pbk)
ISBN: 978-1-315-75595-3 (ebk)


Typeset in Bembo
by Apex CoVantage, LLC

For Julie

# CONTENTS

*Acknowledgements* ix
*Prologue* xi

1 Introduction 1

2 Ancient Greece 9

3 Ancient Rome 25

4 The Gothic 39

5 The Renaissance 55

6 The Enlightenment 71

7 The Industrial Revolution 87

8 European Modernism 103

9 American Modernism 121

**viii** Contents

| | | |
|---|---|---|
| 10 | Postmodernism | 139 |
| 11 | The future | 155 |

| | |
|---|---|
| *Further reading* | 167 |
| *Index* | 171 |

# ACKNOWLEDGEMENTS

First, my thanks to all those immediately involved in the production of this book: Emily Forgot, Julie Cook, Julia Dawson, Tom Wilkinson, Scott Fitzpatrick, Grace Harrison, Fran Ford, Will Hunter, Matthew Barac, Kit Allsopp, Jennifer Schmidt and Felicity Good.

Second, thanks to all those mentors past and present: Catherine Slessor, David Dunster, Jeremy Melvin, Paul Finch, Lee Mallet, Mark Cousins, Belinda Flaherty, Mark Rappolt, Ed Winters, Jonathan Hill, Jon Goodbun, Karin Jaschke, Tim Pyne, Simon Smith and Michael Brooke, Donald Wilson, Torsten Schmiedeknecht, Steven Spier, Cliff Nicholls, Richard Patterson, Shumon Basar, Rowan Moore, Joe Gardiner, Paula Bendall, David Rickard, Grant Gibson, Gareth Gardner, Joe Kerr, Paul Shepheard, Sherry Bates, Graham Addicott, Mary Jane Rooney, Lilly Kudic, Jessica Kelly, Michael Robbins, Katherine Shonfield, Paul Grover, Alex Zembelli, Kevin Rhowbotham, David Greene, Mark Wells, Anne Boddington, Andrew Dawes, Steve Bowkett, Clive Sall, Andrew Lane, Jon Buck, Sean Griffiths, Jo Hagan and Matt White. To those who have passed away, I raise a glass, preferably in the New National Gallery Berlin or at Cleopatra's Barge Caesars Palace, wherever the most appropriate. Then there's mum and dad, who rather provided the grounds for this adventure in the first place, and my brother, Rob, who first played me *Led Zeppelin II*, and my aunty Bid and my uncle Jean, late of Houston. Finally, to the cleaning and security staff at LSBU, who consistently make that early start for a nine o'clock lecture just that little bit more bearable.

# PROLOGUE

If we were to read a general architectural history written a half-century ago, say Pevsner's *Outline of European Architecture*, it would feel a lot different from this one. There would be more of it; it would be denser, more technical and harder to read. Even during this research I hesitated to pick Pevsner up from the dusty bookshelves of a secondhand bookshop in Oundle, the sort of place – these days – you'd expect to find it.

So I do not expect students of our age to dip happily into such historical volumes, despite their authority. In our mix-and-match, jumbled-up age, our technology makes us butterflies. Students jump from this to that. Authors jump from this to that, too. As a consequence, ambitious academics strive to complete world histories across vast digital platforms to keep up. Instead, I like to think of this contribution as a kind of horrible history with attitude or as a classic story abbreviated, and it is intended that this book might be read alongside those digital sources so that various images and further investigation might take place while reading it.

There is much to be said for the old grand narrative; it reminds us where we've come from and what we have achieved. To my reasoning, Western architectural history needed to be retold with more cultural infrastructure and less comparative detail, in broad sweeps rather than intricate distinctions. Retold since of course all the material here has come from somewhere and retold because it is necessary to remind ourselves that we have a history not so much to be plundered as secured back in the mind's eye as progress. This is a term that has almost disappeared

**xii** Prologue

from our lexicon but is nevertheless something that got people interested in the built environment out of bed every morning with a mind for something other than estate agency; which of course, in my more despairing moments, is precisely what I fear architecture might become – that or some inadvertently pretentious parlour game.

Furthermore, I tell it as a human story – mine as much as everybody else's – for human is what we are and because that's what makes history alive and neither some dull abstraction nor an idiotic fairy story. Meanwhile, knowing Mies van der Rohe kept a stash of Edvard Munch prints under his bed tells us a great deal. The personal story is always illuminating if you can get to it, and despite the unfortunately rarefied atmosphere of the great architectural bookshops, architects are not supreme beings, even if some aspects of our academic industry demand we kiss the hem and figure out their parallel universe over thousands of pages of difficult words.

The book derives from a lecture course given to eager undergraduates when they first arrive at a London university to study architecture in the twenty-first century – a basically chronological story explained in the context of a culture – but it should become clear to anybody that there are many crossovers that belie a straightforward tale and many levels to the notion of culture and architecture. In general I have placed material where I think it fits best and selected the most entertaining examples.

There are always flaws to the construction of history, and I have chosen almost the autobiographical method, opinionated in the sense that presently I may be rather down on Ruskin and up on Morris but with the lurking feeling the situation might possibly reverse with time. The working title of this volume was *Architecture: The Unauthorised Biography* for quite a long time, until I got fed up with the question as to what might be unauthorised about it or, for that matter, biographical; hence *Architectural History Retold* is better.

The list of what's left out is scary but serves at least to educate us as to what others include by comparison. In no particular order, I remove everything I haven't yet got much of a clue about but some that I have: Byzantium, Ottoman and Moorish architecture, large swathes of the Rococo, Russian Constructivism, postwar British architecture, Deconstruction, German Expressionism, Italian Futurism and Nordic Classicism, just for starters. I hardly mention four of the five architects James Stirling thought were the *only* great architects Britain had ever produced: Mackintosh, Vanbrugh, Archer, Hawksmoor and Jones. Only one of these makes the fulcrum of my discussion. I even leave out John Soane, whom Stirling left on the bench as a substitute. There is certainly no mention of the

Catalan monk Antonio Gaudi. This bizarre reasoning I hope will become clear as the reader progresses.

To make it relevant (a dangerous word), I do one thing that Pevsner would never have done: I say the past never goes away, it just mutates. The historical sense is always here even if you don't self-consciously cultivate it. Our media continually re-represent the past to us, and students need mechanisms to decode what they absorb, to gain a critical perspective, to understand something approximating a road map. This book is my attempt to provide such a thing.

I'm sorry there are not more women in our pantheon of flawed genius, but that will change. Denise Scott Brown was lovingly pictured with Robert Venturi in a volume commemorating the National Gallery Extension in 1991, but the caption still read 'Robert Venturi and His Design'. It was pathetic. But I haven't gone out of my way to be revisionist, either.

Neither do I dwell on particular race or colonial issues, these being subsumed in to the larger project. When I was studying in the mid-eighties, it was still the ambition of one of my best friends to become the first black partner in a major architectural practice in the UK. At least, thankfully, that's exactly what he became.

And the architecture I'm talking about represents a tiny percentage of the work done by architects. This may not have been true of Michelangelo, but these days, however elevated in reputation, architects work in teams, so when I discuss an architect as if it is one person, I do it only for convenience. Looking at some Mies van der Rohe blueprints, a flag set used on site in the construction of the Fellows Building, IIT, Chicago, in 1956 – fragile, light-sensitive dyelines that I unroll only once in a blue moon – I think not just of Mies but also of the person who drew them. I'm transported into this unknown person's world, what he was looking forward to that week, his Friday night and what he was dreading – perhaps Mies himself looking over his shoulder that afternoon.

I have the advantage of not being a specialist, I can't hide myself away in the details of eighteenth-century doilies. Architects are traditionally generalists and know a little about a lot of things. So don't ask an architect to lay a brick wall, but expect him to know a little about the business of doing it. This is what makes teaching and writing about architecture so interesting. Hence a huge number of popular and academic sources form the understanding in this book, and I include the briefest of bibliographies, rather hoping readers will look up particular references as they go.

Being such a generalist is not easy, but we fight for it. Lecturing in a university school of architecture, I have seen deans, schools, faculties and xiv Prologue

chancellors come and go: planning, civil engineering, urban policy, design, even special effects have all come and gone as our faculty partners over the past twenty years.

For myself, I suppose I'm known for the years I enjoyed lecturing on the subject of Las Vegas. Las Vegas showed me how things really were, how late-capitalist processes really worked, and my application to the understanding of the Las Vegas phenomenon was almost a moral obligation as well as a lot of fun. Of course, as the times changed – with 9/11 especially, when I gazed at 'Alison' dancing to 'Living on the Edge' in a stars-and-stripes bikini in the White Horse, at around 1 p.m. the day after – I realised the writing was on the wall and another task was to hand. This book is the consequence.

So here's my attempt to explain our history, in not so many words, to interested listeners, in the hope that more people might get our subject than presently do.

On the beach. Still the mud lark on Mersea Island, where I was born.
*Credit*: Julie Cook

# 1

# INTRODUCTION

There once was a town in eastern Czechoslovakia called Poruba. I've never been there; I read about it in a book one afternoon. I don't even know how big the town is, but I can be confident it exists because it's on Wikipedia, except now it's in the Czech Republic. Some of the images on Wikipedia even correspond to those in the well-illustrated, good, but rather dry book. It's dry because it's an academic book, probably developed from a PhD dissertation. The book is titled *Manufacturing a Socialist Modernity: Housing in Czechoslovakia 1945–60*. See what I mean?

I have to wade through books like this, because sometimes bells will ring in my head and, well, you know you've got something interesting; you read something quite dull, but you are busy reinterpreting it. This is what I assume lecturers try to do all the time, especially if the lecturer's slot is nine on a Friday morning and the subject is history; that's how to get students out of bed. The primary means to do this is by filling out the context a little. It's all very well knowing all there is to know on Czech housing 1945–60, but what happens if you compare it with what happened in St Albans at the same time or, for that matter, what appeared on yesterday's news?

One student chirped up that these days Poruba is better known for its party scene. *Quelle surprise*! I can picture it already: it was originally built in an industrial landscape for industrial purposes; they proudly checked to be sure that there weren't any coal seams beneath it before they built it, since it was at the coal seam that most of the inhabitants worked. Being part of the USSR meant championing of the worker, so the Minister for Heavy Industry asked: 'Don't you want the miners, who spend all day

**2** Introduction

digging out coal without a ray of sunshine, to have at least enough sunlight in the hours that they have for a little bit of rest?'

The town was built in the 1950s in the Social Realist style: monumental, Neoclassical and grand. The West has dubbed it 'wedding cake', a term at once both accurate and snide. There are grand layouts of boulevards with pilasters and capitals and reliefs in the stucco and statues of workers; there is even the rather hopeful idea that, in the architectural transition from home, courtyard, street, boulevard to eventual countryside, the greatness of the socialist community is made manifest in continuity, from field to table. The entrance to Poruba is even marked by an inhabited triumphal arch, worthy of the precedents of Ancient Rome, or at least eighteenth-century St Petersburg.

But this is not the image we have of housing in Czechoslovakia 1945–65. The image we have is of drab prefabricated identical blocks of housing with little care for the sophistication of ideas such as an architectural language symbolising a greater socialist community.

So the question is about how we got from the grand landscape of the former to the drab landscape of the latter, and the answer is numbers. As the grand socialist enterprise matured, with its centralised power structure and superstructural bureaucracy and dedication to plans and targets, it conspired to turn everything into numbers, and, within it, architecture became a totally technically orientated task. Not a whiff of sentimental grandeur could be tolerated. Numbers of units were more important than what the units were, and there you have one big lesson for not only architecture but a whole political system. By the end there were no architects in the architectural offices; there were just technicians. Architects were superfluous.

But, of course, meanwhile, what was happening in St Albans or Crawley or Basildon? Well, you can guess this. Local councils were building lots of individual little houses with gardens that looked pretty much the same, with evocations of both roses around the cottage door and every man's home as his castle.

I've just been listening to *Any Questions*. I did it by accident, but it certainly struck me that the contemporary debate in the UK, such as it is, is also being driven by numbers. There are quests for so many 'low-cost' homes. Will reform of the planning system save the economy? That is, can we build on that meadow or another for the good of all? There's a lot of squabbling – that's why we set up the planning system in 1947 in the first place – because we couldn't quite bring ourselves to nationalise land itself but we could nationalise the right to develop it. It was a start. Now it's gone back to numbers – or, in our case, money – where so-called

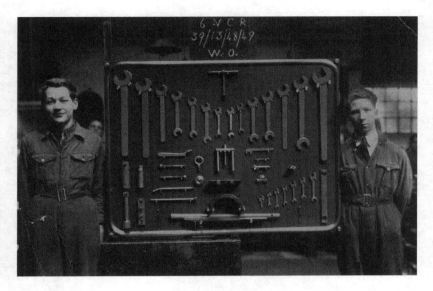

PHOTOGRAPH 1 My father (right) as apprentice of the month, Ruston & Hornsby, Lincoln. 1940.

affordable homes will be built to lower specifications than those that float at market rate; bringing the disturbing image of the most vulnerable placed in the flimsiest accommodation.

At my university I'm told that my office space, my library of books, is valued at £350 per square foot. I don't think it has crossed the mind of the administration that perhaps the value of the books themselves is well above that figure or well below or perhaps that that figure cannot easily be calculated at all. Of course, the value of individual books can be assessed at any one moment, based on rarity perhaps, but, on a broader scale, how might you compare the value of Plato's *Republic* with that of *Harry Potter and the Order of the Phoenix*? The numbers sometimes don't establish value at all.

You can't theorise growing flowers, but you can theorise creating buildings. You can't have Marxist or post-Marxist tulips (for that matter, you can't have Conservative-thinking tulips either), but you can have Marxist and post-Marxist buildings; they would just need some explaining. However, most of the language used to describe buildings these days (I'm thinking of TV programmes such as *Grand Designs*) is indiscernible in tone of rapture from what might be used in *Gardeners' World*. Certainly flowers are things we consider pretty, and Kevin McCloud continually enjoys space as 'lovely', but really we might enquire deeper: 'Well, just

**4** Introduction

what does he mean?' Such questions have vexed me ever since I began my own architectural education.

There are very few architects who regard architecture as a thing. The modern American architect Louis Kahn was one, and he sent everybody spinning round in circles as to what exactly he meant by it as he was trying to define it. Most of us see it as a result of processes; these are not mysterious but explainable. This is the route I have taken with this history, that in general people do things because the environment (physical/ political/social/personal/technological) facilitates them in doing them. Then comes the magic.

What the story of Poruba illustrates for us is that of cause and effect, and the cause and effect illustrated there is not the mere husbandry of flowers but the whole creation of a world, a sociopolitical construction, a human idea for humans, or series of ideas, in consecutive operation for generations of different humans under variously auspicious circumstances.

Both architecture and cuisine prefigure any culture's destruction. As soon as you've got architecture or cuisine, it could be said you are doomed, and henceforth it's a struggle, a struggle to hold it together. Take the aborigines, living in perfect harmony with their surroundings for thousands of years with never a thought for the stuff, not so much as a shack but, then again, a fairly challenging diet. Or the Inuit, stuck in the most inhospitable of surroundings but daring to take a similar view. It's as if they say 'don't come anywhere near us' while chewing happily on two-year-old whale blubber inside freezing in blocks of ice.

If you want harmony with nature, you do not need architecture, and you probably don't need humans either, for civilisation, such as it is, is the antithesis of nature. If only this were something that architecture students had drilled into them on their first day (Architecture 101: Architecture Is *Not* Nature), it would render much heartache unnecessary later on. There are of course other things that should be taught on those first days: a course in first-order logic for instance and, perhaps, a course on cookery. That would set the students up just fine for the endurance course ahead.

Alas, this is a mere pipe dream. In reality those students will take their first steps on a long, arduous and meandering road through one of the softest subjects in the curriculum via the hardest of possible paths, with many dead ends, U-turns and false starts. By soft I mean that architecture is culturally defined but scientifically and economically built, so it is inevitably both a compromise and a battle of wills at the same time. They will learn a very little about a lot of things and eventually, after many years and much out of pocket and slightly out of mind, become a professional Jack of no trades, but apparently the sexiest one, albeit the worst paid. Logic might decree you couldn't have both at the same time.

Just as we might put food in a restaurant, we build architecture in to a tradition. T. S. Eliot's essay 'The Artist and Individual Talent' (1917) makes considerable play on the fact that the term 'traditional' is usually derogatory but maintains that an artist presenting mere novelty is bereft of the necessary historical sense to offer something truly valuable. It is true we live in a world of novelty all around us, but what of our historical sense? Our technology promotes a certain amnesia as we flutter from this to that, but what of our abiding ambitions, the enduring pursuits in the name of humanity itself?

So this is a strange history book to start from such a premise, that of the blind leading the blind through what I shall purloin rather grandly as 'The Great Enlightenment Project': two and a half thousand years or more of catastrophe, terror and general calamity in the honourable, in the entirely human pursuit of a better world. It comes of a desire to reaffirm that project, and particularly to those now least able to understand it – undergraduate architectural students and those casual observers of interest, whose embattled nerves, bedazzled with moments, twittered out, can simply no longer see the wood for the trees.

It is an unashamedly grand canvas; I want to provide the big picture. But I am no Géricault, who first shaved his head and then shut himself in his studio (in all revolutionary ardour!) for seven months to paint *The Raft of the Medusa* in 1818. I am the sort of person who would have liked to be gossiping about him doing it while sitting in the bar round the corner. What I have in mind is more of a jigsaw, and the first piece has me climbing a hill somewhere in the Vosges Mountains of eastern France.

I have climbed this particular hill several times, so I'm very familiar with it. I have been whisked up it in fog in a Renault 21 on a late January afternoon by some boy racer, strained up in sunshine in a Renault 5 packed with university friends; I have crawled up it in a Citroën loaded down with all of a colleague's worldly possessions. I have been up this hill two-up on my Moto Guzzi 500 with a girlfriend on the back, and I have walked it, sweated it, perhaps as it should be done, by myself.

At the bottom of the hill is a little town called Ronchamp, and at the foot of the road – or what used to be track – that leads up from the main road is a bar-hotel-restaurant called La Pomme d'Or. I know that well too; I've played babyfoot with the local youth there, I have dined solo amid heads of wild boar on the wall, I have stayed in one of its bedrooms leaden with Haute-Savoie rusticity.

Halfway up the hill, and it's a substantial hill, there is (at least was) a second hostelry, called Les Acacias. I have stayed there too, with my friend who was moving to Turin with all his worldly possessions. It was a bit musty with the ghosts of so many architectural visitors, a bit haunted.

**6** Introduction

Now this was the last time I was there, and I noticed something – the building, in French chalet style, sported just a few 'Le Corbusier' details in the disposition of some tiny windows scattered across its porch wall.

Amused, I trudged with my friend up the remaining hill. At the top used to be a very ordinary café and gift stand. Both were welcome by the time you'd climbed that bloody hill, and they also sported odd but endearing little L–C motifs. However, the final ascent was to the right, where through a wrought–iron gate and between yew hedges you began to comprehend the billowing shape that is Le Corbusier's majestic Ronchamp Chapel (1954).

Now this damn thing is a bit special, and much has been speculated about it. Why is it this shape? (Nun's hat? Seashell? Ship?) Where does it come from? The funny thing is it's not difficult to explain Ronchamp in quite rational terms. First, there's that bloody hill, and in the '50s it would have been a lot harder to ascend it with equipment. How powerful was a truck back then? On the summit lay the remains of the original chapel, bombed in the Second World War, this being a bitter area of conflict through late 1944. If you are piling up rubble curved walls are stronger than straight ones and battered walls are stronger than plumb ones, especially if you are doing so around a concrete frame. In actuality the swooping south wall of Ronchamp is hollow, so making this piling up a rhetorical device, but it's no less effective for that. Add to this a dash of Le Corbusier's more elemental fascinations: the passing of the day, the weather, the formation of the landscape over time, some notion of the sacred landscape, his notion of 'visual acoustics' (or visual echo), which may or may not be something to do with punning, and the origins of architectural form itself (see Ancient Greece), and you may get somewhere.

You can see this information painted by Le Corbusier on the enamelled doors of the chapel, but not that easily. If you have read L–C's groundbreaking if rather peculiar book *Towards a New Architecture*, you might recall his enthusiasm for Roman vaulting in the lofty side chapels; meanwhile, the roof has something dramatic going on, such as an aircraft wing or a boat, items he also enthused over. If you've tried technical drawing with a T and set square you will wonder at how exactly he managed its multiple curvature, since such things are now commonplace only with computing.

And we haven't even considered the brief yet, which demanded both interior and exterior congregations but not at the same time. Then you will understand why the statue of Mary is mounted on a pivot in the east wall, to face either way, and why the east wall embraces the space outside it so vigorously. Consider all these things and more (I've left plenty out) and you are some way to understanding the whole composition.

Introduction **7**

Of course I've sat and drawn Ronchamp rather picturesquely, just like any student does, in crayon white against a blue sky. Look the thing up on Google Images and you'll find plenty of silly sketches of this wonderful object by bemused students making an absolute hash of understanding it in rational terms. Perhaps they don't want to understand it in rational terms; it is the mystique they are after: the mist of genius.

However, as I descended the staircase at home this morning, I was relieved that I'd also drawn the handrail detail of the little staircase that runs up the outside of the north wall, because that's what I copied when we refurbished our flat, and on my last visit I realised something else that had nothing to do with mystique.

It is something so obvious and rational that it qualifies as my first revelation in this book: Le Corbusier did not design that rather ramshackle café, the souvenir stand, or the coach park. It was not within his conception of the object to imagine such things, and probably not within the conception of the client either. Swarms of tourists, religious or otherwise, crawling all over the thing – it just didn't enter into their psyches in any way. And, in that sense, Le Corbusier clearly would never have understood consumerism, or perhaps he saw it on the horizon, and as he did so, he decided to kill himself. Now that of course is overly dramatic conjecture; there were plenty of reasons for L–C to kill himself in 1965, as we shall find out, and we cannot even be certain he swam out to sea that morning with the intention of doing so.

But, whatever the case, fifty or so years later, Renzo Piano would be commissioned to provide a big brand-new shiny visitors' centre: coach park, gift shop, café and so on. The trucks cruised up that hill. Materials might come from all over the world. Just think, everything seemed to have changed while all the time the humans stay the same. It goes without saying that the result was generally considered disappointing. Perhaps it was the shock of such a magnificent (dare I say human) 20th Century acropolis being shoved so abruptly into the commerciality of the 21st. Certainly exiting via the gift shop never felt so conspicuous.

# 2
# ANCIENT GREECE

You might be thinking, what about the pyramids of Ancient Egypt? What about Black African civilisation? What about Babylon? The Mayans? The Chinese? Well, there's a wealth of archaeology out there, and we can't say there might not be many things to learn from these great civilisations, but for now, let's leave them for volume two, to consider alongside all the other stuff I've left out.

This is an inherent problem with the grand narrative, leaving stuff out, starting in the wrong place. It is clear you can shoot a million holes in this kind of narrative if you have the determination and an adequate university research grant, plus a sufficient belief in history as an artificially constructed project that needs continual readjustment, new inclusions (previously unforgivably excluded) and so on. However, just walking down the street, a Western European street, past a museum for instance, you will be struck with Ancient Greece as a foundation, just as you might study 'classics' in traditional school curricula. It is unfortunate that these days even the word 'classics' carries connotations of class and privilege, and it's even tempting to see this as a conspiracy against the rest of us, for as far as we should be concerned, understanding how we got to where we are today means starting with the Ancient Greeks, around 1000 BC. They represent the beginning, and even then their stories were more ancient than that. Scholars of the West have consistently harked back to this period with great enthusiasm, so we need to understand why.

The Ancient Egyptians represented absolutism, the power of the one deity over all. That's not really us. Anyway, as Osbert Lancaster observed

**10** Ancient Greece

in his cartoon volumes of the 1930s and '40s, the pyramids are a bit boring, very expensive to construct and of little practical use. Meanwhile, while you have the right, it's unlikely you worship Ra. I know of only one modern architect who has studied Ancient Egypt, the excellent Walter Segal, who drew archaeological discoveries on site when he was strapped to do much else within some twentieth-century hiatus, but even that was the result of a particular hiatus we trace back to the Greeks, not the Egyptians.

Sixty thousand tourists climb that agonising path every day of the Athenian summer up to the Acropolis, to the Parthenon. They are wearing Benetton outfits; at least that's what it looks like to me. They, at least, are branded. I am, too. I'm wearing the sky-blue shirt that television presenters wear because I'm being filmed talking about it, and sky-blue shirts are recommended for all TV presenters.

I'm not really supposed to know what I'm talking about. That's how contemporary TV works; you have to know enough but not too much, you need to have perfected some kind of spontaneity and you need to project effortless enthusiasm. According to my producer, I possess this magic art in spades. According to our fixer, a figure who begins to represent in entirety the whole crisis of contemporary Greek culture, I just get things wrong, and she keeps interrupting for the sake of authenticity. It's a bind, making all information transmit like a cookery programme. You have to remember Le Corbusier spent six weeks up here trying to work out what was going on and probably left thinking he was sure, but the latest Classical scholarship, at least in my cursory glance, seems to veer towards not being so sure. Across the Classical world there are too many variables and too many vagaries. The word 'indeterminate' crops up a lot.

Now you could say that the Parthenon looks pretty expensive and pretty useless, too. But it has found many uses – as temple, treasury, ammo dump and so on. Lord Elgin bought the bits of it he could 'rescue' for the British, just as the Germans and the French rescued their own bits of ancient Classical remains too, sometimes whole buildings, all in the name of 'culture'.

If the Parthenon weren't such a miraculous building, a building they are still reconstructing as if it were some kind of spaceship – using titanium fixings and laser technology (when in the first place it wasn't even drawn) – you would think, from a cursory reading, that the Ancient Greeks were basically ruthless, bloodthirsty pirates.

We get this impression from the Homeric stories. Homer's *Iliad* is, after all, pretty much a long snuff movie with a treatise on ethics threaded through the middle. Achilles, the hero, who is by the way half-god, most curiously sits on the beach by his ships for most of the first half,

PHOTOGRAPH 2  Age 19, with my first motorbike, bought during my first year at university, where for some reason I was known as 'Hairy Paul'.

sulking against Agamemnon, who's on the same side but has stolen his girl. Agamemnon has been advised 'by the gods' to sack Troy (but even this was a trick to favour the godlike Achilles). Eventually, with the death of his immediate friend (somewhat his fault), Achilles decides to go on a rampage of revenge, eventually chasing his valiant adversary Hector around the city walls of Troy (this is almost comic, like *Tom and Jerry*) and finally slaying him. Then there are games afterwards, as if anybody would have the energy.

In the companion volume, the *Odyssey*, the hero Odysseus chooses the pain of mortality over immortality. That says something about the

**12** Ancient Greece

profundities of the human condition the Ancient Greeks manage to amplify; after all who wouldn't want to live for ever?

From these books we understand the relation of the Ancient Greek gods to man. The gods are immortal; man is not. There is no absolute god; there are many of them, with the master of the god household being Zeus. They live in real places, Zeus atop Mount Olympus, for instance, but not quite; let's say they inhabit the land, the air and the sea, we decide. I remember getting very confused about Hercules; he seemed to be all sorts of things to all sorts of people. Meanwhile it is not a happy family; the relationships between the gods seems not unlike those between the characters of our own long-running soap operas *Coronation Street* and *EastEnders*. Humans of course beg for the gods' assistance at almost any opportunity by making sacrifices, and we spot signs of godlike activity in the world around us and in our dreams. An eagle flying with a snake, then dropping it in your path: that's an omen. We all have bad dreams; imagine what the Ancients made of them before Freud.

Meantime, as demonstrated by 'godlike Achilles', we have half-gods, mediators between the world of the gods and the world of humans. People, in short, stand a chance, and with that you have the advent of some kind of free will. These guys are called heroes. With free will come culpability, responsibility and regret. The last of these especially gnaws – we are not cats, dogs or horses – we do not just play to our instincts, we think about things.

This marks humans out as different from nature. Meanwhile, the Ancient Greeks further recognised the subtleties of the human condition in the difference between head and heart. While the head and the heart are obviously not so separate at all, we often think with our 'head' and feel with our 'heart'. The Greeks put the one down to Apollo and the other to Dionysus, illustrating the constant battle between rationality and instinct, order and chaos.

Embracing the battle between these two, and the origin of tragedy itself, is something essential to the understanding of even twentieth-century heroes such as Le Corbusier. When considering his Plan Voisin (1925) we don't quite know where to put ourselves; are we looking at a doomed utopia or an optimistic plan? Certainly L–C understood there was a necessity to do things knowing they would be undone and misunderstood – already knowing their failure while wholly promoting them – since this was an elemental life force and not something to be ducked. After all, humanity's great literature (Shakespeare, Flaubert, Tolstoy and so on) is suffused with this stuff, suffused with tragedy.

The curious business of being a half-god might remind us of our own conception of the superhero. In our own culture, superheroes appear to

Ancient Greece **13**

be multiplying, our cinemas and games consoles are positively jumping with them, but they also represent this kind of duality – that Superman is boring old Clark Kent, who can't get the girl by day and who turns into a massively attractive man who saves the world as his alter ego by night.

I find myself watching the sequence where James Bond goes on the rampage through the streets of St Petersburg in a tank in the film *Golden-Eye*. Here 007 is 'godlike' in Ancient Greek terms. Miraculous escapes, great acts of heroism, the fight against treachery, the duplicitous behaviour of women, the sadistic violence and a huge dose of the absurd (it's all ficti-tious) make Pierce Brosnan's chase, his fierce gaze as he pops out of that huge tank, intent on the Russian general who's stolen his girl in a Russian runabout, no less ridiculous than Achilles's climactic and merciless pursuit of Hector around the walls of Troy. Except of course they put the film sequence at the beginning of the tale to get our excitement up so that we do not lose concentration, whereas the Greeks would have had to wait rather a long time for the action to unfold, since the Homeric tales took days of performance.

It's clear we need this stuff; James Bond can cheer us up from our humdrum lives, remind us of our potential and of the possibility of excitement, power and luxury. Meanwhile, if we see through his quests, we read political propaganda. Ian Fleming was telling us the USSR was bad. We are being told stuff in the process.

Which brings us to goddesses. We have continually reinvented our goddesses, too. We have also become them. Female desirability and power, which you have to read between the lines in Homer, became fully fledged living marble with the arrival of the stars of the silver screen with their nuances, inflections, pouts and stares. Roland Barthes described the phenomenon very well in *The Face of Garbo* in 1956. Of course, screen goddesses notoriously felt the effects of their actual mortality – think of Gloria Swanson as portrayed in *Sunset Boulevard*, think of Jayne Mans-field or Marilyn Monroe. Marlene Dietrich, Jean Harlow, Rita Heyworth, Bette Davis, Elizabeth Taylor all brought their own brand of dreamy intoxication, their own glinting eye, to our perception of what a woman was. They could be coquettish, difficult, angry, sultry, deceitful, but all the time they were sexy (and often lit from above) and all the time a mirror of their Ancient Greek counterparts.

Perhaps today's stars are not quite so starlit; as they sparkle on Twitter for a while and are then mercilessly 'trolled'. Think of our porn stars – these screen gods and goddesses perennially find it difficult to cope. The porn star Savannah committed suicide after just breaking her nose in an accident in her Corvette. Being a hero or heroine is tough and, what's more, fabricated. But when you complain about all this, throw a bit of a Gwyneth Paltrow

**14** Ancient Greece

or a Madonna once you've made it; it will inevitably mean a glance at the other traditions, the Eastern mystics. Maybe they'll suit better.

Meanwhile, the *Iliad* is a useful historical document. It reads like a jazzed-up version of a war memorial for those already ancient Trojan War campaigns. To help, the text is not really a text at all but more a lyric poem or song, with many refrains or phrases that repeat themselves. After all, how else should you remember the illustrious dead of long ago? Who got it in the nipple? When? Who was plain sliced up into the brain through his neck? By whom? It features this very graphic portrayal out of respect. Many phrases we associate with today come out of these traumatic descriptions, like 'bite the dust' (after all, it is something you might actually do in the situation), and once Achilles even calls Agamemnon 'dogface'.

The social structure of the Ancient Greeks is very much one of tribes, tribes that are away from their homeland plundering treasure in their long black ships. Their organisation is quite democratic, as it is with pirates in general. Agamemnon is king, but he does discuss his plans or at least has to persuade his army to follow him, and he does consult those around him. But of course the signs of the gods, such as those that appear in dreams, are powerful if unreliable and open to interpretation. He has to employ judgement. How do phenomena occur? Why does fog descend at an inopportune moment? Why do rivers flood? This site for the work of the gods is an early form of what we would call psychiatry in advance of our more scientific understanding. It is not surprising Freud dwelt so long and hard on Greek mythology and made his first major treatise *The Interpretation of Dreams*, since the Ancients invented his subject.

What the culture of the twenty-first-century Western world has largely forgotten is a basic terror: recrimination, warrior spirit, plundering, adultery (but the women are never sneered at), sheer violence and a web of deception alongside these curious moral imperatives that, when you read the *Iliad*, suddenly characterise Ancient Greece as 'our' world. Scholars have consistently tried to remind us of this, notably Friedrich Nietzsche. This brings with it the notion that terror might be somehow intrinsic to civilisation, that life is not a bowl of cherries and that it might be simply a case of terror in the name of what?

There isn't much architecture in the *Iliad*. The eventually victorious Greeks have their 'huts' by their long black ships. All the major characters seem to have a hut to sleep in and to store their armour and weapons in, but we don't know about the others. In the *Odyssey*, Odysseus's marital bed is a tree stump, but he often finds himself sleeping on porches, and there are plenty of doors. In Troy, a few habitable rooms might be

Ancient Greece **15**

strung together, and there are city walls. To make sanctuaries, religious or otherwise, you need walls. Walls were the archetypal act of ancient city-making. According to Cedric Price, we can think of the form of our cities as we might our breakfast eggs – ancient cities being boiled eggs (hard edged), industrial fried and postindustrial scrambled (multicentred or diffuse). However, they would have to be very unusual ancient eggs, for the layout of the protective wall was utterly dependent on the lay of the land. Within the walls, aggregations of buildings came and went. Leonardo Benevelo suggests, in *The History of the City*, that domestic life in, say, the Athens of Pericles and Phidias was marginal because life was largely spent out and about in the polis, and treasures were dedicated to public rather than private magnificence; also, the use of the grid in the layout of streets within the walls reinforced civic identity, but of everyday life little remains.

It would not be until around 500 BC that we see a flowering of Ancient Greek culture in artistic terms that we might be able to understand beyond archaeology and into architecture; even though you could hardly see Ancient Greek architecture as a whole as inhabitable, it tends towards a 'safe' (as in bank) rather than the 'interior' (as in living space). I have a suspicion that this is the reason for the comparative lack of success-ful movies depicting the Ancient Greek world, for, compared with the Roman world (and Romans were very big on the interior), there seems so little to dramatise apart from fantastical apparitions in the landscape and general slaughter.

So the story of architecture is that of accretion. The sacrifices had physical sites – they were done in particular places and related to the immediate environment with presumed meaning. The laurel tree for instance: 'Where's me [*sic*] laurels? . . . Ooooh I'm sitting on 'em!', quips Kenneth Williams in *Carry On Cleo*. The laurel crown was awarded to a victor at the games in the name of a particular god. 'Sitting on your laurels' is a joke we make at the expense of those we think might be languishing too long in victory. Of course Williams is literally sitting on them – that's what makes *his* joke – and there were many other gods with many other associations with particular plants.

So when someone's wife loses her baby or crops fail and everybody's dying – matters largely inexplicable to today's devotees of tabloid media but no doubt easily explained by our scientific community – the superstitious Greeks would make an animal sacrifice, and that soon demanded an altar, which was, in practicality, a kitchen table. You can't carve up a pig's head without a kitchen table, and you can't dissect an ox liver for omens without one, either. Meanwhile the analysis was a

**16** Ancient Greece

primitive form of medical diagnostic; if you practised it enough times you'd learn to read the signs. The kitchen table preceded the operating table. Gradually the trees, the adornment of trees for memorial, just like flowers today at sites of murders and accidents by the roadside, become places of commemoration. It's a small step from those ephemeral flowers to a permanent memorial made of stone with an altarpiece. Just remember Lady Diana.

Once we have stones, we have to ask where the designs, the architectural language – the Doric, the Ionic and the Corinthian styles – come from. How were they derived? The answer, just as with the *Iliad*, is language and song. The origin of language may be song – it's what we first did when trying to cheer ourselves up when we were living in caves, or maybe it started as a howl or tonal moan of misery or lust or as an accompaniment to dance – but in giving birth to language, names for things, great complexities emerged, and eventually architecture happened because the meaning of things, the sound of things and the shape of things became interrelated. Similarly, when we lived in caves, we understood, at least, the concept of 'Mother Earth'. Mother Earth was the fountain of everything. As we conquered and thrived, our range of gods expanded, and as we became more confident, our vocabulary enlarged.

The easiest way to explain this concept (called punning or troping) is via a straightforward example of a very complicated thing like a Corinthian column. Around the base of that column runs a band of stone. It is given the same name as that of the rope used to drag an ox to slaughter at an altar and is the same thickness and shape. It may or may not be a bundle of a collection of upright spears that moulds the fluting of the column. It takes great scholarship to get to the exact meaning of it all, but meaning there is, since the same can be said of all the complex curves and figurations that go to make up the whole Corinthian column; they relate to myriad things, and, once they are established, all that has to be done is to decide how big the column will be and where to put it. Indeed, this is one of the most convenient things about Classical architecture, for while it is not exactly functional by our understanding of the term, it does come as a 'ready-made', just like humans do. They can go anywhere, so where?

Despite the clear sophistication, we do not get much technical experimentation. This could irritate modern minds. The Greeks stuck to their elaborated but straightforward post-and-beam structures (trabeation) where, if we look at the plans, all the potential spans for stonework are the same. They didn't seem too bothered about innovation at all. This conceptual stability remains intriguing. The physical stability does rely on something still relevant to almost any construction today, the datum, for

Ancient Greece **17**

to build a temple, wherever they wanted to put it, the Greeks first levelled the ground with a stone plinth.

There is a story, perhaps apocryphal, that when the Ancients of Delphi deemed it the centre of the Ancient Greek world and decided to mark the exact spot, they knew exactly what to put there – a round temple structure called a tholos – but it took them three hundred years to work out where to put it because the priests and oracles had to work out where the exact centre of the world was. This is complicated by the fact that if you go to Delphi, the attractive tholos structure is not actually the centre of the ancient world; that is now deemed to be a large egg-like rock further up the processional route to the Temple of Apollo, and even that is fake, for it was replaced by a copy so that unruly crowds of schoolchildren could climb over it without causing damage. The real centre of the world is now in a museum. However, given all this, it is hardly a surprise that the centre of the world, birth of the world perhaps, should be a rock shaped like an egg. After all, what came first, the chicken or the egg?

Delphi is a good place to understand the purpose and placing of Ancient Greek buildings. First, we must understand it as a place of pilgrimage and procession, at the summit the theatre and the games arena, with the Temple of Apollo housing its famous oracle slightly below. At first I understood that she sat in a pit underneath it, but now I understand she sat on a tripod above her visitors. In actuality the oracle performed only one day a week in the summer months, and she sat high on a tripod in her sanctuary as ethylene, being lighter than air, rose to the ceiling. Ethylene was the natural product of earthquake fissures below, and mildly hallucinogenic, and it was bottled up for a single day's high times. The Greeks understood they needed this kind of irrationality to explain the unexplainable, rather like '60s hippies taking LSD. We still believe in the mind-expanding drugs, of course, that we might gain some great insight if we escape our humdrum world, even if usually our enthusiasm is misplaced. However, all in all, this explains why the oracle was very popular for a very long time.

And the oracle was as much an excuse to meet politically as to receive divine advice; it might be compared to a twenty-first-century Davos. One imagines the conversations:

'You going up this year?'

'Nah, did her last year, but, as an aside, what do you think about . . . [very important political issue]?'

In fact, what with all the tourism (before it was tourism), oracle, games, festivals and conventions, it's easy to see Delphi as a kind of ancient Las Vegas.

**18** Ancient Greece

Leading up to the temple is the processional route populated by individual shrines, storehouses or banks, depending on how you look at it, where offerings to the gods, tributes – for instance in thanks for being smiled on to win a race – were deposited. The most famous of these is the famous charioteer now in the Delphi museum. Meanwhile, the procession, the ritual, is marvellously depicted in a relief known as *The Goddess of Victory* from around 408 BC. I prefer not to think of her as a goddess at all, because the subject is doing something so ordinary. Projecting this image of a lady pausing to adjust her sandal, reaching down past her flowing robes to remove that irritating, perhaps painful bit of grit, transports a lecture room full of students back more than two thousand years. You pause and draw breath; they are stunned, it's a kind of magic, the empathy we suddenly share with this woman and her world.

The buildings along the processional route were simple rooms; we call them megarons. They could be strung along in a straight line with a line of columns in front; then you would have a stoa. You could put columns on the front or back or both or around the whole thing if you wanted the form of a temple. Ancient Greek architecture is all variations on a theme.

The main instance of complication in the planning of individual buildings comes when you encounter the Erectheion on the Athenian Acropolis. Here several rooms seem to have been joined together in a far more complex way, probably acknowledging a complex site with several religious spots all alarmingly close together. For instance, this building has to acknowledge a fall in the land across its width, and since the ground is sacred, that's what it has to do – it has to step up and down. There is no plinth! It is also 'fronted' by a small portico featuring caryatids – columns that are female figures – the meaning of which has fascinated scholars for centuries.

The seriousness that the Ancient Greeks brought to the business of siting their buildings has had profound consequences for all of us. Since the landscape was inhabited by the gods, offerings to them or eulogies about them had to be made in the right place; after all, pleasing them was essential, and the temple was our human offering to them. What at first seems rather quirky site planning is hence the result of much contemplation. What a thing looks like in the landscape, how it fits into it, is crucial. Delphi, first and foremost, is an incredibly dramatic landscape. One is tempted to wonder, even today, that they made the right choice despite the physical impracticality of the steep slopes. The Acropolis in Athens must have looked like a sacred place even before you thought to put a temple on it.

The relationship can be seen right from the start in Crete, where the Minoans appeared to situate their settlements in response to particular

Ancient Greece **19**

geological forms; notably, in the distance there is usually a mountain with two peaks with a valley in the middle and a softly rounded hill. The symbolism seems obvious if we remember Mother Earth, and we must presume that such natural occurrences, along with other practical considerations, of course, would precipitate occupation and inform 'design'.

The distinguished American academic Vincent Scully has even gone so far as to note the implied axiality in the famous fresco of the girl preparing to vault over the length of a bull (grabbing the bull by the horns) at Knossos. I suppose bulls do charge (when they get going, and with some forbidding on our part) in a straight line, and they come from somewhere. So if you were planning a space in which to perform this spectacle, it would likely be long and relatively thin in plan, just as we need for its present-day derivative, vaulting the 'horse' in gymnastics. *Voilà,* the axial plan!

However, as the civilisation developed with the Dorian invasion, we see the human race asserting itself in more complex relation to nature. If you visit the ancient theatre at Epidaurus, you will note that extraordinary way such a mass of raked semicircular stonework sits neatly in the undulations of the surrounding hills. You will also note how precise it is, wonder at the perfect acoustics and marvel at the view. Meanwhile, visit Olympia and you will be relieved to see the Temple of Zeus orientated almost exactly east/west (as you would expect reflecting sunrise and sunset) with all the other surrounding buildings set at slightly jaunty angles for whatever reasons.

Later, we shall soon see that this issue of 'context' is a very thorny and continually problematic one for architects, and how we view context changes with the tools we have at our disposal. Looking at a building via drawn plans and sections will bring a different outlook than if you don't have them, and it seems likely the Ancient Greeks didn't have them at all. It seems likely that they talked their buildings up as much as anything, and they must have talked for a very long time.

The post-Hellenic, late Ancient Greek culture, roughly two centuries BC, threw up one of the most dramatic altarpieces of the ancient world. By now, the 'kitchen table' analogy becomes irrelevant. This building, well, half of it, now languishes in Berlin in a museum specially cut to size, where it was first taken by the no-doubt triumphant German archaeologist Karl Humann after its discovery in Asia Minor – although the Soviets shifted it as war plunder to Leningrad after the Second World War. It is the famous Pergamon Altar.

The building itself is in plan the shape of an 'H' with dramatic steps up between the side wings to the altar itself. Around the base is an incredible

**20** Ancient Greece

frieze depicting war between the Olympian gods and the Giants. Some of them are climbing or falling down the stone steps themselves, such is the virtuosity of the sculptor's work. The tale itself is as old as the hills, as old as the Flood and as relevant today as any newspaper.

But it is a difficult tale, and the connotations have had vast consequences. While in Greek mythology it represents one thing, the fight of the Titans against the Greek gods, in Judaeo-Christian history it translates to an antipathy between the Jews and the Germanic tribes. Tacitus, the Roman scholar, seems rather the culprit, explaining that while the Jews escaped the Flood on the Ark, those who remained and survived played in their own excrement – which, of course, we might consider as fertiliser – and hence became giants, and presumably these 'giants' waded through the water to survive. The mythology of the 'giant' northern tribes continues among reactionary circles even today. When an ultra right-wing gunman shoots eighty-five kids on their holiday island in Norway, he proclaims himself the inheritor of this tradition, a kind of supreme being, and in doing this he shares the Nazi view.

Of course there are some conspicuous examples of how this thread of history is periodically subverted and misread. In the twentieth century, Albert Speer, Adolf Hitler's architect, designed and modelled a colossal Germania – the visualisation of the thousand-year Reich modelled on sacrifice and heroism, which within ten years proved catastrophic to the German people. 'Blood and soil' runs uncannily ancient, but surely it was twaddle by the time of the Third Reich. The Neoclassical architecture here, tainted with the horrors of the death camps and tyranny, acquires strongly negative associations, and it is interesting that, having very few apologists, Albert Speer is seen as a rather vain and foolish architect who was actually just a brilliant organiser.

But Speer's role still haunts the contemporary architect's conscience. Given he was in charge of slave labour on a massive scale it is now charitable to believe his Nuremberg testimony, that he was responsible but not guilty, as anything but elastic with the truth. This may not have been the impression we got watching the original TV series *The World at War* in the early '70s. Since his death, in 1981, the 'good Nazi' has been tarnished by the build-up of facts. But even this has not stopped the Classical cause in terms of architecture. The Postmodern period saw renewed interest in Neoclassicism as a reaction against the perceived evils of Modernism and disowned the Nazi connotation to the point where Leon Krier could write a fresh appreciation with *Albert Speer: Architecture 1932–1942*, first published in 1985.

For, on the other hand, the rather restrained Neoclassical architecture of the Scandinavian countries of roughly the same period has very much been seen by the British as symbolic of our continuing democratic

Ancient Greece **21**

tradition, symbolic of a kind of gentleness that brings with it images of afternoon tea and scones and the self-deprecation of Sergeant Wilson against the pompousness of Captain Mainwaring. Many an English town hall from the first part of the century evidences a strong enthusiasm for a pared-down Scandinavian classicism; attitudes were upended by the social and technological upheavals of the 1960s.

So what makes Ancient Greek architecture so enduring? There can hardly have been a year since that hasn't seen a Neoclassical building. I suppose the first thing is that we marvel at the precision and the delicacy of Ancient Greek art in general. A relief of a woman pausing on a processional route to adjust her sandal, maybe getting rid of that irritating bit of grit, is extremely touching. We had never made art as real as that before, nothing as subtle or humane. This is the art of ourselves and of our feelings as much as it is to do with rituals and the gods.

There also seem to be technical matters that endure; Pythagoras decoded proportional relationships rather like those harmonies of the musical scales. The musical scales may be ignored – you can make contemporary atonal music – but in the fact is that it is termed atonal; it is defined with respect to that which is considered tonal. In Ancient Greece the lyre was a symbol of political harmony as well as musical.

The third reason must have something to do with the taboos, stories and ethics, not always pleasant but nonetheless powerful, that come out of this world. Our cultures have many strange customs, some of which turn out to be very sensible (such as realising incest as a bad idea) and some of which might appear rather arbitrary (such as not eating pork). These taboos to some extent differentiate one culture from another, and because the Ancient Greeks spelt so much out to us, bringing us democracy, philosophy, ethics, mathematics and so on, we start here because they worked these codes out. Moreover, they oversaw the birth of our conception of tragedy. We could have started without it, we could, like the Chinese, have started with a very non-Dorian notion of transience and flow, of Zen, but we didn't; we fight for things in the name of things and die trying.

So back to the Parthenon, back to its virtuosity. If all of its columns were projected up into the sky, they would meet at a height of thirty miles. Each of the columns is slightly tapered out in the middle to correct an optical illusion that, if they were plumb straight, would have them looking thin in the middle. In the British Museum, itself a Neoclassical symbol, this time of English imperialistic pomp by Smirke, I can scrutinise up close the entablatures 'rescued' by Lord Elgin in their specially designed room. I notice in particular how the Ancient Greek sculptor dealt with the difficult bits, the acute corner spaces as the roofline hits the horizontal. In one he places a horse straining to drag the sun up and in the

## 22  Ancient Greece

other opposite corner, the visibly tired beast dragging it down again. Well, something had to explain what brought the sun up each day and made it fall at night, and it is a moving and poetic sight.

Meanwhile, in front of me on this desk is propped a plan of the site at Olympia, origin of our Olympics, where all the tribes met to suspend conflict and play out the games. I note an extraordinary arrangement, this time with the entablature(s) of the Temple of Zeus. It's a simple observation but a satisfying one. The entablature facing west, towards the accommodations such as they were – the Olympic village, if you like – shows a scene from a battle between the Lapiths and the Centaurs; it's the scene of a wedding going badly wrong. The Centaurs have got drunk, and they are busy molesting the Lapith women. The message? Don't get too drunk at weddings, or don't invite drunks to weddings! The second entablature, facing east, the arena, has a different but equally beguiling message: don't cheat!

# 3

# ANCIENT ROME

While Alexander the Great got as far as India and Hellenistic art reached the heights of expression and technique, political union eluded the Ancient Greeks. While Alexander was marching east, it was Rome that would step by step engulf the Mediterranean tribes from the west, imposing the state – one state – with worse art but better facilities.

The state of Imperial Rome, in the popular imagination, is organised in triumvirate (as well as periodically by a triumvirate). We are vividly aware of their organisation, arches, orgies and plumbing, also of caesars, centurions and straight roads, and, third, of bloodthirsty theatre. Each of these to some extent facilitates the others, and they work almost seamlessly together. However, most important, states need infrastructure, and we have historically been less concerned with the merits of the individual buildings or palaces of Ancient Rome, even at their most grandiose, than with an idea of Ancient Rome as a whole, as a system. At the hub of the system we have what we begin to read as the city – the 'eternal city' in the case of Rome itself, which grew from little more than a village as a result of the expansionist mettle of its progeny.

Although we have an author of sorts for the Parthenon in Iktinos, we believe the Ancient Greeks were hardly specialists when it came to building, painting and sculpture. But the most famous architect of Rome is Vitruvius (born *c.*70–80 BC), who was responsible for organising architecture into a particular set of rules (the *Ten Books of Architecture*) borrowed from the Greeks and inherited from the Etruscans. Vitruvius was also an artilleryman.

There is no doubt that the Ancient Greek world was chaotic; it seemed to work on the model of piracy. This may not be such a bad thing;

**26** Ancient Rome

pirates, after all, are not distracted by the whiff of nationhood, and they are famously unspecialised – they do everything themselves – and also notoriously democratic. As a bunch of cut-throats, they have to agree on matters.

The Ancient Greek world was based on tribes, and to unite them under Rome demanded the unique selling proposition that life was better if you joined in. Of course, at the margins, you were perpetually, or almost perpetually, at war. Peace was cause for celebration. This size of the Empire led to a large, efficient and expensive army at the front and a chain of command from the emperor and Senate on down deciding what to do with them from their base in Rome. Officially we tend to see Rome as a republic, but for long periods it was actually a monarchy, and, in general, to prove yourself as a member of an elite family, you went out and became a successful general (or married one) and then you returned to play out life in and around the Senate.

Thinking about Roman culture therefore conjures up images very different from those we have of Ancient Greek life. There is a good deal more plotting, intrigue and politics at home, simply because things have to be run in terms of the state, and the state can be overturned by mutiny and defeat and the much-feared march on Rome. In his book *Mythologies* (1957), the French philosopher and popular essayist Roland Barthes notes in his essay 'The Romans in Films' that the predominant characteristic of Roman antagonists is sweat, nervous sweat. This is not just because they were enjoying the bathhouse. In *I Claudius,* the novelist Robert Graves takes on the persona of Claudius, a 'sick, stammering, lame fool' within the Imperial family. Nobody thinks Claudius of any importance at all; he's good for nothing but barren history writing. However, this becomes his unique advantage. One wise friend even encourages him to ham it up a bit, because that is the only way for him to remain safe. At home, along with the intrigue, we are also presented with conspicuous luxury, but sometimes the luxury is literal poison, and therein lies a certain moral of the story.

The people are subservient to the sacred Roman eagle – symbol of the greater Rome, or for that matter the sacred tribune (from which the soldiers are addressed) or even the sacred shrines where the legions' eagles were stored. We are still in a world governed by superstition, but Romans have it better, and, if they aren't already, the conquered can become Romans too. Hence Rome conquers and converts lands it needs to exploit, and eventually it stretches from Scotland to Syria, from north of the Danube to North Africa and Egypt. It sustains itself on both booty and trade. There were 'onions from Spain, cheeses from Holland, and stones from Gaul, as Kenneth Williams says playing Caesar in *Carry on*

Ancient Rome 27

PHOTOGRAPH 3 In front of 'the world's biggest sign', outside the Hilton Las Vegas, where I gave my first academic paper (rather badly).
Credit: Julie Cook

*Cleo*. Meanwhile, his earlier line speaks the political truth: 'Infamy, infamy, they've all got it in for me!'

Rome certainly educates us on our duties as citizens. The original tax-and-spend economy was subject to some unfortunate extremes; the spendthrift emperor Caligula soon spent so much on exotic and blood-drenched games that he raised a tax on marital sex. One of his ways of making money was simply to condemn nobles, have them killed or make them kill themselves and seize their estates. All public positions had to be paid for, and there was no way you could turn down the offer. The sweat was real: the higher you rose, the worse the knife edge of approval. More cautious emperors behaved frugally and amassed very considerable funds, with which they could reward the army for loyalty and the crowd for endurance.

It is the construction of this state that fascinates historians when it becomes clear, from the 1700s on, that we are doing somewhat the same thing. Claudius is even found debating the alternative approaches

**28** Ancient Rome

to writing history that I mention in the prologue to this book. He is asked to decide between Livy, who is what you might call 'discursive', and Pollio, who is more factual. The Roman state became a model for our own, even though Rome itself had been left, sacked and culturally abandoned, only to be rediscovered in the Renaissance. Meanwhile, twentieth-century fascism was born in Italy, and a more calamitous attempt at recapturing the Roman Empire can hardly be found than the Third Reich.

It was Edward Gibbon, with his monumental, highly readable and stylistically brilliant *Decline and Fall of the Roman Empire,* who articulated this for the growing, rationalist, intelligentsia of the eighteenth century (see chapter 6). He found himself standing in the ruins of the Capitol one evening in October 1764, listening to the call to vespers and realising the incongruity of it all. Here began his participation in much argument about the relation of church to state: the debate as to whether events were purely the will of God, the cause and effect of human action, or something in between. But he had to do this from the physically neutral ground of Lausanne, where the clerics were less downright dangerous than elsewhere.

Hence we do not think of Ancient Rome as physically chaotic either. Our commonly held view of the streetscape implies cool, calm order – just look at the *Asterix* comics. The first pages of *Asterix and the Laurel Wreath* show a comparison between the streets of Rome and those of Lutetia in Gaul. In Rome, by decree, traffic is not allowed by daytime, sellers proudly sell 'Good Fresh Fish', 'Cakes!', 'Nice Wholesome Veg' and 'Ripe Juicy Melons!' and tourists of the world visit the Circus Maximus accompanied by a pompous guide translating Latin into Egyptian hieroglyphics. In Lutetia, people are simply shouting at each other 'Moron!', 'Idiot!', 'Half-wit!', 'Fool!' and similar epithets, and the traffic is going nowhere. Meanwhile the power of Rome lies in unity – in *Asterix and the Olympic Games* the Roman athletes all win together; you can't pick one from the other.

Of course these are idealised images. Robert Hughes is quick to point out that while we think of the Imperial Rome as all white marble (with gold trim) and fresh white togas (with gold trim), it might have been closer to a Calcutta of the Mediterranean: filthy. The vast majority of the population lived in hovels; overcrowded six-storey primitive shacks; *insulae* (islands), a sort of rickety tower block with little or no sanitation and no chimney. The original Romans may have piped *in* their water here and there via the eleven aqueducts and lead piping, but while they had a sewerage system of sorts, they appeared to have put a lower priority on getting their waste *out* – there was no waste

Ancient Rome **29**

collection, and people generally just threw it out of the windows. There were periodic 'shit carts'. The Roman poet Juvenal recommended the use of padded headwear as protection against the threat of continuous careless projectiles.

But that was by the by to your Enlightenment thinker, to whom overall philosophy, organised trade and military enforcement mattered most. That Rome cultivated an impressive merchant as well as military fleet that cut crossing times across the Mediterranean considerably, and that it laid 85,000 km of roads linking the Empire was kernel. Meanwhile, one traded product, papyrus from Egypt, may even have been the reason for a profound transformation in the possibilities for architecture, the 'encapsulation of space' as well as the extension of it via maps. Marshall McLuhan, the '60s theorist, coined this term, and to make sense of it we need to go back to those straight roads.

To make straight roads you need maps, and those maps need to be lightweight and durable – making papyrus very useful – and it also helps if your landscape is flat. Along these roads you march legions and ride chariots, and all roads lead to Rome. The legions know where they are and how fast they can go by the mileposts along the road. McLuhan even asserts (but we might be suspicious here) that the Roman Empire declined just as the papyrus crops failed and Egypt stopped exporting. Without the roads, he wistfully reminds us, you are likely to need the ancient version of a 4x4, commonly known as a horse. Hence the cavalry was born, or at least that heavily armoured warrior on his warhorse – well, just as long as you've invented stirrups to get him on and off it.

There may be more to this than meets the eye, for the Roman Empire was predicated on the art of war, by the legion: that meticulously ordered fighting machine drilled to perfection night and day in the gymnasium (with arms twice the weight of those used in battle) and marched with equal perfection along those straight roads to wherever trouble lay. It was ruthless (you should fear your own officer more than the enemy) and the vehicle of patriotism (pride should be such that internal punishments were dealt out by soldiers themselves). It was also a mechanism of social mobility, for it was your local farm worker, smithy or carpenter, used to arduous work, who was the obvious feedstock for the legion, then trained and in other ways Romanised to gain honour by valour in the field and be rewarded when discharged as a form of citizen, usually after sixteen years but often – when times got tough – far longer. Of course there were other auxiliary groupings in the army (and there was a cavalry), but the image of the legion is the symbol of Rome itself.

The Romans buried their dead along their straight roads. Who was buried where indicated the class of a certain district and the identity of

**30** Ancient Rome

the town. Imagine arriving at a town you had never visited before (maybe you are not Roman) and being greeted by all these tombs and tributes and unable to read the signs. It would be disconcerting, at least not exactly 'Welcome to St Albans'.

Presumably once you have papyrus, you might draw on it. The Ancient Greeks may or may not have had papyrus; they did have chariots (it says so in the *Iliad*), but then again the landscape is generally too mountainous for straight roads. Do you need a drawing to build an arch? You might if you want to string multiple arches together by drawing a straight line across a map in either plan or in section and also when you put arches together internally and begin to make complex spaces clearly demarcated for particular uses.

So drawing predicated such utilities as bridges and aqueducts (the most famous of these being the Pont du Gard near Avignon), and the invention and utilisation of the arch became preeminent. So while we can enjoy great urban objects such as the Maison Carrée in Nimes, these are essentially Greek derivatives (and architecturally meaner versions featuring only one portico), and it is the promulgation of the arch that is more important.

I once asked my fourth-year tutor what I should do on a visit to Rome. He said, 'You should go and sit in the Pantheon all day long'. Well, I didn't manage a whole day – it got rather cold – but over the years I've seen his point, made with his typical impish humour while sucking on his pipe and eyeing up a glass of wine. The Pantheon represents the first time we made architecture as we understand it today, as a functioning thing for us, as an interior. It is even dedicated to all the gods (and there were a good many of them by this time), so by making a room for all of them under one roof, you sort of eliminate them. All the Pantheon really does is mark the passing of the day, not by the efforts of horses dragging the sun up and down but by a simple oculus in the centre of the dome which casts a moving spotlight across the interior. The measure of time is thoroughly architectural: the last book of Vitruvius's *Ten Books of Architecture* – the Roman architectural text on our Greek architectural origins – focuses on timepieces and sundials. Meanwhile, since the Pantheon can really be understood only in section, it surely had to be drawn on that papyrus so as to conceptualise the massive thicknesses of wall needed to support its dome, to organise the materials on the basis of the laws of statics and furthermore to figure out how to lighten the weight of that dome and how to do the hole in the middle. You would seem to have needed to draw it to do it, because we can *understand it* only by studying a drawing of it.

Ancient Rome **31**

Looking at the remains of a Roman wall is unimpressive – a lumpish coagulation of stone, brick, flint and tile, but it is the essence of concrete. These lumpish masses would then be clad, when the occasion befitted, in marble and carved for decoration. The Pantheon features finer, thinner grades of concrete as it reaches its apex, and this reveals what we might call a tectonic graduation of part from part. This is no Stonehenge, and, what's more, the sophistication is not immediately apparent, so it's not like the Parthenon, either.

It seems unlikely that the fall of Rome corresponds singly with a lack of papyrus, although we should note its dependence on a global economy of sorts, but it is worth thinking about it as a symptom. Gibbon actually holds the fall of the 'generous' Roman Empire to the rise of self-righteous Christianity. For him, engaged in the eighteenth-century battle for reason, the monasticism of the medieval world was anathema. To him, the pluralism of belief he saw in Ancient Rome, the social virtue he saw embodied in it – the semisecular state – was utterly compromised by the Christian Church, the main thrust of which he seems to view as unbearable Christian stubbornness and intractability. He writes on page 34:

> The policy of the emperors and the senate, as far as it concerned religion, was happily seconded by the reflections of the enlightened, and by the habits of the superstitious, part of their subjects. The various modes of worship which prevailed in the Roman world, were all considered by the people, as equally true; by the philosopher, as equally false; and by the magistrate, as equally useful. And thus toleration produced not only mutual indulgence, but even religious concord.

We can empathise with Gibbon when we look at the contemporary etchings of Giovanni Battista Piranesi (1720–1788) showing the giant ruins of Ancient Rome up to its waist in detritus (human or otherwise), overgrown with creepers, crumbling to pieces. The views at first seem horribly exaggerated (as if Piranesi felt just like Gibbon) with rustics scuttling about, looters quarrying marble and squatters cowering in the shadows of rotting theatres; while gentlemen stand by pointing and gesturing, wondering what on earth could have happened. One of Piranesi's most famous works is an imaginative reconstruction: the *Campo Marzio* of 1762. In it, he's dreaming of the eternal city grander than ever before. This large lithograph is tellingly hung on the wall of the twentieth-century architect Louis Kahn's office (see chapter 9), and we will encounter

**32** Ancient Rome

the phenomenon again, in reverse, when we come to scrutinise Albert Speer's rather absurd 'Theory of Ruin Value' in the doomed architecture of Hitler's Germany.

In Gibbon's view, when Constantine created the Holy Roman Empire with the Edict of Milan of 313, which legalised Christian worship, he, unwittingly sealed doom to eventual medievalism. He has a point, even today; as President Obama battles for budgetary leeway, far-right Christian organisations threaten to fatally destabilise the United States and wish to decide who is guilty on the basis of pure suspicion without due process of law, and of course they throw in a bit of creationism as well. History repeats itself, unfortunately.

However, it is clear the Roman system was not exactly foolproof. Power corrupts and absolute power can corrupt absolutely. Augustus acquired god-like status while remaining essentially modest and good humoured; Caligula embraced that status and was the opposite. Emperors could become deities, and the worst made themselves deities. In such circumstances, gossip could then become blasphemous, history could become suddenly blasphemous, and you could find yourself amid state control as ruthless and arbitrary as that we might recognise in the worst segments of our contemporary history.

And you can understand Constantine's position. He had a battle to win and, if blessed by victory the next day, promised this U-turn on policy towards the Christians. Having everybody worshipping every god at the drop of a hat was proving most inconvenient, and limiting the number of gods to three – Father, Son and Holy Ghost – might be seen as welcome and efficient. Hundreds of years later, Gibbon, who saw religion primarily as a manifestation of suspicion, didn't take kindly to the decision, while at the time Constantine understandably was not in a position to appreciate the political consequences for the machismo of the Roman state that came with the recognition of the Lamb of God.

Whereas the fantastical apparitions of the Ancient Greek world seem rather underrepresented in our modern media, quite the opposite is true of Rome. I grew up to the salaciousness of Frankie Howerd in *Up Pompeii!* By the 1960s Rome was associated not with revolutionary virtue (as we might see in the painting *Oath of the Horatii* [1784] by David) but with bawdy fun. A funny thing happened on the way to the forum.

But I enjoyed one of my first visits to the cinema to see *Ben Hur*, and when I was sitting in the pub the other day a man sold me a film called *Centurion*. It was predictably terrible, but that is not the point; I was just wondering what we do with the myth today. What was clear in

Ancient Rome **33**

this case was that it was a story about our troops fighting at that time in Afghanistan. The analogy was with those Roman legions in Germania. It was set in Roman times, but it was an absolutely contemporary story. This is why we cannot consign our understanding of history to a kind of historical waste bin, for we live it and breathe it every day, even via pirated DVDs.

This is as true for the world of architecture as it might be for fashion or hairdressing. And when we consider Roman architecture we are immediately aware of two main themes that would seem to be contradictory: engineering and showmanship. The cities were served by aqueducts and made-up roads and, certainly in the settlements built up from scratch (for instance in North Africa), sewers. All of this was organised within a strict grid pattern with gates north, south, east and west. Entertainments were often sensibly placed outside the city walls for fear the combatants might wreak havoc if they escaped.

On the other hand, the image we have of Roman architecture is something rather bombastic, rather brash, rather stage set. It doesn't matter whether we are considering Caesars Palace in Las Vegas, the Golden Palace of Emperor Nero (featuring the first revolving restaurant) or a spot of nouveau riche appliqué of a Classical portico to a bungalow in Peterborough or a mansion in East Cheam. The Romans never lacked application and built marvels to prove it, but aesthetically they suffered from an inferiority complex and copied. Roman poets even considered themselves dull by comparison with the Greeks. Hughes points out that the Roman aptitude for statuary was what we might call Warholian; perhaps as many as fifty thousand busts of Augustus might have been fashioned all told. It is a characteristic we can't get away from; in this sense, Caesars (no apostrophe) is as Roman as you're likely to get. In Caesars Palace, I have even seen teams of actors masking real building work to make it more entertaining.

And I have sat for many a pleasant hour at the bar of Cleopatra's Barge there, relaxing on the black leather-padded bar stools, watching the hookers sip their nonalcoholic drinks with their little purses and sensible shoes, listening to the thump of '80s disco music coming from the actual floating barge of a dance floor, endless renditions of 'Celebration', 'Music and Lights', and so on, all aimed at the suddenly young hearts of middle-aged businessmen who, if they have any sense, are about to get themselves into trouble. I became on very good terms with one of the bar staff there, a lady from Arbroath whose husband was in the military. You see, it all rings true – lavish entertainments, orgies, visitors from the Empire, the military, even superstition at the craps table. Notwithstanding the tremendous infrastructure and organisation that back up a machine

**34** Ancient Rome

like Caesars Palace, you'll never see so much as a dustcart. The original cartoon advertisement for Caesars Palace, from way back in 1966, shows a girl feeding grapes to a rather portly, toga-clad, balding gentleman.

Part of this second enduring theme resides in the fact that the Romans, when they weren't creating feats of great engineering or marching their legions, were sticking on bits of Classical Greek architecture to whatever building they wanted. Even Asterix shows us this. When we encounter the 'original' Caesar's Palace in *Asterix and the Laurel Wreath*, we see a formidable multistorey building that is essentially a pile-up of what we now call 'Classical motifs'. However, this pile-up, whether it constitutes itself in elevation, plan or section, is the raw material for the art of composition, and presumably composition is a rather high-minded term for putting elements together in an agreeable, auspicious, practical or splendid way, and architects have been trying to do this with varying degrees of success ever since. Meanwhile, the set designers of Hollywood have relished the opportunity Rome provides with high-camp zeal. The set of *Cleopatra* (1963) was the most expensive ever created and the scene where Cleopatra (Elizabeth Taylor) arrives in the capital is as unforgettable as it is delightfully preposterous, even if Caesar did once return to be greeted by forty elephants with torches held in their trunks. It does not help that the Romans enjoyed giant phallic monuments such as Trajan's Column and were very fond of triumphal arches, each an apparition representing a subconscious carnality to civic theatre.

Meantime there is the Coliseum itself, with its vivid, exotic and murderous entertainments. Caesars built one specially for Celine Dion, and originally the target audience was crowds of orgiastic women shoppers; the catchphrase for Forum Shops (an adjunct of Caesars and one of the most successful shopping complexes in the world) was 'Shoppus Till You Droppus'. And there are plenty of Las Vegas strip clubs which enjoy the Roman motif, whereas I suspect their successors (the Goths) would have hung the exotic dancers from the gibbet.

But thankfully we employ Rome only as a motif. The Roman temperament employed excessive cruelty with some nasty side effects: that you might get a taste for it. As to whether that cruelty was necessary or otherwise, it is no surprise that the Roman ideal suffused the art of the French Revolution – perhaps its actual practice during the Terror – and conditioned twentieth-century fascism. Conquering armies, slavery, sadism and bloodlust are all linked. Prostitutes, whose lives must have been nightmarish, would throng around the Circus Maximus to profit (if that can be the word) from the appalling spectacles within. The bacchanalia

Ancient Rome **35**

(by reputation originally a harmless vineyard cult) transformed themselves into festivals where cult members assured themselves that nothing but nothing was a crime. The Senate legislated against the bacchanalia in 186 BC, and its members were liquidated – largely because their activities mirrored those of the state.

To miss this point and idealise Roman society, as so many of the subsequent purveyors of Graeco-Roman Neoclassicism have done, is a case of so it goes, but recognising the fact does explain that fondness for life in Ancient Greek Arcadia, often bewilderingly misrepresented (with the startling exception of Nietzsche) as one of largely innocent and unbridled fun. Meanwhile, it also highlights the sophistication of the painter Nicolas Poussin, who named his idyllic scene of rustics around a tomb of 1638 *Et in Arcadia ego* – suggesting that his audience, amid their luxury, if they had a mind, might be reminded of death. Death was not what you were supposed to find in the bushes of Stourhead.

So the orgy business is problematic – not quite the free love one might imagine, not necessarily 'a night of the senses' (of gaiety and laughter and potential orgasm) with the likes of Ammonia, Senna, Erotica and Lurcio, but rather one of acute pain, ritualistic humiliation and possible death. At least that would be the case if you found yourself invited to the wrong party. Only in very unfortunate circumstances might this happen in contemporary Las Vegas, and these days we consume even these possibilities virtually: by watching *CSI*.

Once inside Penthouse, a former large car garage, we found ourselves in a Speeresque foyer with giant breasts. Like the colossal Constantine in Rome, where you get just bits – a head, some toes – here you got just giant 2D breasts. Once past them you would enter the darkened arena. By technical necessity we always shot the interiors with the lights up, to show them off, but in reality, once in use, the architecture was insignificant, reduced fairly much to the sound system, the multiple and multiform stages, the chairs and the dancers, all of which were of course intricately worked. For instance, in Minx the plush chairs (with more than a whiff of California Modern style about them) were on rollers – since the dancers expend considerable effort shifting them about for privacy. Meanwhile, the banquettes in Jaguars seemed specifically designed, almost anthropometrically, for the guys to 'kick back' and let the dancers do their stuff to maximum efficiency. However, it was incredible just how much was spent on décor, considering its utterly synthetic task, and even some of the exteriors, for instance that of Jaguars, could stand comparison to the Maison Carrée.

But should we take this sort of observation seriously? Am I being serious when I employ observations of *Asterix* cartoons, Caesars Palace Las

**36** Ancient Rome

Vegas and the city's strip clubs? Well, of course I am, because presently I'm watching a documentary on the National Geographic Channel, which in between advertisements for insurance and personal injury claims is broadcasting *Rome's Greatest Battles*, and I have to say, since they try to make it realistic by dramatising the action with 'real' actors or at least very good CGI, the set designer has looked carefully at the *Asterix* version of the 'original' palace of Caesar.

All of this seems at odds with the notion that Ancient Rome actually represents a stable sense of order. Funnily enough, Caesars Las Vegas is also physically an accretion with an underlying sense of order but aesthetically a bit of a mess, as was Rome, which grew from a village under the threat of order but didn't as a result end up looking ordered at all. That sense of order is an idea rather than a resultant fact. Le Corbusier was shocked that the real Rome was such a mess. But remember, such urbanity just crept up on the Romans; they had only just got around to stringing some rooms together. When Le Corbusier went looking for solutions to a highly industrialised economy in 1928, he had an idea of Roman order that just wasn't there.

We can particularly see this new conjugation of inhabited forms, composition, in Hadrian's Villa, which builds in such curiosities as an island for sulking. We can see it particularly in the plan, because what we have here is much more advanced than any Ancient Greek accommodation built around a tree trunk. We can see that rooms are constituted and stuck together using particular forms of arched roof, either barrel or dome or a combination of the two. Le Corbusier famously sketched the remains of these barrel-roof structures and employed them himself: they leant themselves to a concrete construction applicable to the twentieth century as much as the first. One of the lasting legacies of Ancient Rome, accepting that the know-how was lost during the Dark Ages, is something as straightforward as concrete construction.

So in Roman architecture, we find the first popular evocation of what might be pleasant to live in if you were highly privileged. Pliny the Younger wrote a series of letters outlining the design of commodious villas in the country, deemed the Laurentian and the Tuscan, which have inspired myriad built and unbuilt interpretations ever since. It is conspicuous that he never seems much interested in building material and construction (so to some extent he misses the point of Roman achievement), but as a diplomat perhaps he found such considerations below him, and perhaps it is with pointed relief that he described instead the subtleties of presence, outlook and atmosphere.

Ancient Rome  **37**

This pursuit of the agreeable architects will not shake off, despite herculean efforts, for the next nineteen hundred years. In the early nineteenth century, the German architect Karl Friedrich Schinkel, in particular, seemed to take Pliny to heart, especially at Glienicke – when he was building a retreat for a prince on an idyllic spot south of Berlin overlooking the Havel as it broadens into the Jungfern See – and in a series of buildings where complex aspects (rather than forms) are the key to their pleasures (see chapter 6). Meanwhile, the Postmodernists (see chapter 10) found Pliny, as an enthusiast for the experience of architecture, rather a saviour and antidote to the aggressive functionalism of Modernism. Hence a project titled 'Pliny's Villa' has periodically been a stalwart in the architectural curriculum as a chance to test both students' powers of literary interpretation and their poetic sensitivities ever since.

Pliny was so obsessed with the genteel that he took time to elucidate, at considerable length, the soothing contribution of particular flowers, shrubs and trees. It is not as if he were doing the weeding or enjoying the symbolic importance of the laurel or the oak – here we are presented with buildings that are definitively in relationship with the landscape for the purposes of enjoyment by a refined class. It is tempting to say the concept of landscape architecture is born here, to be exploited fully in the great villas of the Renaissance, such as the Villa Giulia in Rome (1555), an ensemble piece par excellence that includes thirty-six thousand particular plant specimens amid the orange blossom. Of course, all this is rather at odds with the ruinous monumentality we experience at Hadrian's Villa or the Palace of Diocletian (which makes up most of the Croatian town of Split) and that has inspired quite the opposite: a sense of Roman mass and volume and the detritus that mired the streets of Rome.

# 4

# THE GOTHIC

We are all aware of 'the glory of Rome', but we are less aware of the extent of Rome's reach. We get a bit vague as to exactly how big it was or exactly how long the Empire lasted. If we set the epitome of Ancient Greek civilisation at around 500 BC and we understand the Gothic period to have germinated at AD 1200, that gives us a bracket of 1,700 years, that allows the glories of Rome (including Byzantium) to occupy, conservatively, half of our human history as far as this text is concerned. But the Western Empire collapsed in AD 476, leaving seven hundred years very dark indeed. However, the geographical extent was enormous, from Scotland to Africa, from Persia to Spain, divided into two empires, and all under some or other notion of a republic. It is not surprising that the Roman enterprise has preoccupied our minds; it's almost as if we can forgive a bit of indulgence in the lion feeding.

The sacking of Rome, the collapse of such an apparently well-organised, boringly efficient civilisation (we do not gasp at the wonders of Rome; we more likely stand to attention), still occupies the mind. Was it debt? Was it Christianity? Was it decadence? Was it immigration? All these worry us because our modern world looks fragile too. Meanwhile, most of us aren't precisely sure who the barbarians who sacked Rome were, what, precisely, they stood for or whether we've now got them as neighbours.

This is an unauthorised history, and it's also biographical, and under both rubrics I'm leaving the late Eastern Roman Empire, Byzantium, out. This is of course a huge mistake, but I'm reminded of the chapter 'Mistakes I Have Made' thoughtfully included in the Marquis de Sade's memoir *120 Days of Sodom* or, more parochially, of rock writers like

**40** The Gothic

Chuck Klosterman who might routinely admit they have been remiss in omitting the influence of, say, Nipple Squeezer on the nascent Wisconsin hair metal scene.

The present trend is to attempt to let everybody play a part in the construction of history, to be inclusive. Great tomes seek adequate inclusion of everything and everybody, especially in such a conspicuously globalised world. But this is a technically insurmountable task, and one of the paradoxes of our technology is that those big important books tend to get read by fewer and fewer people. Biographers, meanwhile, face the very special task of empathy – they would give their eye teeth to know that Jesus winked at Judas; at least I would.

This book does not attempt an all-inclusive history, but to hardly mention Hagia Sophia, one of the greatest constructions of all time (or, for that matter, Córdoba, that apparently sublime orchestration of shade in the heat of southern Spain), still seems almost criminal. It pricks my conscience that my only experience of Hagia Sophia comes from repeated watchings of *From Russia with Love*.

In his *Journey to the East*, the great modern architect Le Corbusier visited a good deal of ancient material to set him on his way, but even he didn't get much beyond the Bosporus. A good friend of mine confirmed the sentiment one day – this confident Californian was driving through Europe with a group of friends in the late '60s, and when they reached that memorable strip of water, he just baulked; he wouldn't go any further. This could have something to do with our youthful entertainments, rumours, where we situate Istanbul as the extremity that will undo the Western traveller. The cloak-and-dagger stories of Rider Haggard, John Buchan and Eric Ambler come to mind – here drug-induced frenzy lurks, the beguiling sorceress, a land of strangeness and magic.

But actually I have experienced similar undoing myself. On a field trip to Venice, another crossing point of East and West, I found myself perilously drunk on a mixture of vodka and valium, plied to me in some bar or another. I didn't believe the bar was particularly unsavoury, but I was alone, and I woke up the next day with a black eye and a broken camera and as a consequence headed straight to the railway station for Vienna. So you won't find much of Venice here either, except later, when we go to Las Vegas.

So I am skipping the treasures of Byzantium ruefully, noting that even though I have marvelled at the early Christian mosaics in San Vitale in Ravenna, the Eastern Roman Empire's Western outpost (it's easy to forget that Hagia Sophia is an early Christian church, representative of Emperor Constantine's conversion and Istanbul as Constantinople), I find

PHOTOGRAPH 4   Cleopatra's Barge, Caesars Palace. In my mind terminally associated with the lounge act's '80s funk.
*Credit*: Julie Cook

no drawings of it in my sketchbooks. Serendipity plays its part; you can't have everything – some things are in, some things are out – so the early Christian Byzantine empire slips into the shadows, while a true northern phenomenon, the darkness of the Middle Ages, looms.

The barbarians may have been Goths, but we associate the Gothic with the northern Christian Church. The relationship overall is more complex than we might think, but to understand the churches we have to take some lessons (some diagrammatic planning moves) from the earliest basilicas, an eventual consequence of Constantine's Edict of Milan. Imagine taking two Greek stoas and putting them together in plan. What you suddenly have is a central space between the two sets of columns that we can call at first a market but later a nave, with two parallel outrigging enclosures we can call aisles; put an altar at the top end and shelter it in an apse of some kind and you have the basics of every village church. Why do this? Because the Christians needed to be saved to go to heaven – and saved weekly at least – in an organised way, so you have clergy and congregations and this all has to happen in an obvious building, perhaps with

**42** The Gothic

a bell tower reminding the populace of their obligations. Then you have to keep the rain off with a decent roof – one over the nave and two lean-tos over the aisles – and decorate the interior to get your message across, and there you have it.

The Christians were not predisposed to worship willy-nilly. They would not beseech Jove in the street when they burnt the toast. Christianity demanded lifelong commitment, and that gave the Church increasing power, grandeur and wealth. All that piety had to be looked after, and cleverly the house always got its percentage without ever having to deliver the goods. In fact, the more mysterious the goods were and the more all-encompassing the project, the better the Church was going to do. It is no wonder then, that St Francis ended up trying to convert animals and birds. Like capitalist business, Christianity had to grow to survive and thrive, and that's what it did.

No one should doubt the practical advantages to society that such faith brings. Supplicating a potentially rabble-rousing bunch of individual maniacs into a body of believers in basically good things seems like an excellent idea. Indeed, when this doesn't happen (see Postmodernism) we might worry. Christianity might take an ungainly chunk out of your Sunday, but it will make you feel better about your terrible desires.

So back in the land of the ice and snow; Kenneth Clark, in that milestone of arts TV *Civilisation*, notes that there can be no planning or use for great works of architecture. We make the best of what shelter we can in what is essentially a wasteland. We won't get a lot of architecture. Clark compares a Viking longboat to a Classical temple, something the moderns would understand (just as they enjoyed aeroplanes). But he is sure the Vikings lacked something, and presumably this is one of the constituents of civilisation: that the Dark Ages were indeed dark – dark with fear and superstition, unsettled, where beauty was best handheld, portable in the form of embellished gold, and the monasteries remote, isolated, so even kings couldn't read.

Whatever the 'Dark Ages' were, Clark reassures us that by the twelfth century, 'man may (once more) rise to the contemplation of the divine through the senses', in short, enjoy life or at least the prospect of the afterlife. Those were the words of Abbé Suger, and with him we rise from the gloom of the Romanesque into a new lofty luminosity, exemplified at St Denis and Chartres cathedrals, where apparently even the carts bringing the stone and provisions for its great rebuilding were drawn by knights and ladies of the nobility as well as by the peasantry.

This seems peculiar, certainly sudden, as does all the mythology of a golden age that pervades a certain conception of the Gothic era: the myths

The Gothic **43**

of damsels and knights and fairy castles and crusades, which we corroborate with the reality of angelic female figures (carved in stone) suddenly appearing on the west portal of Chartres and even the cultivation of the cult of the virgin herself.

But we fantasise. As a kid I would dress up in a sheet with a red cross on it and wield my sword – a bit of wood and cardboard – in the garden and under the stairs, just as I would later move on to homemade tommy guns and battles with the Germans. When I was a child, medieval dramas such as *The Black Knight* and *Camelot* were all the rage. Who's to say these ludicrous stories from Sir Walter Scott didn't provide that appropriate nickname for Margaret Thatcher, 'The Iron Lady'?

Some of these confusions over chivalry have had even more disastrous consequences, Nazism for instance, but they may also inspire youth's pilgrimages to Glastonbury (Avalon) and even the appropriate chapters in *Civilisation* ride high on an amplified respect for courtly love, perhaps Clark's own. For Clark, the chivalrous knight is the antecedent of the gentleman he was taught to be at public school. Schools, especially the new public schools (that are confusingly actually private schools) that sprang up as a function of the Industrial Revolution, instilled chivalry with great fervour.

Clark was enchanted by the period to the extent that he bought a castle in Kent and married a countess, but if we understand his background as the son of an industrialist who reputedly broke the bank at Monte Carlo and retired to the life of the idle rich, we shed light on his appreciation of St Francis as the saint who gave everything away, even his clothes. The filmmaker Pasolini (in *The Hawks and the Sparrows*) expertly parodies St Francis and his attempts to bring the faith to animals, but Pasolini was a Marxist; Clark was no such thing, and he loved dogs. Medieval courts were full of dogs, and the Clark family loved dogs so much that when Kenneth's son, Alan, was dying, he expressed his joy to be joining his favourites once again in the hereafter. Perhaps Clark's bubbling enthusiasm for medieval art, where women smile beatifically, should be viewed with caution, because they might be smiling because they had to. Instead, images of the burning of witches might come to mind.

Such romantic conceptions also led to the worst excesses of the Pre-Raphaelites, the home-decorating tastes of Jimmy Page and our own Houses of Parliament. They inspire Laura Ashley wedding dresses and leaded light windows. Indeed, the Gothic Revival is an all-pervasive Victorian English style, leading (by railway rather than charger) from the Houses of Parliament via St Pancras Station to Manchester Town Hall and

**44** The Gothic

beyond into Wilmslow's suburbs and my teenage bedroom. All of it is ponderous and pious and mega-gloomy.

Mentioning the Houses of Parliament twice, I went along to have a look, through the airport-style security, right into the corridors of power. Of course they are preposterous, leaden with gloom. You can hardly move for a knight here and a maiden there. If you were an architectural determinist, somebody who believes that buildings directly affect behaviour, you would be both appalled (realising that Great Britain is mired in baloney) and relieved (because you're a determinist who has just been proved right).

Religious Gothic labours the vision of both heaven *and* hell; it relies on redemption to one and fear of the other, and even as a believer (compulsory) you were permanently on the balancing scales. Our original barbarians, as well as our contemporary Goth tribes (for Goths do not go away, they simply reinvent themselves), probably were not originally concerned with (and have now probably given up on) heaven. They were and are diverse druid types. Today they might bond over Hollywood special effects, dark-side computing, fetish fashion, Walpurgis Night, Nosferatu, death cults or simply an overly operatic dress sense. The Leipzig Goth festival, held every year at Whitsun, embraces inclusivity to such a degree as to offer the umbrella 'all things dark'.

It is hard to imagine such a thing in the UK. It's not because the UK didn't spawn Black Sabbath, doesn't have its share of Cure fans or readers of Dennis Wheatley, but culturally we have not been encouraged to see the principal significance of the Middle Ages as 'dark'. Instead, we rendered it as our heritage. Hence UK heavy metal is, by and large, enriched with the ironic – dark *and* patriotic. Think of Saxon: led by Biff Byford (from Barnsley), Saxon manage to throw all the clichés into the mix at the same time; they ride fiercely patriotic wheels of steel. Their albums include the titles *Lionheart, Call to Arms, Sacrifice, Power and the Glory* and, best of all, *The Inner Sanctum*. There is a video of them somewhere perched precariously on the ramparts of a castle singing about maidens. You cannot say Saxon don't have a sense of humour. Thank goodness UK metal does not tumble freely to the depths of Death or Black Metal unless it migrates to Germany (or Norway) or LA.

But if Britain represents its dark side through either rose-tinted glasses or a sense of humour, Germany does not. German culture has fully embraced this dark side of humanity, for better and worse and in the name of the best and the worst. The Hanseatic churches are

The Gothic **45**

stern brooding essays in control; there's nothing light about them. Clark noted a sense of tawdry chic in the sixteenth-century paintings of Lucas Cranach. I read them as spooky/deathly. Cranach's allegories of Christian stories are populated not by the idealised figures you find in the southern Renaissance but by people who are clearly real people. As reformists (Cranach's company even printed Luther's Bible), they offer no distance; people are assuming the position, and most of them appear scared stiff. Who would even want to paint such a grizzly picture as *The Seven Ages of Woman* and who would hang it on a wall – unless you want to show that vanity is the work of the devil.

Too much at home with their dark soul, the Nazis (Himmler in particular) were steeped in the occult – the search for relics, the worship of the reliquary. This horrible fascination did eventually come to provide us with *Indiana Jones and the Temple of Doom*, but there I go again, illustrating my cultural difference and thinking of the Holy Grail primarily in terms of entertainment and not as something to be celebrated on a daily basis in a castle deep in Westphalia.

Whatever, the churches got bigger and bigger – they had to. New heights, more splendour (in England and France), more glory to God as these towering edifices rose above a confusion of shacks. Other than the cathedrals, monasteries and castles, what was there? Matthew Collings picks out, in his *This Is Civilisation*, the Hôtel-Dieu in Beaune. It is a polychromatically jolly giveaway. Hotel is not the word; it's a doss house provided by the richest merchant in France at the time, Nicolas Rolin. It is a pretty upmarket doss house for sure, but it reminds us of the importance, to Christians, of charity rather than entitlement. It's a leg up, a chance to pull yourself together; it's work ethic, bootstraps. We are not too far from these means of provision today. In a Gothic world, to show you care, and for the sake of esteem and a shot at heaven, you donate.

So this is a fine context in which to view TV Clark's rather nervous (anxious, as Collings observes) appreciation of the Gothic world. The alternative, the creeping socialism, the Reds under the bed, are a threat to *him* and all he holds dear, especially in 1968. Meanwhile Clark somehow finds himself in bed with our heavy metal artistes. The 'they don't like us and we don't care' attitude of, say, Bruce Dickinson of Iron Maiden is the corollary of Clark's privilege, and howling absurdity and strutting machismo have brought Iron Maiden vast riches, their own jets.

Meanwhile, post-Enlightenment, a desire to live in a castle finds us in interesting psychological territory. Even HRH the Duke of Edinburgh

**46** The Gothic

complained of the privies at Windsor. The draw must be the airs and graces of Camelot but include the fantasies of Cinderella, Sleeping Beauty, and perhaps 'mad' (but not) King Ludwig. But surely Dracula, Himmler and (at least in my case) Colditz come to haunt, and certainly 'money pit' looms large, as confirmed by Alan Clark's amusing diaries and the despair of many a foolish celebrity. In the medieval world, the castle was merely a hell of a lot better than everywhere else.

Money was no object to the Earl of Bute when he employed William Burgess to reconstruct his medieval heritage. A visit to Cardiff Castle (circa 1880) is highly instructive. We first note its distance from Cardiff Bay, where the dirty business of wealth creation was done, and the dark isolation and introversion the sumptuous interior provides (literal protection during the Merthyr Rising of 1831). It is authentic down to a room playing homage to the Crusades. Thankfully modest in scale, if not in detail, it is also comic: a monstrous absurdity incredibly well done. It would clearly be awkward to read a book in the darkness of a castle library.

But, having despaired at the social world of the Gothic, be it in Westminster Abbey or heavy metal, we have to admire the technical virtuosity. It still rocks. Those architects particularly interested in the material qualities of things (some call this materiality, but be aware that materialism carries a different interpretation in both the philosophic and the economic realms) will find themselves gravitating to the complexities of Gothic vaulting because it's fabulous. One is tempted to make a comparison to James Hetfield's fretwork.

Make those silly comparisons all you like, but we have to remember that for all the grandeur in Gothic architecture there is no bombast. Because (excepting those castles, an antisocial but no doubt necessary provision) it's all for God, and it is full of craft, anonymous craft: the embodiment of meekness. Meanwhile it pushes the envelope, then stretches it, always going one step beyond. It is also full of the spirit of doing it over and over again. It's not for slackers. Beauvais cathedral collapsed six times, but they kept going.

Students should be wary of merely liking the Gothic: as an instrument of propaganda we can hardly be ambivalent. The Victorians Pugin and Ruskin were certainly fervent believers, and enjoyment would seem dependent on understanding the theological iconography as much as the ruthless technical virtuosity. This view may become controversial later on, but in the meantime Chartres is hardly background. It is not something that should be playfully and picturesquely sketched; with experience it becomes a projection of heaven one either believes in or

The Gothic **47**

mocks. Meanwhile, of course, the Gothic also appeals to lovers of dreamy intoxication and fearful of the republic who might happily draw away for hours.

So personally, because I still believe we can do life another way, my favourite Gothic is the more plastic kind. And all of this guff provided the best name for an eatery in the most extraordinary outpost of Post-modernity in the world, a place where the house does occasionally have to deliver the goods and pay out. When I first saw it I wept tears of joy. Deep within the monstrous and brilliant fairy castle that is the Excalibur Las Vegas, the visitor used to be able to dine (not so finely) in Lance-a-Lotta Pasta before no doubt mooching down to the jousting show in the basement. Now that was funny, Lance-a-Lotta Pasta. That's life-giving spirit to folks like me — if we laugh at it, we can digest it. King Arthur would at least bring out the best in Monty Python. This is the bright side of dark side.

So I'm sitting in a bar in Charlottenburg in Berlin. It's a real vintage bar, and I come here every time I come to Berlin because it's around the corner from where we usually stay, but also it has come to represent to me what Germany is at its best. That is, while Germany may be the 'engine room of Europe', 'strongman of Europe', 'Champions of the World' (at football) or 'the banker of the Eurozone' and all those other clichés, it is also a place where human satisfaction is represented in order, insurance, assurance and total calm. It is quite uncanny. No matter what technological hoops BMW and Mercedes are jumping through for technological change and profit, here the beer is the same as it always has been, the sausage is the same as it always has been and, goddammit, that old couple over there who come in three times a week for their beer with a brandy on the side, if they aren't exactly the same as they've always been as well. The bar is painted dark as a cave, the silence is almost religious, punctuated only by occasional antique rock 'n' roll from the jukebox.

To me this is both charming and historically fascinating at the same time. People often ask us why we keep coming to Berlin for our August holiday. If I were to say that Berlin represents just about the most colossal hangover of all time, I don't think I'd be getting it too far wrong. For much of its history, Germany has been a calamity; for its relatively recent history, it has been in cataclysm.

Germany is the centre of the Gothic. The Goths, east of the Rhine and north of the Danube, proved a step largely too far for the Romans. Yes, they did occupy Dacia, north of the Danube, but Germania largely remained the territory of the warring tribes of the north. It makes sense if you think

**48** The Gothic

that 'forests' were just about the worst place for legions. Legions needed straight roads facilitated by maps that needed papyrus; Goths forged stirrups. The fact that the Visigoths, the Ostrogoths and so on sacked Rome is slightly bemusing; you can hardly imagine them wanting to leave those forests or forging empires, if by empire we might mean civilisation.

For us, forests are the land of danger. Bad things happen in forests, from bears to Buchenwald. If you want to hide something, you hide it in the forest; that's where the dead bodies go; Little Red Riding Hood. In forests you become disorientated, you lose your sense of direction, you become confused, it's dark and so on; you cry. Think of the fairy tales we consume as children; the vast majority seem to concern themselves with difficulties of getting 'lost' in the forest. However, for pagans the forest is a land of wonder, the home of Pan and a source of magic. The druids of course predate Christianity by thousands of years.

There are many ancient myths linking pagan and early Christian thinking that have consequences for our image of Germania, one of the most pertinent and most monstrous being carved into the Pergamon Altar – the first formulation of the Jews versus the northern tribes and of the notion of the strength and power of those northern tribes with their occult ways. This notion underlies Adolf Hitler's concept of a new Germania reinvented thousands of years later, but we should not forget the ongoing persecution of the Jews through the Reformation and Inquisition, when they were always defined as rootless and somehow not belonging, not at home in the forest or for that matter in the republic either. It is easy and rational to say this stuff is nonsense, but one day as I stared out of the window of that Charlottenburg neighbourhood bar, I saw a father playing like a giant with his child; she was hanging on to his thigh, and he was taking these giant steps with her hanging on. I couldn't believe my eyes.

After such dour thoughts it might do well to be sensible. The only thing remotely Gothic about Germany today is the guttural language and a few choice typefaces that you might still just find on remote railway stations. But aside from my excursions into the semiotics of heavy metal (which may be too much for aficionados), Goth fashion, a penchant for wearing black and strange hairdos certainly count. Western youth appears to have a secure enthusiasm for the Goth as a symbol of teenage rebellion and as a secure depository for teenage anxiety. I take a (very brief) look at a dating website for German Goth youth, which features lots of ridiculously huge boots and moody looks. It understandably makes me feel a bit peculiar, but I still want to go to that festival in Leipzig.

It is also peculiar to note that Leipzig is the spiritual home of the new Europe – where the first demonstrators gathered in St Nicholas's church

The Gothic **49**

against the DDR in 1989 – as well as being a centre for German culture in general. This festival, with its confluence of Goth streams (bit streams?) could perhaps become a Goth river, a Goth estuary, an all-pervasive darkness: 'rivers of evil, swimming in sorrow', as Ozzy sings. Or maybe it's just like Disneyland, where on a particular day, under the Californian sunshine, Goth kids don heavy black coats and boots and clamour to make signs of the cross at Snow White.

Our original Goths were in a world away from this indulgence in contemporary floating signifiers. It was a life-and-death business of life and death – on the doors of the basilica of San Zeno in Verona there is a prime example. On these giant front doors, cast in bronze, were instructions to the faithful that you could actually touch. Generations have rubbed their hands over special guidance regarding everyday events, such as chastity and childcare. The pregnant woman's tummy positively gleams with evidence of centuries' worth of hope and faith.

Alongside the church you would find a monastery. Knowledge had to remain the domain of the Church, especially dangerous knowledge; in fact, the containment of dangerous knowledge is the name of the game for those hundreds of years, and it is not until we get to the Renaissance or the Enlightenment that we can see things any differently. Think of a story such as Umberto Eco's *The Name of the Rose* for a populist evocation of such dark arts. Think why Leonardo da Vinci had to write in code, perhaps to keep his thoughts to himself and to avoid the charge of heresy.

Note that in the plan of a monastery as presented even in Banister Fletcher's *History of Architecture* there is nowhere to do anything which is not strictly prescribed. You can pray, you can sing (to God), you can weed the vegetable patch, you can sleep (but only in a dormitory and not for long), you can look after the chickens, but from there on your horizons are strictly limited. There are no baths. Contrast this with Rome, where we associate so much with bathing, with the pleasures of the flesh. Here the naked body is one of dread and prohibition, the devil's temptation, and aquatic enjoyment suddenly a vanity and dirt the mark of sanctity. The monks could travel, but only under necessarily filthy, therefore spiritually pure conditions, since water, especially the sea, was an unknown full of evil monsters. This was no beach holiday.

Instead, they worked for God. The carpenters and masons of the Middle Ages proceed in leaps and bounds. Consider the development of a church roof – consider that roof over the nave of San Zeno basilica in Verona. Understanding the components of a church roof, starting with the smallest component (a tile and its fixing), to the biggest, will tell you a great deal about architecture. Here matters are not mystical at all, merely practical.

**50** The Gothic

You can fix the tile along with other tiles to form a weatherproof covering only by overlaying them. It's worth looking out for the many ways of doing this and for the varied types of tile that have been developed for the purpose. But the upshot is clear – the tile is fixed, probably with nails, by a roofer and is the smallest component of the roof, probably because the clay can be fired only so big or the slate economically used so big. The tile can span only between and over other tiles and is fixed to the next component up, the batten. The batten spans in the other, horizontal, direction, whereas the tile spans vertically or, rather, to the angle of the sloping roof. The batten has to span a distance too, a bit longer than the tile, and it spans between the rafters to which it is fixed. While the batten spans horizontally, the rafters once again span vertically, or to the slope of the roof. The rafters are the next component up, spanning much further than the batten but still not far enough, so they span between purlins, which again are spanning horizontally. The purlins are much bigger than the rafters, and they span between the biggest component, the truss, the things you are likely to see articulating the space of that roof as you look up from the interior. These triangulated structures have to span all the way between the supporting walls and support the purlins, and because of their size and the demands put on them, even if there are relatively few of them, they can get quite complex, with so-called king and queen posts and hammerbeams.

The width of the nave is determined by the size of truss you can build, and since trees grow only so big, the length of the log or the extent to which you can join the logs together to make the truss will be the determining factor.

The only way you can go bigger than this is to vault the nave in stone. This has the advantage of being fireproof but the disadvantage of weight. And for now we've forgotten concrete, a Roman invention now lost. However, once we can make holes in walls by making arches, it is only a matter of perfecting technique to turn a two-dimensional arch into a three-dimensional vault. Vaults of ribs with infill characterise the development of the medieval masons and allow bigger spans than the length of a tree between supporting walls. But the masons soon discovered that the problem with vaults as opposed to trusses is that the vault pushes to some degree horizontally. The truss sits squarely on its supporting walls and all forces are resolved in the downward direction, but a vault to one extent or another pushes them out, so the walls have to be buttressed. Then, if you put holes in the buttresses, you get flying buttresses, and if you need more downward force on the buttresses you pile pinnacles on top of them, and you get a cathedral such as the one at Cologne, which

The Gothic **51**

from the outside looks like a huge porcupine, but that doesn't matter, because inside, with all those holes filled with elaborate stained glass, it looks like the kingdom of heaven itself.

A great deal of trial and error went into these structures. What we would call disastrous failure regularly occurred. The masons became secretive, they moved from job to job and met in their own hut where the clergy were kept out for fear of interference. They became quite naturally a kind of secret society, the origin of freemasonry and the ancestry of the professional status of the architect.

Cologne cathedral did not fall down, even when the Allies dropped thousands of tons of high explosive and incendiary bombs on it. Cologne was victim to the first 'thousand bomber' raid, in May 1942, and we can imagine on the one hand a sensitive colonel in the briefing room, reminding his bombardiers that the precious cathedral stood next to the railway station right in the centre of the city, and on the other, in this context of total war, some hours later, a steely rationalist bombardier drifting his B17 right over that same cathedral and pressing the button in preference to bombing the surrounding civilian population. We can also imagine that the fact that the cathedral survived (demonstrating almost supernatural power) might have severely spooked him.

The great cathedrals dominate our understanding of the Gothic. Domestically nothing much survives because much of the populace lived in hovels. Of course there are castles, whose design evolution depended largely on keeping up with the latest measures for assault. It would take the Italians to realise that being at war didn't necessarily mean you had to fight, and the business could become more symbolic. Eventually, general improvement in the social order would breed charming fortified houses, such as Stokesay Castle on the Welsh borders, to provide ideal homes for today's Conservative MPs.

So in England today we are blessed with Gothic lite, from the humble village church – iconic feature of the English landscape – to the triumphant cathedrals of Ely and Salisbury. But we have the medieval map of the world, the Mappa Mundi in Hereford, that in its accurate depiction of a psychology as well as a physical geography shows us just how horrific the medieval world really was – a world which could aspire heavenward but hardly map the coastline. There is a distinct kink in the choir at Lichfield cathedral demonstrating how well the gothic masons enjoyed going up rather than across.

We've categorised Gothic architecture politely into phases – Norman, Early English, Decorated and Perpendicular – each representing that ongoing struggle heavenwards, culminating in the jolly smart magnificence of King's College Chapel in Cambridge. We've adopted it as the

**52** The Gothic

style for the Houses of Parliament and dressed suburban homes and post offices and pubs in 'Gothick'. We've believed in it as representing us true Brits. Dotty but highly influential writers such as John Ruskin have championed it, William Burges created fantasy castles with it and Waterhouse Victorian town halls and railway stations with it. We have certainly overdone it, even if I still love those Sisters of Mercy records.

# 5

# THE RENAISSANCE

The Renaissance could not have happened without developments in trade, a certain rather fresh enthusiasm for the mercantile economy and a certain questioning of the role of the Church, all in a day's work as far as our civilisation goes.

This despite the fact that such a large number of Renaissance buildings are idealised church buildings, since people still wanted to prove how godly and righteous they were compared with everybody else. The standard example illustrating the birth of this phenomenon is Florence in the fifteenth century, as Florence became the centre for wool – English wool as it happens – coupled with the dyes that came from the East. But, as well as associating the Renaissance with Florence, we could associate it with Bruges, since that city grew the first bourse, and it was the banking houses that benefited as a consequence of trade, given their innovations in the world of international currency exchange, and that drove the Renaissance.

There were suddenly international ties to be considered as well as local disputes. You were unlikely to jeopardise your newfound wealth by wasting a further hundred years debating whether angels had wings; there were more practical matters to address. It was a tumultuous period, with Italian city states, principally Florence, Milan and Venice, and foreign powers, France, Spain and even Switzerland, along with the Holy Roman Empire, in continual competition and dispute. Sometimes they would actually fight, and sometimes they realised a standoff. There was fragility in governance, and it took Niccolò Machiavelli, a Florentine, to produce the one work symbolic of both the period and another birth of modern times: *The Prince*. *The Prince*, an amazingly readable book, simply gives

## 56 The Renaissance

advice to the modern prince on how to conduct affairs. It is practical rather than idealistic and hence witnesses a rebirth of politics. In the eyes of the Church, it came very close to being heretical, since, despite many passages reassuring the reader of the author's motives, it clearly puts man back at the centre of things. Quotes such as 'it is much more secure to be feared rather than loved' could after all relate to the Church at this time as well as to any prince, but that was not exactly the consequence of such a thought; the general consensus became 'the end justifies the means', clearly not an idealist, godly sentiment but a practical political one.

A system of continually warring families, states and nations was hardly ideal. Despotism would provide material and artistic gains at the great expense of others, and it would take the second great writer of the Renaissance, Michel de Montaigne (writing fifty years after *The Prince*), to write in mordant humour (both writers are enjoyed for their nonesoteric writing style) on the delights of scepticism, so setting us on the road to the Enlightenment (and Rome again).

However, Renaissance Italy did provide us with the most fabulous art and architecture, even if it appeared to come out of chaos. Filippo Brunelleschi began life as a clockmaker in Florence. Remember that Vitruvius wrote of timepieces and that the Pantheon in Rome measures, to some extent, the time of day, but by this time we are talking of the ratchets and weights of mechanical timepieces, demanding the skills of the silver- and goldsmith. Skill in such small balancing machinery was transferable to the siege engine or the pulleys and cantilevers of cranes and scaffolding. It was by this route that Brunelleschi found himself an architect, as a man of fiendish ingenuity.

Alongside this knowledge Brunelleschi also cultivated an interest in the architecture of the Ancients, travelling with his close friend Donatello to Rome, by now a place largely to be avoided through superstition and inhabited by derelicts. Travelling incognito, with a staff and a basic knowledge of trigonometry, he could calculate height by the length of a shadow; Brunelleschi hence began to reconstitute notions of order and proportion of ancient times, almost working archaeologically amid the long-plundered remains, excavating and measuring things right at his feet.

Brunelleschi also pondered the beauties of the eye as he formulated the rules of perspective via a curious little handheld device. Previously it was widely held that the eyes were like ray guns, outward sensors, and that whatever you saw was real. If you saw goblins, there were goblins. What Brunelleschi understood was that the eyes were passive receptors, that light travelled in straight lines and behaved mathematically. Goblins were an illusion.

PHOTOGRAPH 5 Our wedding at the Las Vegas Fantasy Wedding Chapel. Married by King Tut, with a belly dancer from Brighton and four schools of architecture on a field trip.
*Credit*: Susan Perry

He was also rather ugly, devious, antisocial, an excellent mimic and prone to playing practical jokes. One evening he got a particular enemy drunk, then slunk away to hide in the man's bed. When the victim arrived home, Filippo pretended to be him. Since the victim believed what he heard through his own locked door, he was driven mad; he believed a magic show. So Brunelleschi presents a rather classic combination, practical ingenuity meeting the reinterpretation of Classical sources under the auspices of an extraordinary personality. And he is our first modern architect.

And what ingratiates Brunelleschi's architecture to our eyes is a quality we cherish in the architecture of the modern period, for it is extremely modest. It can be playfully articulate in plan (look at the plan of the Foundling Hospital in Florence), but in appearance it is uniformly strict, stripped, with a colour palette of purely grey and white: ordered, calm. Both the churches of San Lorenzo and Santo Spirito in Florence exemplify these qualities. It is definitely not a reincarnation of the operatic splendour of Rome, and it embodies none of the strenuousness of the

**58** The Renaissance

Gothic; it does not have to try too hard and offers, despite the social context in which it was created, spaces of great repose.

The development of perspective certainly helped this sense of repose, and it began to be applied to the urban landscape in general. Ideal squares, ideal cities came out of the previously ramshackle. If we were created in the image of God, the idea seemed to be that we had now fathomed some of his tricks. Humanism was born. We could create places in the image of God-given harmony; more than that, we could dream of a sense of unity in the conception, all the pieces fitting together in this harmony. This harmony might be derived from mathematical ratio or music, then applied to plan, elevation and section. It might be less easy to commodify harmony in three dimensions, but the laws of perspective at least centralised vision. All this despite the fact that in the actualities of life (Brunelleschi no less than anybody else as a goldsmith), it meant working in appalling conditions of filth and stench.

Leon Battista Alberti, who had enjoyed a precocious early life as an athlete, linguist, pornographer (writer of fruity poetry), antiquary, art critic and diplomat, became the propagandist for this reinvigoration of the ancient Classical architecture with his *Ten Books on Architecture*, which became the first printed book on architecture, in 1485. This was essentially a reworking of Vitruvius with added zeal. Where Vitruvius seemed to see himself as a custodian of ancient knowledge, Alberti was overtly promoting the display of Classical virtue to the vulgar citizenry. In this sense it's a precursor to something we would see in the twentieth century – its machine-age counterparts, Le Corbusier's volumes *Towards a New Architecture* and *The Radiant City*. In his work Alberti sets out fascinating and useful information on when to fell trees, how to choose neighbours and the mechanics of pulleys, as well as redetermining the rules of elegant building, just as L-C railed about the stupidity of traffic wardens while setting out his five points for a new architecture.

The stratagem proved popular: there are rafts of examples, but Bramante is considered most representative of the mature reinterpretation of the Classical, even if it's for the tiniest of reinterpretations of a circular Roman temple at San Pietro in Montorio of 1502. Of the others, Vignola, Romano, Sangallo and so on, I'm going to deviate; I don't want to list.

Deviation, repetition, hesitation – that's how you got lost in *Just a Minute*, my favourite radio programme as a boy, but also that's what made the show. When lecturing you may lose your thread, pace up and down a bit, fill in with something else – you never really know what you might say next, and certainly I never read from notes. I think of the lecture hall as almost sacred, a locked room of initiates, of participants. In a book it's easy

The Renaissance **59**

to dry that sort of thing out, become too academic. That is why this book is drafted without reference books to hand, with conflict in Gaza and Ukraine and documentaries on wild boars on the TV, with the whirr of a small fan that struggles against Berlin at the end of July, and with only minimal use of the Internet (the Internet, of course, is the kiss of death to something as vital as lecturing to a group of real laughing, crying people). So we pause, and I pace up and down a bit.

Sometimes this book's questions revolve around conversations I have with my wife, Julie, in the bar around the corner. Things like:

'What music did they play in the Renaissance? . . . what did they have for breakfast? . . . what was the ideal shape for a woman? . . . was Brunelleschi homosexual?'

'I have no idea', I reply and then think about it.

'I guess . . . lutes . . . wine for lunch certainly . . . all the scaffolders on the Duomo [Brunelleschi's technical masterpiece] in Florence would have a flagon of wine for lunch even at such dangerous heights, and anyway the water was foul. I guess the shape of the ideal woman was "rich". . . at least potentially . . . and homosexuality was so rife that the prostitutes of Florence were asked to wear bells on their heads to remind the gentlemen of the "correct" orientation . . . it was thought to be (sapping the army) . . .'

And with such musings we get a renewed sense of an arduous, highly competitive daily life. Benvenuto Cellini (more of him later), also a goldsmith, complains of being charged with having sex 'the Italian way' and his need to keep a girl in his back room ready for his every pleasure. His exploits include swordfights with ruffians sent to hijack gold he's only just been given to carry out a commission. The level of double-cross, intrigue, pettiness, deception and duplicity that seems to mark those times is extraordinary. Casanova seduces his mistress while the husband wants to watch, from the vantage point of a secret cupboard; Casanova falls in love with a young girl, or is it a boy? When we see politics as it was then, it is not the same as the politics we see now, which, while venal on an international scale, rides a platform of our supine resignation at home. This is ducking and diving for high stakes every time you leave the house.

No doubt if I'd read the Ancient writers, the Romans Plutarch, Cicero, Seneca and so on, Greece and Rome would become more alive too, but even Claudius fights shy of detailing Tiberius's bestiality. Above all, history is a work in progress. It unravels before our eyes, and over the years, and over the centuries. Mies van der Rohe, the great twentieth-century architect, was known to prize the thoughts of St Augustine, but Philip Johnson (see chapters 9 and 10) claimed he'd never seen him read a book. So as I sit here I want you to realise this is a live document; you must forgive my lack of reading of Seneca and Plutarch (or St Augustine), but at

**60** The Renaissance

least savour the fact that I know by this stage in my life that they might be important and that they may become so to you.

That out of the way, let's get back to our impression of Michelangelo – Michelangelo Buonarroti, the original artist diva. There's a funny scene in the 1965 film *The Agony and the Ecstasy* where Rex Harrison (playing Pope Julius II this time, rather than Caesar in *Cleopatra*) is about to go into battle having laid siege to Perugia or Bologna or some such place and is confronted by Michelangelo, played by Charlton Heston (who also played Ben Hur), brandishing his roll of cartoons for the Sistine Chapel. While his commanders keep running up to him urging the pontiff to get on with it and with cannonballs raining down around him, the pope instead spreads the drawings out on the ground and proceeds to haggle over Michelangelo's fee. The scene seems so outlandish it appears ridiculous to us, but perhaps it wasn't at all. Pope Julius II was a good military campaigner, forger of alliances and great patron of the arts, and here we just see him doing it all at the same time, condensed.

If you'd been watching the whole film you would have seen Michelangelo himself, in rather camp fashion, receive his inspiration for the ceiling from a dramatic configuration of cloud forms he witnesses from the summit of the quarry where he is cutting his stone. And we are confronted by ongoing hysteria; his *Pietà* (1499) – a sculpture of Mary holding the dead Jesus, found just inside the portals of St Peter's – is as well known for the sobbing crowds that continually gather in front of it. In 1972 an enraged geologist even attacked it with a hammer while shouting, 'I am Jesus Christ!', so it's now protected by bulletproof acrylic.

The *Pietà* represents the astonishing combination of naturalism and Classical composition under the auspices of a religious theme. It is perhaps the pinnacle of high Renaissance. It is important to realise that in Gothic art the general rule was that the most important figures were shown the biggest; here such a basic conception has been utterly overturned, and in this marble we do feel the pain. Michelangelo was so proud of it he signed it, something he would never do for any other work, for he suddenly felt it one step too far for a man.

But Michelangelo the architect is also temperamentally theatrical; his combinations of motifs are so fluid and unusual as to demand the term 'mannerism'. His Laurentian Library features a fairly outrageous entrance stair, while his entrance gate the Porta Pia (1565) for Pope Pius IV features an unusual feature in the decoration of the upper round windows, which appear to be draped in fabric. These are barbers' towels, reminding us of that pope's worthy origins. His Piazza del Campidoglio atop the Capitoline Hill not only features a domed and richly patterned floor; it

# The Renaissance 61

arranges the buildings to inversely exaggerate the perspective on reaching the top of the grand steps leading up to it.

We might view divine inspiration as contradictory to the order and proportion we associate with Renaissance architecture. It's hard to imagine the passionate artist who had just completed the Sistine Chapel finding the manipulation of mere Lego-like blocks sufficient. It wasn't. Michelangelo disturbed the language and emphasised the sculptural dimension, so the Laurentian Library antechamber is tall and small like a pit, with that overexaggerated stair bulging out, while the library is long and thin like a tunnel. Pevsner compares this stretching to a similar exaggeration we can see in Tintoretto's painting *Finding of the Body of St Mark* (1548), so others were doing this, too, but then Michelangelo jumbles up the components so that they no longer make logical sense. This is why Jacob Burckhardt was more inclined to think his moves 'an incomprehensible joke of the great master', somebody who was confident enough to bring it off. Meanwhile we can imagine him as impossible to work with, demanding at every turn. We might also think it all a bit over the top, but that gives us another lesson, that nothing ever reaches stasis, that somebody always pushes things on, or over, the edge.

Michelangelo appears as the darkest philosopher within the famous papal room fresco *The School of Athens* by Raphael. There he is brooding in brown while Plato points upward to heavenly purity (perfect circles) and Aristotle down to earthly facts (imperfect circles), both surrounded by clumps of all the other thinkers, collected in the grand embrace and perspective of the Church. Perhaps this is the summit of the Renaissance; too, this representation of largesse, the grand accommodation of ideas all in one. While we can envy this state of affairs, all balanced and correct, we soon realise this is not quite the case anymore. Michelangelo's precociousness prefigures the Romantic, the madness of Goya or Velázquez – who painted royal figures with the faces of doughnuts – or our twentieth-century Francis Bacon, who painted those tormented popes like salivating animals. Once 'God is dead' we shall certainly reap the whirlwind. But nevertheless we stand in front of *The School of Athens* in awe, for what was in Raphael's grasp and not our own.

Times were certainly not dull. The Villa Giulia was the party residence of Pope Julius III. Vasari might credit himself with the overall design, Vignola the main villa, Ammannati the playful waterworks; even Michelangelo pitched in.

It features a delightful nympheum at the bottom of the garden running three storeys into the ground: a land of the frolicking nymphs, possibly literally frolicking nymphs if this pope's reputation is believed, frolicking nymphs usefully hidden behind a large wall. Of course such grottoes mimic the Roman excavations of the time, where wild pagan scenes were

**62** The Renaissance

found painted on the subterranean caverns. They were functional, too, for the cool waters of the nympheum soothed the pope's gout.

So the representation and control of nature, the taming of (wild or otherwise) nature, as well as historical reference, was now the very subject, and obviously this resulted in various contortions when it came to relation to God's will, the Church and the Garden of Eden. At the Villa Lante at Bagnaia, near Viterbo, in central Italy (Vignola 1564), we can see that man's control of nature is represented by the channelling of water – from the gurgling spring of the grotto to its passing over a series of obstacles to its eventual presence as delightful fountains and playthings. With the world more secure, the world of gardening extends beyond the cloister and extends across the landscape as a series of formal open-air rooms. A narrative is established that demonstrates how far we've come, so where do we go next?

With such power came a problem. The Reformation, the reaction against the hegemony of the Catholic Church, was much facilitated by a northern invention of Johannes Gutenberg around 1439: the movable-type printing press. This machine – just as the computer has done across the Middle East today – facilitates rebellion. The dissemination of information is sometimes more provocative than the understanding of it and is often sufficient to provoke anger among the already aggrieved. It was Martin Luther who took pubic offence at the Church for the selling of indulgences (indulgences were one step on from the promise of heaven; they were actual tickets), and he wasn't afraid to say how un-Christian this practice appeared. Meanwhile, he translated the Bible into a vernacular that ordinary Germans could understand.

He was excommunicated in 1521, but in the north the Reformation gained sway. Some found it personally advantageous (Henry VIII of England, for instance), but for the Catholic Church principle was at stake (the cumulative formulations of Church practice); there was no way you could have people running around saying that the teachings of the Catholic Church were no longer consistent with the teachings of the Bible. Hence the Inquisition, memorably explained in the chapter 'The Grand Inquisitor' in Dostoyevsky's *The Brothers Karamazov* or by Monty Python in 'Nobody Expects the Spanish Inquisition'!

In architectural terms the Counter-Reformation, the Catholic Church's response to the Reformation, was a beano. The public had to be convinced of the need for discipline and the power of the Church just in case they turned heretical, and new churches would become more operatic and more extreme in their depiction of the rewards of correctly pursued faith. Ignatius Loyola (1491–1556) founded a fanatical Jesuit order that undertook a series of arduous spiritual exercises to the higher

The Renaissance **63**

truth. This can be seen physically manifest in the Loyola chapel in Rome (1722), which demands you stand on one spot to comprehend the whole of God's world in all its rollicking glory. When you leave that spot, you don't get it any more – a perfect metaphor. Loyola's fanaticism (or the notion of Opus Dei) was thoroughly exploited in the blockbuster *The Da Vinci Code*.

This retaliatory swing is commonly termed the Baroque (around 1600), where architecture – even church architecture, especially church architecture – would turn into a veritable ice cream cone of complexity and movement. We should remember that the Roman Church was everything. No event, no medical calamity, no birth or death, no affair of state, not even the buying of a bun seemed to preclude its intervention. The Inquisition courts held numbers you might find at bullfights through the sixteenth century. You needed the Church for everything, to become a lawyer, a doctor, a teacher, anything. And the Church became very wealthy (while all the time, according to Luther, it shouldn't be).

Remember Jesus turfing out the traders from the temple? Remember 'usury'? The making of money without personal effort, this was a spiritual crime according to the Holy Bible, but it was exactly what the new currency exchanges engendered. Once merchants had developed a system of international exchange, where invariably currencies were valued higher in their place of origin than elsewhere, variable exchange rates would inevitably make money without any effort. To stay on the right side of the Church, the merchant bankers donated vast sums of money, and, as the cash rolled in, the Church decided to continually fudge the issue (or build more glory to God), something anticapitalist campaigners note even today. Only Savonarola, with his 'bonfire of the vanities' (when even Botticelli burnt his own paintings), took a stand, only to be very quickly assassinated in 1498.

The Catholic Church was rich, but just like our multinational companies today it needed to be richer, since it had competition. Meanwhile, the mercantile economy brought more wealth, and opulence impressed clients. Baroque architecture was like advertising; it was rabid self-promotion to the masses in an age before television and magazines, and its masters were Borromini and his foil, Gian Lorenzo Bernini.

It's best to think of Bernini as a Hollywood stylist, maybe Warren Beatty. You go to the right parties, you have all the right connections, you can do something this way or you can do it that way, so what do you fancy? Probably Bernini's best-known work is the great colonnade in front of St Peter's in Rome – giant arms to gather the flock – but his most representative is probably the *Ecstasy of St Teresa* in the Cornaro chapel of Santa Maria della Vittoria. This is far better described as St Teresa in ecstasy

**64** The Renaissance

because that's certainly the state she seems to be in. We almost enter the world of special effects. It seems part stage set, part sculpture, part painting, part simpering sentimentality, part gushing ornament and part orgasm. It is certainly something, but it is also so OTT as to leave us rather a longing for simpler fare. Goodness knows what Bernini would have served up if he were a cook; probably he'd work it like Heston Blumenthal.

Borromini, on the other hand, is the crazy man in the attic, a reclusive genius who hated everybody and probably didn't eat anything at all. In a Baroque world, I believe Borromini to have had positively Gothic inspiration. Borromini spends most of his life working on one building, San Carlo alle Quattro Fontane, also in Rome (Rome, with the Vatican, has now recovered). The planning alone is extraordinary, for on an irregular site he squeezes all the elements together, eating every inch of spare space as well as constituting balance and symmetry, even in the slightly oddly shaped major volume. This need to constitute a series of major volumes within irregular sites is now common as the city becomes more constrained. We use the term 'poche' or 'pocket' to stuff all the awkward bits in. For a small church, this building provides a dizzying experience even when encountered for the umpteenth time.

It remains to squeeze in another phenomenon, but a highly significant and influential one. Without the poise of Brunelleschi, the drama of Michelangelo, the operatic onslaught of Bernini or the craziness of Borromini, Andrea Palladio worked in the opposing Venetian republic, with much of his work being villas for the wealthy landowners or, better, farmhouses. So this marks him out, for we don't really consider him a city architect – even though the city of Vicenza is a World Heritage site in his name. Of course he did city buildings, but that's not what we think of when we think of him; we think of the Palladian villa.

And he wrote the third book in our story, the *Four Books of Architecture*, in 1570. It became, over a considerable period of time, highly influential and especially influential in England, so I'll return to him later.

Moving on from the Baroque, I get into uncomfortable territory. The Baroque spreads north to confront the reformists, right up into Austria and southern Germany, not without fabulous events – Guarini in Turin, for instance – but slowly morphing into Rococo. It is tempting to think of the Rococo as ormolu done by dwarves or Tiepelo by the yard.

The mechanism it is constructed upon – the collusion between the Church and the nation-state and a mercantile explosion for the benefit of the great families of Europe – makes it a particularly distasteful environment to talk about, let alone walk through. These are the great palaces of the new royal families of Europe (see chapter 6) that nonarchitects think of as architecture.

The Renaissance **65**

Students walking into architectural school with an enthusiasm for this sort of stuff – for Versailles, for example – will certainly be tolerated but could quickly find themselves ranked with enthusiasts for Ceausescu's palace or Imelda Marcos's shoe collection. Usually there is at least one smidgen of an architect's soul that wishes to improve the world. There is a conspicuous morality to the business after this period. Today's conscience still makes architects generally painful to be with, a bit pious: Bernini's life as one long lunch seems ridiculous. So your architectural student is soon more likely to be captivated by Borromini than by Bernini, since he was starving and mad – although absorbing the lesson of Bernini would buy that same student a better car. That is, unless the student is a contrarian, like Robert Hughes, who preferred Bernini for kicks.

So much of what sightseers and parents think of as the great architecture of Europe unfortunately falls into this category: really sightseeing and theatre. Even so, some of it is pretty good; even Le Corbusier loved the Petit Trianon.

First on the list would be St Petersburg. Go to St Petersburg in winter, say February, and make it a Sunday, when the snow still falls and the Neva River is frozen over, and stand on the bank that looks back at the Hermitage. Make it around noon. Well, you won't be standing; you'll be hopping up and down on the spot and very pleased to have your strong boots, big coat and proper Russian fur hat. Watch the stream of walkers as they trudge across the river with their prams and dogs, disappearing like dots into the buildings on the horizon, buildings so gently composed in their pastel colours against the white that you cannot help but think: 'Yep, that's what a city should look like' and then, just as you are indulging yourself, a gun will go off – a real artillery piece, mounted on the fort behind you – making you jump two foot in the air. They fire it every Sunday at noon to remind everybody of the horrors of the Siege of Leningrad, when people ate the leather from their own shoes and licked the dried wallpaper paste off their walls. The combination of all those things makes for quite a moment.

We were filming in St Petersburg. A particular hound would turn up everywhere we shot as if by magic, like some mystical thing. The hotel bar was full of hookers, the corridors would flutter with them, and it was vodka for breakfast. I felt this very civilised indeed, except it wasn't; as in all things Russian, there was another Russia. They would build the fronts of those palaces in stone and stucco, but behind lay old Russian squalor, the hold on civilisation very tenuous. We lapped up what we could and made a souvenir of the shell casing from the gun, stinking of cordite. The airport security took no notice at all.

**66** The Renaissance

St Petersburg was the creation, from nothing but swamp, of Peter the Great (1672–1725). Peter lived a colourful life not without incident. As a young man he travelled all over Europe, even living in London's Deptford for a while. He was not afraid to mingle with the masses in disguise, generally be rather badly behaved with his companions – drinking, gambling and womanising – but when he returned, and realising the need for a strategic Baltic port for the Russian navy, he decided to build St Petersburg. The conditions under which it was built were atrocious. Thousands and thousands died, but his creation became the jewel of the north, not for individual buildings but for the way it all fits together: in fact a composite of all the architectural delights Peter had savoured across Europe, a bit of Amsterdam, London, Paris, Vienna and of course Venice. Dare I say a sort of eighteenth-century Las Vegas? One of the best moments is the cathedral, a miniature St Peter's.

St Petersburg became the fountain of high society. Actresses and actors from all over Europe were summoned to the court of Catherine the Great, including Casanova's mother, from Venice. Architects too: one in particular, the Scot Charles Cameron. From 1600 on, people were on the move, be they intellectuals or opera singers. Those who could do so migrated among the great houses on a continental scale. Talent was imported and exported among the great palaces. It's a sort of globalisation, if not quite on the scale we see today.

English gentlemen and women took to the Grand Tour to acquire an aura of sophistication from the natural glories of the Alps as well as from the cultural delights of Italy. One of the most fortuitous was the English architect Inigo Jones, who was particularly struck by the work of Andrea Palladio.

Pre-Jones, England was prone to architecture as gaudy spectacle, often *by* Jones in the form of the masques featuring mechanical intricacies and special effects that made his reputation as he presented them to court. The content of these masques was often Classically themed (and written by Ben Jonson), paving the way for the architectural version. Once in charge of solid building as surveyor to the king, Jones took to his Palladio and substituted outward dignity for Tudor exuberance. Nowhere can this be better appreciated than in his rebuilt and, at the time, radical Banqueting House of 1622, where those fantastical masques were sombrely accommodated in an austere box we now hardly notice, since its Classical language was almost universally adopted for officialdom across London's Whitehall.

One of the reasons Inigo Jones enjoyed Palladio was that he was more readily accessible; his pupil Scamozzi was still showing people around Vicenza. Except for the Vatican, Rome was comparatively more difficult;

even Montaigne referred to it as 'not so much a ruin as a sepulchre of ruins'. The Grand Tour was still a tricky business, and to make off with a couple of Titians and a Tintoretto or two took a patron, connections and a good deal of perseverance as well as a pocket full of gold coin.

In the Renaissance the excess wealth, once gleaned, stayed put. There was no international investment market as we see it today, so the glories of Venice come out of the money that Venetian merchants made and put back into their own limited back yard. Inigo Jones and his ilk represent a shift, an investment market in art objects whose use value is overwhelmed by their exchange value. A pot that was once used becomes definitively unused – as unused as it possibly can be, but highly valuable – when placed in a museum.

Palladio's country farmhouses would become as appropriate to the landowners of England as those of the Veneto; they were cheap but looked expensive. Meanwhile, London developed quickly. Charles I, without Parliament behind him, lacked funds, so land was sold to individual noble families, eventually leading to the London landscape we know today, developed under the Bedfords, Tavistocks, Grosvenors and so on. In 1630 the fourth Earl of Bedford commissioned Inigo Jones to overhaul Covent Garden (the old convent garden of Westminster Abbey), which occupied the squeeze between the City of London proper and Westminster. By developing the Classical piazza with a cheap church (the 'finest barn in England') and surrounding houses where the newly institutionalised leasehold and freehold preserved the rights of the original family, the Bedfords were able to remain rich in perpetuity. The Duke of Westminster is still the richest native Englishman as a consequence of this formula.

Jones started the modest Queen's House at Greenwich in 1613, and we can immediately see the usefulness of Palladio. Wait a hundred years and you've got the ultimate Palladian copy – Chiswick House, built by Lord Burlington – but cast your eyes further and you will see Palladian country houses springing up everywhere, from Stourhead to Mereworth. We might presume, simply on the look of them and a certain English conservatism, that the style caught on because it was relatively cheap, preserving modesty with commodity in more ways than one. 'Firmness, Commodity and Delight' is the English translation of Vitruvius's definition of architecture, brought to us by Sir Henry Wotton in 1624.

However, there is more to it than that. Classicism ingratiated itself as intellectual. We construct our landscape, but we also read it. Palladio was building on what was essentially drained swamp. His advice in the *Quattro Libri* says some very straightforward things in such difficult physical circumstances: for instance, put your villa on a hill (for ventilation and health), put it in the middle of your estate (for observation purposes as

**68** The Renaissance

well as practical convenience), put it near a river or canal (for convenient transportation of yourself and trading of your produce, which is likely to be stored within the villa compound), and make it close to a good straight road (a pleasant legacy of the Romans).

Importing the image might not garner all significance, while contemporary artists would cleverly adapt to the fresh circumstances. We should note the influence and enthusiasm for the Neoclassical paintings of Claude and Poussin. These are all constructed landscapes, but beneath their lyrical constructions lay subtle messages. There is supplementary information to the extent that T. J. Clark has written a whole book about just two Poussin paintings. Looking at Poussin's *Landscape with a Man Killed by a Snake* (1648), we see that our notions of horror are merely a function of proximity. Once we've got that idea in our heads, CNN TV news and drone wars become rather more interesting than they might have previously. Just as he did then, Poussin pricks our conscience, so paving the way to enlightenment.

# 6

# THE ENLIGHTENMENT

I scratch my head as to exactly how the great empire states of the next two hundred years formed themselves north of the Alps – how the Hapsburgs spanned from Vienna to Lisbon, how Italy was gobbled up and how three people being thrown out of a window in Prague led to a thirty-year war. I wonder at how Cardinal Richelieu managed to consolidate the French state at the expense of his nobles (but then run out of money) while the English contrarily established theirs with Parliament (priming a golden age).

Richelieu dallied with the Protestants; so as far as Reformation and Counter-Reformation went, the ends really did justify the means. Whatever the case, the New World was a source of funds, since Columbus had turned the world around, and the gold of the Mayan found itself transported into the king's new cruet just as soon as Cellini had disposed of his ruffian muggers.

The concentration of power allowed building on a vast scale. The Baroque cities of Paris, Vienna, Naples, Barcelona and Turin and the newly commercialised London and Amsterdam show us what centralised, or at least cohesive, planning can do. At Versailles, the whole landscape as far as the horizon is crisscrossed by the Sun King's expression of order, while 129 windows per floor look out over it. Such set pieces can come over as bombastic, overbearing, antagonistic to the spirit, but sometimes they are a relief, well handled, as in the Plaza Mayor in Madrid, commissioned by Philip II of Juan de Herrera, one of the more delightful urban experiences in Europe.

Overall, what were just straight roads became vast boulevards extending way beyond the confines of city walls. Baron Haussmann drove them

**72** The Enlightenment

through Paris for Napoleon III, so as to disrupt a rabbit warren of revolutionary enclaves but also to provide overall better utilities. Meanwhile, Amsterdam boasted an organised municipal plan designed around the infrastructure of four-lane canals with regularised house frontages, and London became an agglomeration of streets, squares and mews with their characteristic section.

When the English king ceded lands to the English nobles, he precipitated not only the streets and squares of Georgian London but also the country houses of the National Trust, and we begin city building, no longer in an *ad hoc* fashion but ordered for the rich if not yet for the poor. The history of city building is beyond the scope of this book, but in Europe we see the beginning of palaces as city blocks divided into apartments, with many enterprising configurations of plans to squeeze the appropriate multiple occupations and functions within. In England and America, the block is subservient to the terrace, an altogether easier job. Any casual observer will note that negotiating the corner is generally a more elaborate architectural puzzle in European cities than it tends to be in London or Chicago. But we are getting a little ahead of ourselves, for the pace of city building will not accelerate until the mid-nineteenth century and after with the Industrial Revolution.

The silversmith Benvenuto Cellini's *Autobiography* and Casanova's *Story of My Life* present us with a cavalcade of brigands and distress, pomp and imprisonment, piety and party. Both proceed from the sublime to the ridiculous, as if the era were ready-made for parody in *Carry On Henry* and *Carry On Don't Lose Your Head*, fine evocations bracketing the period. In fact, seeing as Casanova's story runs to ten volumes in the original and even Cellini's is indulgently dense, you might do well to spend just an hour or two giggling at Sid James as he plays the effete Sir Rodney Ffing, who describes himself as 'bored with balls' while attempting to sell life insurance to the Duke de Pommefrites. Other enduring popular references would be *Dangerous Liaisons* and *The Three Musketeers*, and even Ian Fleming gives more away than he might in relation to the bad and the beautiful when, in *Live and Let Die* (1954), he has the villain, Mr Big, setting the highest standards of 'subtlety and technical polish so that each of my proceedings may be a work of art, bearing my signature as clearly as the creations of, let us say, Benvenuto Cellini'.

With absolutism across the continent, power was now centralised at court rather than in the monastery, and these gilded cow sheds, or mirrored cages, were now everything in one: entertainment centres, universities, offices, garrisons, residences, chapels, casinos and theme parks. Indeed, there was a merry-go-round of travelling among Paris, Madrid, Potsdam, St Petersburg, Venice, Vienna and Stockholm, all

PHOTOGRAPH 6   One of the most magical views in the world. As one student put it after a lecture, 'the only poetic thing you've said all evening': filming across a frozen Neva River, for *The Treasures of St Petersburg*.

*Credit*: Julie Cook

in the thrall of kings' and queens' and courtiers' cash. These courts showed mastery of the universe in a grand, self-conscious performance, that is, until the balloon went up with the Montgolfier brothers, and suddenly our perspective on the world changed, just as it would do with the aeroplane and the moon rocket, much to the annoyance of Louis XIV.

Why absolutism? It is the conjugation of many things: gunpowder made armies bigger, there was a disconcerting awareness of power for its own sake (and therefore of vulnerability at the other end of it), there was the necessary divvying up of world treasures in empire, even a knowledge

**74** The Enlightenment

economy to be controlled. We might be reminded of Marshall Berman's comment: 'the narcissistic will to power, most rampant in those who are most powerful, is the oldest story in the world'.

But as soon as this happened, you had the birth of its nemesis – the revolutionary. Edward Gibbon had to be spirited out of Oxford to more liberal Lausanne. Eventually Gibbon's critique, almost but not quite heretical, called Christianity's bluff, encouraged thoughts of the rights of man and of life beyond one's station or the hereafter.

The most top-heavy would fall first, as the new spirit of reason entered through the stage door. Voltaire epitomised that claustrophobic atmosphere where wit collided with virtue. Within absolutism, any notion of identity is dependent on rank within the court, yet suddenly the rights of the people were a subject of debate or at least entertainment.

The excesses of Louis XIV may have been legion, but they were also axiomatic of the role: he required at least two hundred servants to enable him to run France by himself, and that does not include his advisers. Indeed, he was 'France' even in bed; meanwhile, he was no slouch, a hard worker (it was his descendants Louis XV and XVI whom we associate with ruin). To us, understanding the difficulty might lead us to consider a contemporary pop star's sycophantic dressing room and publicity machine.

When it comes to enlightenment we should think not just of England, of Newton and Gibbon or even of Scotland (Hume and Smith) but also of Holland, where Descartes roamed about avoiding people, Rembrandt painted anatomy classes and Vermeer those cool, studied interiors. All this while the Rococo swamped the Danube. And in Holland, Spinoza was not only a great thinker but also the manufacturer of the best lenses for those new inventions the telescope and microscope, and that in the age of the Inquisition. And in Vermeer we see those maps, a fascination hardly surprising in an enterprising trading nation.

'The design and construction of mechanical instruments', 'astronomy', 'Latin' and 'the works of Aristotle' are all packed into the Wikipedia entry for Sir Christopher Wren, who went to study in Oxford in 1650. He turned his hand to architecture and made a naval hospital one of the grandest buildings in all England: a naval hospital, illustrating of course the importance of the navy and respect for the victims of global exploration and booty. Meanwhile, when London burned down, it provided the opportunity to plan – not entirely successfully – or at least to implement standards, and Wren got to build his great churches as a political

The Enlightenment **75**

instrument. Wren's London churches (fifty-one of them) especially demonstrate his dexterity in planning on what were often difficult sites.

Wren has an equal but opposite figure (just like Bernini) in the figure of Nicholas Hawksmoor, and if you asked a general question of architecture students as to who they preferred, they would again say Hawksmoor rather than Wren. Hawksmoor got to do only six London churches, but they show more curious and arcane juxtapositions than Wren's and are far more intriguing than the efficient buildings Wren designed. And of course Hawksmoor was the underdog.

In France, Montaigne and Montesquieu led fairly directly to Voltaire. Voltaire was trouble, but he was still invited to the royal court at Sanssouci (Potsdam) by Frederick the Great as a benevolent gesture of admiration. Predictably, the personalities of the two men were incompatible. They fell out as Voltaire satirised the opinions of the president of the Berlin Academy of Science, and, while on his way home, Voltaire was arrested at an inn in the dead of night.

The Royal Societies were awash with argument. I'm not going to dwell on the philosophers too numerous to mention – Descartes, Kant, Rousseau, Locke, and the Scottish writers Hume and Smith – all of whom interrogated the status quo.

I suppose the excesses of Versailles might be enjoyed before we join the Revolution, but only briefly. Le Corbusier admired the Petit Trianon for its proportion, although I've never heard anybody sing praises of Marie Antoinette's 'Petit Hameau', a revolting exercise in picturesque poverty. The Hall of Mirrors might be accidentally subversive, I suppose, and was copied by Adolf Hitler for his (short-lived) Berlin Chancellery. St Petersburg is amazing, but Charles Cameron's is a cautionary tale.

Connections were everything, and ambitious Jacobite Scots held certain advantages on arrival in Rome, and these could be extended, even if that Jacobite heritage was fabricated, to St Petersburg, where the formidable Catherine II put great store in her Scottish physicians and the Scots in general.

After a spell in Rome groping around the customary choked-up ancient cisterns and vaults as well as plundering contacts and constructing identity, Cameron pulled together a number of 'corrected and improved' drawings for his book *The Baths of the Romans* (1772). This made him something of an architect (since at that time it was still a self-proclaimed title), as he had at least finished off some drawings by Palladio while purloining others, uncredited, from Isaac Ware.

But, while exhibiting the engravings in the correct societies and publishing his book in London, Cameron hit trouble, suing his own father

**76** The Enlightenment

(with whom he lived) over the theft of some books and busts, so that Walter Cameron was detained (and died) in a debtors' prison. Now socially outcast, Charles had little option but to seek work abroad. Emergent St Petersburg, an architectural marvel founded only in 1703 and where Catherine now hired expertise 'like a bag of tools', was the obvious choice. It is not clear exactly how he got the job, but the situation demands immediate comparison with opportunities offered in the Gulf States more than two centuries later. Once established in Russia and experiencing difficulties with the local labour force, Cameron advertised for clerks and brickies in the *Edinburgh Evening Courant*.

Of course the wily empress had to be charmed, but luckily Catherine had fallen out with one of the more truculent of her architects, Clérisseau, and may have been looking for a lighter style, a breath of fresh air, given her palace: one of the more colossal Baroque barns, plastered in ornamental goo, that she was busy 'refurbishing' at Tsarskoe Selo. She wrote, wittily, that her present architects were 'too old, or too blind, or too slow, or too lazy, or too young, or too idle, or too grand, or too rich, or too set in their ways, or too scatterbrained' to do her any good.

Luckily, Cameron didn't get on the wrong side of her. Today the apartments in Tsarskoe Selo that Cameron renovated do not quite give the impression of total lightness of touch that so delighted the empress – think of Adam and Wedgwood combined with a 'mania for building . . . like drunkenness' and you won't go too far wrong. However, his freestanding attachment, the Cameron Gallery, is as exquisite a piece of neoclassicism as you are likely to find.

But the moral of the story overall is a sad one. Given the jealousies within courtly life, Cameron's career died with Catherine in 1796, and even back in England, the hasty decisions of youth still meant he was considered of insufficient moral character to be offered honorary membership in the newly formed Architects' Club, in 1791. Both his predecessor in the Russian court, Rastrelli, and his successor, Brenna, died in abject poverty. Staying in Russia, Cameron avoided that, but only just, via a few royal favours.

When the French Revolution came, it brought its own structural calamities to the processes of building and architecture, never mind style. Guilds were now unconstitutional, sitting uncomfortably between the rights of the individual and the general will, bringing a crisis in production. Meanwhile, the Roman style was predictably employed, speaking so readily of the republic even if it felt a little anachronistic.

There was revolution in America, too. The British Parliament, wanting to tax their colonies, was rebuffed with the phrase 'No taxation without representation' (as immortally delivered in *The Great Escape*). This brought the Declaration of Independence, whose principal author was an architect, Thomas Jefferson. This document incorporates the slightly bizarre notion that people have a right to happiness.

Jefferson chose the Palladian style for his own house, Monticello, since he was immensely practical by nature. He was so practical as to state that the president must have a good wine cellar, even though the new United States was broke. He believed a good wine cellar and decent dining room for the entertainment of visiting dignitaries would conceal the lack of a navy. There is more to this than meets the eye: when you think of American construction in general, you realise that solidity is not one of its strong points. Even the most upmarket homes with their present-wrapping rooms (and whatever) are generally built of balloon-frame timber construction, so named because it was feared they'd blow away. Timber America had plenty of, labour it did not, and this technique lashed buildings together sufficiently. Of course, we soon get back to thinking of Hollywood and set dressing. While this attitude would be all-pervasive, it would later breed, in Sullivan, Wright, Kahn and so on, a strong reaction towards the organic, a longing for something more substantial.

Jefferson was well travelled himself and laid out guidelines for US visitors to Europe on what they might want to see to help establish their own country on firmer footing. The list starts with agriculture, goes down through industry, pointing out the knowledge gap but hopeful the 'can do' attitude will prevail. The list ends with architecture. As for art: 'you might want to look at [it] but don't waste time on studying it'. Even now, we Europeans and the Americans display these stereotypical prejudices. Julie has often found her European photographer friends classed as 'clever Europeans' by her US friends, and it is not meant as a compliment.

Meanwhile, Jefferson also parcelled out the land on a strict grid system. You bought a parcel of it and you could do what you liked with it within reasonable constraint. This in itself explains why New York looks like it does with its ever-competing skyline, but it also explains, as I walked around downtown Houston (with a far smaller business district), why you can still find the small juxtaposed with the extraordinarily large. It is a consequence of that chequerboard and the spirit of democratic liberalism.

Back in France, David might have been painting *The Oath of the Horatii* (1784) for the king, probably a very worried king. This striking picture is about loyalty and duty, impending death and virtue, and once more refers back to the Roman Empire – this time evoked in the service of the monarchy against the approaching republic (the meaning of the picture swings

## 78  The Enlightenment

both ways). The three brothers share a dramatic moment (the dynamism is as palpable as it is slightly ridiculous) as the father presents his sons with the swords of battle. Note that the picture shows the moment before the battle. The brothers pledge themselves to their father while the women weep in the corner (their husbands fight for the other side). It's obvious but powerful.

So you are either with us or against us. Less than ten years later, on the execution of Louis XVI, in January 1793, the revolutionary Louis Saint-Just declared: 'One does not make revolutions by halves'. He declared plenty more, too, classics such as 'A nation regenerates itself only on heaps of corpses' and 'If they want neither virtue nor terror, what do they want?' The French revolutionaries went on and on about virtue. Virtue had a special meaning then above that which it might suggest now, when it could easily be slang for 'a better than average House record'. It is much discussed in the ancient classics, and resuscitating it had some major consequences, since it is a term generally applied to the business of when and how to die honourably. Remember the slogan of the French Revolution: Liberty, Equality, Fraternity. It's the third one that might surprise, for within this quest for rationality there is also imperative to stick together, a warning of the threat of counterrevolution.

So when is revolution necessary? How does it happen? In August 1917 Lenin gave a derisory and necessarily short address to a disappointed crowd because he knew they weren't ready. It wasn't until October that he believed they were, when they seized or, rather, scuttled up the back stairs of the Winter Palace in St Petersburg. So revolution needs circumstances. And it needs an idea.

Back in France, in 1793, it would be good to say that as despotism fell, a new version of events, a new organisation of the people based on the thoughts of the Enlightenment period and notions such as the rights of man triumphed and everybody lived happily ever after. On the one hand that is true and on the other it is not, because the French monarchy was restored at least once and Europe plunged into the Napoleonic wars. The lesson of history is that this always happens except when you are Stalinist about it, and then you are in danger of chucking the baby out with the bath water.

There are always problems. When the guilds, which had previously negotiated rates of pay, were abolished because they represented protectionism, there was no longer effective worker representation in disputes. The bricklayers and stonemasons, already up against it, became even poorer. The imposition of the truth of an idea comes up against everyday life. 'Freedom' might mean one thing to an employer, another to a

The Enlightenment **79**

politician and something quite different to the worker. The problem is that you can't get rid of the idea.

An idea is something based on truth, when something becomes truthfully apparent. I'd like to think that despite our apparent plenitude we still might not confuse ideas with desire. To fancy fish and chips for supper is one thing, but perhaps such musing should be accompanied by the unfortunate realisation that fish-and-chips shops are disappearing while the discount supermarkets, with their unfeasible enticements and unrivalled disappointment, proliferate, in short, that 'real cod' has become a matter of degree. More provocative, when thinking about Claude Nicholas Ledoux's scheme for a brothel (as we shall), we might be reminded of the idea that (at least traditionally) an erect penis is not a crime against humanity but a progenitor of it.

What is striking about Casanova's description of pre-Revolutionary France is the degree of delight, knowledge and wit he brings to the scene. He brings us to it as a kind of epicentre of culture; after all, French was by now the polite language of all Europe. But what is most interesting is that we can suddenly see Casanova as nothing if not a man of contingency, of behaviours and manners. Whatever he might be – charming, intelligent, seductive and hilariously funny, whether he is a priest, a soldier, an ambassador, a magician or a violin player in the orchestra (for he was all of these things) – he is not a man of virtue. Instead of ideas, the court represents the cult of sensibility. Kenneth Clark finds the epitome of Rococo decoration in Amalienburg, in an amazingly elaborate interior done by Cuvilliés, and that's all very well until you realise that Cuvilliés was originally the court dwarf.

Read Casanova's passage when he recalls his meeting with Voltaire, and note not only the subtlety of their manners but also some deep, lurking idea:

> 'This', I said, 'is the happiest moment of my life. I finally meet my teacher; for twenty years, monsieur, I have been your pupil'.
>
> 'Honour me with twenty more, and promise to bring me my wages after'.
>
> 'I promise; but you must promise to wait for me'.
>
> 'I give you my word, and I will sooner fail to keep my life than my word'.

General laughter apparently applauded this initial sally by Voltaire, but Casanova takes the jovial ripostes merely as a symptom of manners and wit.

**80** The Enlightenment

We could take a look at another book, better known through the 1998 film adaptation staring Glenn Close and John Malkovich, *Les Liaisons Dangereuses*. The story is set in the 1750s amid the pre-Revolutionary life of the French court. It involves deception, betrayal, cruelty, sex and wit all at the same time. The bored aristocrats have little else to do with their time. What is memorable about the film is the finesse and delicacy epitomised in the performance of Close and Malkovich. We used to call that decadence.

So take this term 'virtue'. Virtue is thrown into sharp focus when we consider the notion of resistance. To resist the Nazis in Prague in 1942 and to assassinate Reinhard Heydrich held no guarantee of success or even of survival, but, against the prevailing mood, a small group managed it. At the time they couldn't have imagined the outcome of the war, nor can we assume they took it on as a whim. We now think of these people as heroes, and that's the point – we *now* think of them as heroes, in retrospect. Those resistance fighters established something worth dying for, and it was the right thing.

The terms 'stoic' and 'epicurean', despite being ancient paths to virtue (and this is virtue as opposed to the merely good), might now refer to things hardly linked at all. People may react in a stoical way when they lose their job, and 'epicurean' is likely to be a classy way to describe somebody who likes his food. When university students today are presented with the word 'virtue', they might reasonably reply, 'Well, I suppose patience is a virtue!' But look at an earlier text, from Michel de Montaigne talking 'On Books', struggling, but at least struggling, with questions of judgement in a highly self-deprecatory way in the second half of the sixteenth century: 'Knowledge and truth can lodge within us without judgement; judgement can do so without them; indeed recognising our ignorance is one of the surest and most beautiful witnesses to our judgement I can find'.

So amid all the Rococo set dressing, architecturally, this period will look to the setting for virtue. It is rife with projects that might represent new ideas, that look like revolutionary projects. The problem is, its stars, Claude Nicolas Ledoux and Étienne Boullée, were locked up by the Revolution, rather than fought for it. Perhaps they were misconstrued. It's proved easy ever since.

Ledoux's project for a brothel, where the plan is clearly that of a pair of balls and an erect penis, might be considered a very important step away from the Classical language and into something else. Ledoux's work is Classical in the sense it uses Classical volumes, spheres and cubes and so on, but they are stripped of decoration and Roman only in their control

The Enlightenment **81**

of light and their massive scale. Ledoux might then be seen as an architect who makes progress away from Classical stagecraft towards something called *architecture parlante*, or speaking architecture. Clearly the brothel scheme 'speaks' of what it does, its functionality rather than generality, through its plan. This is quite a big step for architecture and foreshadows the pattern books of Durand, where 'type' is carefully analysed. However, asking a serious student to use the brothel scheme as a precedent for a design scheme 'nowadays' has always proved an unmitigated disaster. Why is this? We can't seem to take it seriously.

Ledoux designed and built a very striking royal saltworks at Arc-et-Senans in western France. Best seen from the air, this ideal farm comprises a perimeter circle of drying sheds and other accommodations necessary to the operation, with a central bar of major accommodation running across the middle. It puts the master of the works at the centre of the composition, with all the other elements nicely subservient but correctly unified around him. Only part of the overall plan, which would have comprised a whole circular city of righteousness, was completed. (Whole circular cities of righteousness can be an appealing idea. When the Nevadans needed to build Boulder City for the workers on the Hoover Dam, they didn't want anything to do with the free-for-all evils of Las Vegas up the road, so they went concentric.)

The German court showed greater restraint and practical charm, and there was far less volatility in the populace. In 1824 King Friedrich Wilhelm III employed Karl Friedrich Schinkel to build him a tiny summer residence, not much more than a four-square house, adjacent to his palace in Charlottenburg. Rather like our own appreciation of a simple, rough Chianti, this shows the king at his most sophisticated; it is, after all, a house, not a palace. It is sterner, perfect and disciplined, with lovely details (note the painted star motifs on the underside of the balconies), so delightful as well as very strict. The interior, far from the intricate web of gold ormolu, looks like something you could find in *House and Garden*.

Schinkel's Gardener's House in the grounds of Sanssouci in Potsdam is a masterpiece in the same vein, but this time a low-key rendition of the Classical vernacular, with exhortations to the prince not to drink too much carved in as he dawdled there in the company of his friends (euphemistically speaking, his gardeners). Of course, the glorious complex of the Sanssouci Palace was and is still there, but that is not what attracts us today. We are more likely to be found scouting the periphery of the park, wondering what might or might not be the work of Schinkel, this architecture being so unassuming.

**82** The Enlightenment

This is no Petit Hameau; this is not chocolate box. We might be reminded of how the River Café – originally a restaurant built to serve Richard Rogers's architectural office and opened by his wife and Rose Gray – became successful as the place for the new political caste that was New Labour. It served simple, good-quality food, the sort of thing that might be cooked up on a roadside in Tuscany, and it became very popular with those movers and shakers of the 1990s clutching their first mobile phones. Jamie Oliver graduated from the River Café, and, whether you find him engaging or not, you can't dismiss his efforts for our general well-being. It's the same thing going on, the flag of honesty and understatement.

The Gardener's House is a complex arrangement of modest tower house, pergola and ornamental courtyard, including authentic Classical remains and a small re-creation of a Greek temple, all organised with great poise around an axis reflected across the passing of water from stream to lake to garden to water trough (and eventually to actual greenhouses), recognising – just as at the Villa Lante but in far less resplendent terms – the importance of water to the gardener. And under the pergola the prince would take time off with his friends, no doubt charmed by the rusticity and trying to stay off the booze.

Schinkel was a man at home designing in either the Gothic or Neoclassical style and even came to England to fill his notebooks with its new industrial architecture. In fact, Schinkel's place in architectural history reflects the virtuosity, dexterity and subtlety he could bring to almost anything.

It's good to find architecture that quietly supports human action rather than shouting, be it an operating theatre or a restaurant. One of Schinkel's greatest ensembles is almost invisible – okay, there are a couple of golden lions here and there, some fountains – but if ever there was some architecture that just begs you to chew over stuff for a couple of hours, it's Schloss Glienicke. On first encounter, it elicits little response other than 'is this it?'

The complex is summed up by the Casino, overlooking one of those stretches of water the Berliners have cultivated for their pleasure around Wannsee. It's a large building that looks tiny, for one thing, reminding you that there have been contrary objectives to those of contemporary despots and encouraging inner calm in the dappled sunlight. To us, it's almost a joke it's called a casino.

So with Schinkel, who was so clever as to be appointed director of Berlin architecture at around the age of twenty-five – painter, architect, visionary, technocrat and bureaucrat – we have an architect at the top of all games and, for the first time, master of the understated. But even he

The Enlightenment **83**

had his off moments. His vast design for the portentous (and thankfully never built) Cathedral to the Wars of Liberation of 1814 evokes a tangible sense of some inner darkness, and we can't help but reflect, in retrospect, on some looming cataclysm.

In France, we have foreboding too. Post-Revolution, the new machinery of governance needed administrative technique, and the swashbuckling Baron Haussmann (1809–1891) was no callow figure. He seemed to understand the post-Revolutionary balance of power: 'With all local councils' he said, 'it is all a matter of knowing how to set about things', and set about it he did, and always to his own advantage into the bargain.

He worked his way up the prefecture through the reign of Louis-Philippe, persevered through the revolution of 1848 and was running Paris for Napoleon III by 1853. There was largely modern government, with large ministries and power struggles, and, of course, an emperor. But Napoleon III needed to remain popular, sharing goals for public well-being and their suppression at the same time, lower taxes *and* re-housing. The energetic and nothing if not self-regarding Haussmann was charged with the task of letting the people have their cake and eat it.

Haussmann realised that the ministerial status quo undervalued the revenues that would come with growth, and he was committed to 'transformation' if not exactly free-market enterprise (France was slower to react to the Industrial Revolution than England). Haussmann enjoyed six-hour meetings with the emperor and had a huge – 9 × 15 foot at 1:5000 scale – map of his new Paris built on castors to be studied like an altarpiece.

His subsequent interventions came in three phases, at once an invasion of the geometric and the demolition of the old fabric of the city, undoubtedly the mark of the prime organiser, and cutting swathes out of the admittedly squalid realm of the revolutionaries of 1848. He wasn't an architect and had no great architect to hand, but his dramatic contribution shined 'by dimension rather than by grace and harmony'. The crowning glory was supposed to be the new opera building by Charles Garnier, but there were continual grumblings that it was a bit of a sham.

Parisians must have experienced a certain déjà vu when Le Corbusier exhibited his Plan Voisin in the same tradition in 1923. The experience of political cleansing even tainted both the building of the Pompidou Centre and the redevelopment of Les Halles (originally a Haussmann project) following the riots of May 1968. Meanwhile the *Grand Projets* of the leftist president François Mitterrand in the 1980s

**84** The Enlightenment

were also criticised as crude. In city building all these represent the ongoing dialectic between identity and inhabitation on the one hand and ownership and forced development on the other that continues to this day.

But it is England that was secure enough politically to take advantage of what became known as the Industrial Revolution, building new industrial cities from scratch. And in England we see the procrastinations, distractions and tribulations affecting the new bourgeoisie, or middle class, regarding how to dress their new corner shops of whatever scale: a battle of styles between the Gothic and the Classical but underpinned with iron.

# 7

# THE INDUSTRIAL REVOLUTION

I summon up 'Rockin' in the Free World' by Neil Young, a live version from YouTube. It's 2009 and everything is still all wrong, but Young is relentless, visceral, steady and loud and great, and at that moment sixty-four.

It's splendidly emotive of our whole capitalist enterprise, because we are still in it, this Industrial Revolution, whatever phase you choose to place us in. It's still a world of investors and profits. Its manufacturing phase was home to me, my father being a production engineer, until I left home for university when I was eighteen.

My father was brought up on the Welsh borders, his father rooted in the business of cider apples, with a fledgling transport concern with a Mercedes truck you could hear ten miles away. Leaving school at sixteen, he served an apprenticeship in engineering, learning everything from metallurgy to sales over six years. Now in his nineties, my father tells the story of walking into the works manager's office at Ruston & Hornsby and declaring he wanted to be the best production engineer in the country. The director was so taken aback he took him seriously: nobody was particularly interested in production engineering at that time, it seems; it wasn't very glamorous. My father changed his name from Ashley to Brian, and after a long career performing a close approximation of his ambition in those companies of legend – Paxman, Mirrlees Blackstone and Gardner diesel engines – he retired amid British manufacturing's decline. I always thought he blamed it all on the 'Trots' – the agitators he hated – but later, more sanguine, he blamed it on the bosses of the corporation, by now Hawker Siddeley. 'More profits', he said, 'they

**88** The Industrial Revolution

wanted more profits'. He'd always hated those board meetings when he was summoned down to London's Mayfair.

So there you have it. That's my story. My postgraduate students often ask me why the texts they have to study always mention Karl Marx. 'It's a critique', I say. 'Capitalism doesn't offer its own critique; it thinks it's natural', and therein, of course, lies its flaw. As Marx approximated, it's not enough to observe the world; the point is to change it. There is a sense across the nineteenth century, among anybody who really thought about it, from Goethe through Dickens, and ever on to Neil Young that day in Hyde Park, that the Industrial Revolution had unleashed powers that, unless harnessed, spelt our doom. Remember the most efficient factory in the world, the one with no labour costs, would become Auschwitz. And if you didn't feel like thinking about it, religion and laudanum were there to assist.

Certainly this revolution would not bring tightly ordered cities reflecting the natural order of things. The Industrial Revolution, 1750 onwards, brought chaos.

In that this phenomenon happened in a particular place, Britain, and resulted in the creation of a particular city, Manchester, a wealth of factors came into play. But with industrial Britain we see the fruition of Empire, and in the birth of Manchester we see the modern metropolis and the modern way of life, the like of which we had never seen before. We might say that what Manchester was to the nineteenth century, Silicon Valley is to the twenty-first.

Simple things confuse us here, the northwest of England: damp, wild and full of sheep, the word 'mill' which we associate with flour, and cotton, which we confuse with wool. Cotton a product superseded hemp and flax products like calico (which have rougher fibres) largely produced in Far East. Cotton became Britain's primary import and export of the Industrial Revolution. Grown on British-owned plantations of the New World by slaves, it was imported to England and processed in mills for export. In the post-Napoleonic years, cotton products made up precisely one-half of the value of all British exports.

So the Industrial Revolution is a global business (just like the Florentine wool and Spanish gold), but it relies on entrepreneurship rather than patronage; the aristocracy are hardly involved. Those who became wealthy as mill owners were likely to have invested piecemeal in relatively accessible technology; they might have previously run pubs. The steam engine did not require the services of rocket scientists, and as the population grew there was a larger pot of freely available labour with particular and easily taught skills.

Engineers – a broad term ranging from anybody who whacks something to make it work to those who redesign the whole apparatus – came

PHOTOGRAPH 7 Looking rather Keith Floyd in Delphi while filming *The Treasures of Athens and Olympia*. That was our joke, the Floyd thing. There was always a hair problem.

*Credit*: Julie Cook

into their own. They also embody entrepreneurship. There are suddenly engineers in all fields and at every level. This makes the architect, still raised on the orders and with professional manners, look a little anachronistic. Certainly it's a case of architects dressing the things engineers come up with for the next century to make them look respectable.

England feeds its industry with labour. Exactly why the population grew is a matter of some debate, but think of soap, of medicine, and think improved agricultural production and distribution most of all. Certainly at this time England had a larger pot of labour than France to put to use; the population of England grew from 6.5 million in 1750 to 14 million

**90** The Industrial Revolution

by 1831. For whatever reason, France appeared to maintain what we would now term 'craft' methods of food production for much longer; hence our appreciation of all appellations *français*.

The technological development of the cotton mill happens quickly; a couple of generations see the shift from spinning wheel to 'Spinning Jenny' to 'Mule' and the arrival of the distinctive industrial architecture to accommodate the throng of workers, 80 per cent women and children, who toil as 'hands'. The distinguished German architect Karl Friedrich Schinkel was sufficiently intrigued by this new world to come to take a look in 1825, making notes on the multiple-layer long-span flat-plate structures that became progressively more elaborate as the century progressed. Several remain today, converted to hotels and fashionable loft apartments.

Perhaps used to the perils of gambling, the aristocracy looked on, thinking most of these endeavours too financially risky, perhaps rather tawdry, for them. But they sold their land for mills and railways and enjoyed better prices as their farmlands supplied the growing cities with food. The nub of it is that industrialisation relies on buying cheap and selling expensive. It relies on cheaper and cheaper labour (slaves/women/children), manufacturing costs (mechanisation) and transport (canals and latterly railways), and it relies on markets buoyant enough for manufacturers to sell at a profit. Even after the abolition of slave trading, in 1807, Manchester mills continued to source the cheapest cotton by hook or by crook.

Manchester was the town from nothing. From the banks of the River Irwell sprouted chimneys like mushrooms. Half of it, Salford, was so awful it hardly gets mentioned. Bits of it were holes within holes. The river was black, the air was black, but Manchester's population grew from 40,000 in 1780 to 142,000 by 1831.

With the Industrial Revolution comes a social revolution that we witness almost every time we sit down to watch Sunday evening TV: almost any adaptation of Jane Austen or Thomas Hardy or lesser-known facsimiles such as *From Lark Rise to Candleford* or *North and South*. In these we will always find the arrival of the young man of ideas, usually from the city, who will wreak havoc on the traditional ways of doing almost everything. With country life destabilised and horizons opened, we also see people drift to the city on the basis of opportunity. After all, there's not much for them back in the village. Who has not had that urge to leave the family and make his or her own way? We see that on the TV every day too in the news, in India, in China.

But who wouldn't relish the anonymity, the opportunity and even the necessary alienation of city life – the bright lights? (actually no light; gas-lit mills arrived in 1805 – to extend the working day). I still find myself, after a trip away, arriving at King's Cross with a strong desire to shout

The Industrial Revolution **91**

expletives to the crowd. Nobody will care, that's the point! I'm my own man (except of course I'm not, only if I'm lucky), and of course I want that freedom, but I also want to meet other people just like me, make a new world for myself. Of course I don't necessarily comprehend how difficult this will be. Even the most taciturn of individuals, the twentieth-century master Mies van der Rohe, on first arrival in Berlin was promptly sick in the street, and it's quite possible that on the steps of Grand Central Station, New York, multitudes have sat down and wept.

Goethe (1749–1832) anticipated the whole process of development in his poetic tragedy *Faust*, a story that took up most of his working life. It basically depicts, in all its necessary tragedy, what happens when science comes to supplant the Church as the driving mechanism of human development. This is a big step; God isn't dead until 1877 (and will be revived in 1989), but put it this way: Goethe anticipates certain problems that will only be patched from here on in.

While sounding difficult and German, *Faust*'s initial themes are easily understood. First Faust is fed up – he's in mid-life crisis, if you like. He's off kilter, he considers suicide but does the equivalent of spotting *Led Zeppelin II* on the shelf, so puts it off. But he's up for anything except being ordinary and so makes a pact with the devil (science or mysticism or both) and in doing so acquires great powers (education and riches of all kinds). He makes a pact with the devil because he knows he won't get anything done just by doing good; you have to destroy to create.

He falls in love with Gretchen (a simple country girl) and she with him, but for opposite reasons, he because she represents what he's lost, she for his charm, gifts and knowledge. But Gretchen, if she goes with Faust, will leave her family behind, her support system; in fact, she does this inevitably by just hooking up with him. But when she cannot keep up with Faust, and when she gets a bit clingy and when Faust gets bored, she no longer has anywhere to go. She is doomed to a tragic end.

In any audience there are students who have left behind young love. He wanted you to go with him and grow cabbages in Australia, you wanted to come to London and discover a new intellectual world, whatever. Goethe's is an accurate prediction, and as the story moves on we get a picture of industrial development as a whole and its inevitable tragedies, and it's not only victims who can't keep up that form the tragedy; the process of development can't stop in itself. Such tragedies are the point of ancient literature, too, but with *Faust* Goethe takes us into the serious difficulties of a 'modern' age, why capitalist businesses have to keep growing to stay alive. Enough is never enough. One of the cardinal elements that the Devil, Mephistopheles, brings to Faust's development is the need for speed. Goethe uses six steeds as a metaphor, but think of the horsepower we can conjure today.

**92** The Industrial Revolution

In the end Faust is visited by four angels, named want, need, guilt and care. He manages to banish want, need and guilt but not care, and that is the moral of the story.

Of course this is an absurd description of a masterwork of great complexity, but I'm not here to offer you an in-depth understanding of Goethe's *Faust*. I don't have one myself.

England's production of iron soared from 20,000 tons in 1760 to a massive 700,000 tons by 1830. The value of England's cotton production rose from £4 million in 1750 to £270 million by 1830.

The mechanisation of the cotton industry broke first, but the mining of refined coal and its transportation to foundry-fuelled iron production made for the production of more machines: more engines, more rails, more constructional components for valiant bridging exercises – first celebrated at Ironbridge in Shropshire. Two engineers, Telford and, later, Brunel, were the pioneers.

Ledoux worked on mostly bridges in Paris, now benefiting from iron reinforcement bars infecting the patterns for stonework in ever more elaborate ways, and normative spans were overcome with a little hidden muscle.

Such ironwork would be an invisible component in the polite architecture of this time, evident only in the construction drawings, for most architects were arguing over pattern books of architectural appearance, a sort of exterior wallpaper – think of Nash's terraces in London, notoriously shoddily built but looking highly refined. But iron would make for its own expression soon enough, in the great Crystal Palace of the Great Exhibition and in grand glasshouses where plant species from around the world could be maintained and displayed.

There remains a good deal of interest in the organic in architecture, so it is pertinent that one of the key figures in the developing architecture of the Industrial Revolution was originally a gardener, at least an early horticulturalist. Joseph Paxton, with no formal education, made himself a great success from very modest beginnings. Nature and industry were for him conveniently entwined, and not just because he found inspiration for the roof of the Crystal Palace in the giant lilies he was famous for accommodating. As one of those piecemeal investors caught in the whirligig of development, he invested heavily and successfully in the railways just as soon as he could, becoming a director on the board of the Midland Railway and Member of Parliament for Coventry. He even started a newspaper with Charles Dickens.

This was a man of great industry, a model Victorian, never idle. On getting his first proper gardening job at Chatsworth House, Paxton not only arrived on site at 4 a.m. but had done a whole day's work and met his future wife by breakfast. Later his schedule was sometimes so busy he didn't eat for days. *Punch* put his early death, at the age of sixty-one, down to overwork.

He designed the Crystal Palace on a sheet of blotting paper during a railway board meeting. He drew it up, with the help of a railway engineer, in a week or so. It became as significant a building for the Industrial Revolution as Chartres cathedral was for the Gothic or the Parthenon for Ancient Greece.

Paxton explained his task in the manner of typical enthusiast. First he'd tweaked this, then that (his rafters, his sashes, his sash-bar notching machine, his glass). All these innovations were dedicated to reducing cost and improving performance, and all these things added up until he was ready to conquer the world, solidly and squarely. His greatest innovation, Paxton guttering, combined structural elements  with rainwater disposal and even condensation collection in single elements, so making for economy and lack of clutter.

It comes as no surprise that Le Corbusier mourned the burning down of the Palace, in 1936, in the pages of *The Architectural Review*. He had found 'the spectacle of its triumphant harmony' an inspiration; it had shown the way forward. Not only was it a triumph of organisation, a true work of modern man, but also it was higher than St Peter's in Rome. And Paxton had made full use of prefabrication to the extent that its components, once forged in Birmingham, were generally in place on the building within a mere eighteen hours. Meanwhile, for Paxton, presumably the industrial age and all it offered *was* organic. In thinking so, he escaped all talk of style and its meaning and (unwittingly) consigned academicism to the ash can. Paxton had drawn the sword from the rock.

Le Corbusier would also have sympathised with the burden, for the Crystal Palace was also notable as an event, a struggle. There was almost daily coverage in the press of its miraculous construction, with continual fears that it would blow away or be fearsomely hot. Paxton was no Nietzschean superhero; it was with the support of colleagues such as Brunel and his own aristocratic and business connections that such a blunt, solid, methodical fellow could hold on, addressing the Society of Arts in 1850, pleading for their forbearance, since he'd never had to do such a thing before.

It may not have been academic, but the Crystal Palace certainly meant something: a giant display case of Empire, a phantasmagoria like the previous St Petersburg or the future Las Vegas – the transportation of the world

**94** The Industrial Revolution

to one place for showing off. It was even fitted out with large magnifying glasses overhead offering unexpected, wonderfully disorientating glimpses of the next opportunity just over there, so the experience must have been not unlike browsing a box of Quality Street chocolates.

But it isn't generally the twinkle of sunlight on glass and the warmth of the conservatory we associate with the Industrial Revolution (although Paxton was interested in the amelioration of the appalling conditions with his parks and greenhouses, and he was quick to adapt his greenhouses to domestic conservatories). We associate it with vast outpourings of smoke and noxious vapours, with whole towns built with little thought for sanitation, with tracts of terraced housing built without foundation, forming the terraces and Coronation Streets of our northern towns – think of Bury, Salford, Bradford and Barrow or, for that matter, Clapham, only superficially one step better with a line or two of cornice. The business of architecture was an economic expedient for the most part; industrialists railed against any kind of regulation against the forces of the free market.

So the Industrial Revolution, perhaps unsurprisingly, sees architecture develop as a pattern book. In France, Durand put together a taxonomy of building types to fit the requirements of the vast new bureaucratic state, a bible for students of the Beaux-Arts schools, who, when asked for a library or museum, could simply memorise the appropriate pages and turn out the expected sketch, or *esquisse,* in twenty minutes.

Under the organiser Haussmann, many anticipated the state's financial ruin, but Paris boomed. Opportunistic landlords cashed in on the state-sponsored development to the extent that rents in the centre of Paris doubled between 1851 and 1853. What we now call social provision never materialised; workers could not even afford the attics, and Paris divided into rich and poor. The military defeat of Napoleon III by Bismarck seeded the rebellion of 1871 and the short-lived Paris Commune, whose 'Communards' Karl Marx could now hail as 'a glorious harbinger of a new society'. Haussmann had just made the rich richer, the poor poorer, and had brought down an empire in the process. He had also created what was to become, in Impressionist painting and Realist literature, the modern city of alienation rather than colourful squalor.

As Charles Dickens put it: 'It was the best of times, it was the worst of times, it was the age of wisdom, it was the age of foolishness, it was the epoch of belief, it was the epoch of incredulity, it was the season of light, it was the season of darkness, it was the spring of hope, it was the winter of despair, we had everything before us, we had nothing before us, we were all going direct to heaven, we were all going direct the other way'.

The Industrial Revolution **95**

That's Dickens sounding typically liberal, but militant workers could turn revolutionary. Could the masses seize the moment and overturn the system? Certainly there were regular riots in Manchester. This was the idealist perspective developed by Marx and Engels, the eventual triumph of the proletariat. If the French Revolution had emancipated the people of France and made the Rights of Man contagious, this would seem inevitable; even Napoleon had done his bit.

The capitalists were the enemy, eventually to be overturned, but even Marx was happy to credit the new bourgeoisie with achieving something. The men of ideas had freed themselves from the shackles of the traditional hierarchy and come up with what appeared to be great improvements via their own ingenuity. Marx analysed situations scientifically, in the spirit of the industrial age. Hence his viewpoint dwells on economics, on the logic and the mechanics of change.

Then there were those liberals, practical reformers, and those who spoke out: guilty pastors and sudden humanitarians. There were factions of revolt and factions of reform, with Dickens in the chair. But in Manchester at least, we can't expect to see any local political will for anything but the new status quo; after all, all this was lining the country's coffers as well as the pockets of the daring capitalists. It was not until 1877 that Manchester's civic choices found complete representation at all.

Manchester Town Hall was completed in 1888. The architect was Alfred Waterhouse, son of wealthy mill-owning Quakers. Manchester had achieved city status in 1853, and the choice of lavish Neo-Gothic is representative of the pious front of the new city fathers. It is, as my mother used to say, all fur coat and no knickers, but it has a good plan. The rich interiors feature astonishing murals by Ford Maddox Brown in Pre-Raphaelite style, depicting such laudable discoveries as marsh gas. As if this were their Sunday night TV, these paintings (religiously dedicated to a painting style more than three hundred years old) seem preposterous. In the midst of the horrors of progress we find painters doing this?

The Pre-Raphaelite movement itself represents a kind of psychosis, a retreat into fantasy when reality became too much. All those luscious images of the Lady of the Lake, My Beautiful Lady, The Lady of Shalott and Ophelia and so on by such artists as Rossetti, Burne-Jones, Alma-Tadema, J. W. Waterhouse, Holman Hunt and Millais burn with sexual tension, a tension often associated with Victorian sexual repression. The architectural theorist John Ruskin was notoriously horrified to find that his wife had pubic hair and never consummated his 1848 marriage as a result. His view, explained by his wife (who stuck it out for six years), was that the realities of the female form were not as he imagined.

**96** The Industrial Revolution

Transport, the railway, power, action (Rain, Steam and Speed) transformed the landscape of Britain. How often is it, in those period dramas, that it is the imposition of the railway across estate land that causes so much trouble? How often does it do the same today? People still don't want their Neoclassical views spoiled. But if we concentrate on the more material consequences of the railway – the ability to move materials from the place they were mined to the place of manufacture to distribution and to do it quicker and cheaper – we see it's of crucial importance. Today we call it 'infrastructure'. Previously it was mere fortune to find all the right things in the one place; now industry was free to move, and the workforces moved with it, just as now businesses move globally, and people can't.

The laying of this new infrastructure demanded huge teams of labour in itself. You have only to travel in by rail to Liverpool's Lime Street Station to witness the cliffs of stonework and brick navvies cut into the ground or to go to Baker Street in London to ride the first London Underground tunnel or to go under the Thames for the first time at Wapping. Meanwhile, Victorian railway stations display both technical virtuosity and symbolic power. Since all the railway companies were competing agencies, their termini were the focus of their identity or brand. In London especially, we see a row of northbound stations, King's Cross, St Pancras and Euston, all jockeying for position. Of the three, St Pancras survives as the most architecturally preeminent, partly through an engineering decision. Lines in to King's Cross tunnelled under the canal behind the station; the engineers at St Pancras bridged over it, making St Pancras a larger hulk of a building. Meanwhile they used the large undercroft of the platforms for goods storage, notably beer (from Burton). The architects then made the best of an imposing hotel structure with a Gothic fantasy.

The collusion among nation, Protestant Church and industry ran very deep. In particular it was a convenient political response to rely on the charity of the fortunate to aid the poverty of the less so. Phrases like 'pulling yourself together' or 'pulling yourself up by your boot straps' are typically northern exhortations to self-help, expressing the virtues and guaranteed rewards of hard work. The bigger picture reveals this as a national priority, both to boost the economy and to save on public provision. Certainly this is not an environment our friend Casanova would have understood. For him the Church was more a practical problem, but the Victorian church is a newly minted much-holier-than-thou version, demanding complicity to be merely good. The alternative is revolution: nasty old Marx.

And here I must declare some personal interest in these matters, for these words are by no means those of an impartial, dispassionate observer.

My parents moved to one of the wealthier districts of south Manchester when I was thirteen. The world of Alderley Edge was described by A. A. Gill recently as 'somewhere it would be impossible to be fat; you'd let down your car'. I can't do better than that, except to add that our near neighbours in the vicarage became the soon-to-be-disgraced Neil and Christine Hamilton and that when my parents finally sold up, and after a totally shaming interlude as a marihuana factory, developers, unwary of the name, first levelled 'Willow Spring' and then turned it into a huge multistorey hole in which to float swimming pools and car garages with a precariously balanced footballer's mansion on top. Oblivious to the laws of fluid mechanics, but clearly subject to them, five years on, the project was still a hole.

The whole burgeoning bourgeois class share an image – an image endlessly self-renewing, of success, worth and validation. It might get a bit showy. The term 'snobbery' first came into English usage in the 1820s. Such images take residence over a whole district, at safe distance, in this case well south of the prevailing winds that blew the smoke and stench of the factories northward. Meanwhile, high up on the Edge, from your turret, you could just about see your ships negotiating the Manchester Ship Canal.

I remember going to Manchester's Free Trade Hall to see my first gig ( Joan Armatrading), and I never stopped to think why it was called the Free Trade Hall.

The contrast between these genteel suburbs and the reality of the city of Manchester was extreme. It took Friedrich Engels, stationed there as a representative of his father's company, to picture the squalor:

> Such is the Old Town of Manchester, and on re-reading my description, I am forced to admit that instead of being exaggerated, it is far from black enough to convey a true impression of the filth, ruin, and uninhabitableness, the defiance of all considerations of cleanliness, ventilation, and health which characterise the construction of this single district, containing at least twenty to thirty thousand inhabitants. And such a district exists in the heart of the second city of England, the first manufacturing city of the world. If any one wishes to see in how little space a human being can move, how little air – and *such* air! – he can breathe, how little of civilisation he may share and yet live, it is only necessary to travel hither. True, this is the *Old* Town, and the people of Manchester emphasise the fact whenever any one mentions to them the frightful condition of this Hell upon Earth; but what does that prove? Everything which here arouses horror and indignation is of recent origin, belongs to the *industrial epoch.*

**98** The Industrial Revolution

This is taken from *The Condition of the Working-Class in England* (1844). Indeed, Engels's reaction is one of immediate and unimaginable horror – the stench, the foulness, the pigs, the pitiful conditions repeated over and over. This power of immediacy is not something we can always preserve. Take this piece, written later, an evocation of what Manchester was like from W. G. Sebald in *The Emigrants* and published in English in 1996:

> Contained by hills on three sides, it lay there as if in the heart of a natural amphitheatre. Over the flatland to the west, a curiously shaped cloud extended to the horizon, and the last rays of sunlight were blazing past its edges, and for a while lit up the entire panorama as if by firelight or Bengal flares. Not until this illumination died . . . did his eye roam, taking in the crammed and interlinked rows of houses, the textile mills and dyeing works, the gasometers, chemicals plants and factories of every kind, as far as what he took to be the centre of the city, where all seemed one solid mass of utter blackness, bereft of any further distinguishing features. The most impressive thing, of course . . . were all the chimneys that towered above the plain and the flat maze of housing . . . thousands of them, side by side, belching out smoke by day and night.

We've forgotten. There is still the fact of it all in Sebald, but he can't write it as if he were stepping in it like Engels; it has become almost poetic. Perhaps we should remember the message of Poussin's *Man Killed by a Snake* – after all, we face it every day on the TV – just because you are not stepping in it doesn't mean it's not there, and remember Faust, who when finally blinded is made so by the angel called 'Care'.

'Drains!', said Danni, barmaid at the Old George. She was right. While the preachier commentators were bickering about the representation of truth in Victorian Britain, at least somebody realised it was more about what happened down below and what you did with it. Joseph Bazalgette was the author of London's world-famous (and colossally expensive for the time) sewers. In an act of unheard-of generosity, Bazalgette projected the most extreme total capacity for the new network, then doubled it, and then even managed to convince of its necessity. It is hard to imagine such foresight today, when so much of the twentieth-first-century urban world squats in squalor.

Today, the Pre-Raphaelite style still appeals to middle-class mums and timorous teenagers alike who continually display the same symptoms of dissuasion. One figure unfortunately caught up in all this phoniness is William Morris. Overall there is an impression that William Morris was

The Industrial Revolution **99**

a bit of a dabbler – there is a distinct *woolliness* – and he certainly devoted his great energy to a vast array of things. This impression, it turns out, was somewhat contrived for us by the British establishment, which set about minimising the significance of Morris's revolutionary persuasion after his death. We should not be too quick to rank Morris with the High Church dalliances of the Pre-Raphaelites (despite his lifelong enthusiasm for the works of Walter Scott and his deep association with the Pre-Raphaelites themselves), because it was the family of Edward Burne-Jones that first took it upon themselves to present Morris without his politics and to employ the appropriate biographer. When the centenary exhibition of Morris's work opened at London's V&A in 1937, Stanley Baldwin – Lady Burne-Jones's nephew and the future Conservative prime minister – made no mention of Morris's communist politics whatsoever.

But certainly it was Morris who redefined the architect's mission statement in 1881: '[Architecture] embraces the consideration of the whole external surroundings of the life of man; we cannot escape from it if we would so long as we are part of civilisation, for it means a moulding and altering to human needs of the very face of the earth itself, except in the outermost desert'.

So while his endeavours – stained glass, typesetting, calligraphy, wallpapers, embroidery, tapestry and so on – appear rather lightweight domestic pursuits, we also have a man who, while translating Icelandic sagas, writing poetry and composing futuristic novels (and inventing the concept of building conservation in the meantime) not only ran a business, Morris & Co (with Burne-Jones, Rossetti and the architect Philip Webb) but mounted barricades and addressed demonstrations, gave countless lectures and wrote many incendiary articles to the extent that he meant more to Clement Attlee than Karl Marx. And if in doing so he often seemed a man almost at war with himself, as the epitome of the English bourgeois socialist, at least he knew it. He was certainly ridiculed at the time – 'a money-grabbing hypocrite', said architect Norman Shaw.

Morris is hardly on his own as being somebody who valued architecture as the greatest of the arts but who found his aptitude for it weaker than his ambition. He had decided early on his vocation but abandoned it after a spell working for George Street, famous as the architect of London's law courts. Pressed to other things, he was more manic than woolly and prone to rages; in fact, the whole family suffered illness – Morris's wife, Janey, took to the sofa at twenty-nine and pretty much stayed there, and his daughter was stricken with epilepsy. Whatever the medical conditions all round, it cannot have been easy for Morris – despite his free thinking – to accommodate his wife's affairs, one with his partner Rossetti. She was a famous beauty, a groom's daughter with a pronounced long neck, huge eyes and a mane of suitably pre-industrial black hair,

**100** The Industrial Revolution

and in those days, most professional partnerships and marriages collapsed under such circumstances. Morris carried on. There seems to be a cruel pleasure in the caricatures Burne-Jones made of Morris throughout his career, coming across as he does like Winnie the Pooh crossed with Yosemite Sam.

So to find Morris's Arts and Crafts suffused with radicalism, in an age where it crams commercial museum gift shops and Liberty, is as big a challenge as appreciating Welwyn Garden City as a hotbed of revolution. Morris would agree; his duties running the business often conflicted with his respect for rude, crude, basic décor – to his taste simple whitewash and a tapestry on the wall would do. Indeed, the fact that Arts and Crafts–style architecture has tended to enfeeble rather than energise the English may be distressing, but its intention – although this clearly did not apply to all participants – was deeply significant (even if it sounds a bit kooky), that within the maelstrom of the industrial age, honest work might not be drudgery at all but ecstasy.

It is our impression of Victorian architects that they were professionally astute but artistically dilettante. Robert Hughes, in *The Shock of the New*, boldly puts it: 'for much of the nineteenth century, architecture had nothing to say about this misery'. Morris is the first to clearly articulate (nobody could accuse Ruskin of that) a political rather than a religious conscience, for, as Hughes also explains, while people can live perfectly well without painting, music and cinema, the life of the roofless is 'nasty, brutish and wet'. This marks Morris as such an important character in our story, not least because his concepts caught on. The modest English middle-class house – slap between the squalor of the poor masses and the smug intransigence of the aristocracy – was taken as a model by a German, Hermann Multhesius, and his book *Das Englische Haus* (1904) was to become, in time, a progenitor for the Bauhaus.

So the dwelling of the ordinary human would become the focus of architectural endeavour. Perhaps this is our crowning achievement – to bring the humble human dwelling, the qualities of an essentially private domain, to the table of architecture after centuries of public show.

The battle among art, craft and machine rolled on in many incarnations over the next century and found crystalline expression (and 'crystalline' in a great many senses) in the Bauhaus. It twisted and turned via such diverse harbours as Heinrich Tessenow, who famously explained: 'the simple is not always good, but the good is always simple'; the extravagances of British High-Tech and the karma of Peter Zumthor. It even cracked and shattered as we lost track of Morris's humanity altogether, as our technology ephemeralised to pure information and our freedoms turned over in the interests of avaricious multinational corporations (see chapter 11), where such pleasures are evident only in fancy dress.

When it happened, Victorian attempts at liberal reform naturally (*sic*) had the strongest air of patronisation. The provision of pubs was rare; Thomas Cook set up dry away days. Saltaire, near Leeds, and Port Sunlight, near Liverpool, attempted a more invigorating environment for the employees of Sir Titus Salt and Lever Brothers, respectively. Bournville did the same south of Birmingham for the Cadbury enterprise. But in general the artistic environment of the nineteenth century, excepting the purely industrial aesthetic derived from Paxton, is unsurprisingly neurotic. That neurosis was aesthetically crippling and not, of course, confined to Britain, and to begin to play our way out of it we need to shift to Belgium.

# 8

# EUROPEAN MODERNISM

Perhaps to its credit, Belgium is prone, almost chronically prone, to the surrealistic mentality. Why this is the case I have no idea, but spend any time there and you are immediately dunked into a soup of seduction, poetry and generally bizarre behaviour.

Victor Horta was a Belgian aristocrat. He inherited all that is academic in Classicism and all that might be exotic in the northern European 'Berghaus' Gothic, but he was interested in the new science and the new social world. He was confronted with both Darwin and Marx, plus an internal situation in Belgium that might best be described as volatile, even if not actually boiling over into anarchy. For many present students of architecture perfectly capable of drawing a fish but unable to plan a library, Victor Horta should be an inspiration.

The Tassel House 1893 in Brussels is a magnificent house, quite a marvel of total design. Look it up and you will always find pictures of its main staircase, which appears to weave itself skyward in a triumph of sinuous joinery, amid walls and floors no longer sure exactly which is which, and flooded with gorgeous, tender colour and tone.

But Horta's breakthrough – this Art Nouveau architecture – is actually a combination of good old-fashioned Classical planning with a brand new idea of decoration. Horta even has his own curve, perhaps derived from the passage of a spawning salmon or, for that matter, human spermatozoa, to generate all those decorative shapes, all those handrails. This is Art Nouveau. It can become whimsical and overwhelming at the same time, but, armed with a new interest in biology and construction, you can see the point. However, it was certainly exhausting, and Horta's effort

**104** European Modernism

didn't last; the energy sapped him, and he soon sulked his way back to a fairly banal Classicism.

Henry van de Velde took up the mantle and sobered the language up, straightened it out and made things appropriate for industrial production. In doing so he embraced the notion that design and industry would grow together as an almost organic whole, but led by artists of course. This is a big step, and a contentious one: what comes first, the art or the machine? But it is a step on from Morris, who suddenly looks anachronistic, but only a shuffle on to the Werkbund and then another stride to the Bauhaus.

Marx and, later, Freud made us aware that the scientific, possibly mathematical or weirdly subliminal mechanisms under which the world is organised were now up for rational analysis. They attacked the flawed precepts and dotty arguments that have dogged our human progress. Nietzsche declared in 1882 that 'God is dead'. What he means is, it is not the case that God has not existed in the past, but for all intents and purposes right now (and from here on in) he doesn't. This doesn't stop you believing – by the way – it's a free world, and plenty of quasi-religious idioms will soon flourish to fill the supposed vacuum.

Back in France, Tony Garnier was drawn not to the organic at all but back again to antiquity, but a practical antiquity, a modern antiquity, a mechanised antiquity and an Arcadian one to boot. Garnier was a conscientious Rome scholar, a student in what by then had been consolidated as 'the Beaux Arts', where intricate drawings of Neoclassical schemes were encouraged – by now a default position amid industrial chaos. There are cartoons of him wearing a toga. At the same time, he is likely to have been inspired by the Realism of the literary figure Émile Zola, who in his novels *Nana* and *Germinal* responded to the evils of the second wave of the Industrial Revolution by documenting life in the French coal fields, plus, of course, a whole legacy of French utopian thought including the thinking of Fourier and Saint-Simon.

Garnier came up with an extraordinary set of drawings titled *Une Cité Industrielle* (1904), a new vision for the city and certainly the opposite of that which those Mancunians were used to. It depicts a fresh new city set in the landscape, with dams for power, industrial plant (all meticulously and lovingly drawn), airport, port and living quarters a way away that might remind you of life in an island villa in Greece – a life of languid tranquillity where you might just occasionally pluck a fresh orange from the tree, pause to sense the loveliness of its aroma and then simply explode with joy when you taste it. Garnier was the first proponent of zoning of the city, enabling the peace and quiet of home life to complement the majesty of industry minus dirt. Even the blast furnaces were clean. And if you think this is

PHOTOGRAPH 8  Chandigarh, standing in the space L-C designed for public demonstration with just the one distant circling bicyclist. No wonder; even the hotel corridor was policed by machine guns.

*Credit*: Julie Cook

an extraordinary juxtaposition you are right, but it has been enormously influential. In the meantime, *Une Cité Industrielle* was a utopian project with practical spin-offs: a hospital (composed of rather tidy pavilions linked by a business end of underground tunnels) and an abattoir (a dirty great shed) in a most interesting district of Lyons called Les États-Unis.

Garnier's Puvis de Chavannes Arcadianism ran at odds with the startling and violent realities of the modern world. Many artists dealt with the shock (of the new) by assuming the mantle of some higher plane; they escaped the other way. They said artists were those in touch with higher, more profound truths, and nowhere would this become more evident

**106** European Modernism

than in a more daring approach to sexuality. The advent of photography had encouraged a fascination with the body, bodies over which artists were the traditional custodians. But it is a raw, sexualised body foreign to Ruskin. Pictures of naked girls and boys were not smut when handled by artists and connoisseurs, because artists and connoisseurs understood more. So we see a rise in esoteric religion or cultish behaviour. Think of one of the world's most popular paintings – Gustav Klimt's *The Kiss*. It is hardly explicit, but this swooning eroticism epitomised the breathless, slightly stoned atmosphere of Secessionist Vienna. When Gustav Mahler lay down on his writing-shed floor to listen to the earth for inspiration, one wonders if he did so because he could, or because he should or if he was just a little tired and emotional.

Gustav Mahler's wife, Alma, was notoriously the most beautiful woman in Europe, deeply ensconced in the Viennese whirl, and what we might call a sex bomb. Oskar 'The Savage' (her term) Kokoschka was so devastated when she broke off their affair that he had the first (to our knowledge) love doll made in her image and used to take it to tea.

After a particularly draining tour of the United States with Mahler, Alma was sent into rehab. Dancing and fresh air were proscribed, hardly surprising after their jaunts to find opium dens to salve the pains of touring. On the dance floor she met 'the Silver Prince', Walter Gropius, who was recovering from injury in active service in the First World War. One thing led to another, the sex made her dizzy, the passion found him hiding under a bridge trying to peek into her bedroom and sent Gustav to Freud, the ultimate shrink.

When Mahler died, Alma married Gropius, but not without reservations. He wasn't musical, but he was dependable. Meanwhile, Gropius took the directorship of the newly merged Grand Ducal School of Arts and Crafts and the Weimar Academy of Fine Art, or Bauhaus, in 1919.

The rest, you might say, is history. Bauhaus studies are so lengthy and so all-pervasive they are inopportune here – but, whatever – Alma didn't stick it out. While she undoubtedly facilitated, just by being there, Gropius's appointment of the strange array of teaching talent – especially those of a monkish disposition such as Johannes Itten – that made the Bauhaus unique, she didn't like the all-pervasive smell of garlic mush that they lived on, and she was ill disposed to fidelity. They divorced in 1920.

By 1925 the Bauhaus had moved to Gropius's custom-built masterpiece in Dessau, a building so lean it came down to the door handles. Gropius described it utterly without hyperbole: the windows are glass, the roof is asphalt, the walls are concrete . . . and so on.

So the cultural context, both general and personal, of the Bauhaus is particularly striking. And despite all the mountains of Bauhaus studies, it

European Modernism **107**

is hard to encapsulate the era. One American journalist, writing in Berlin in 1918, talked of 'Germany's nervous breakdown'. There had been extreme and unfair hardship in the army and starving at home at the end of the First World War. The removal of censorship led to violence on the streets by day and transgression by night. Returning troops were able to relate their explosive and all-too-real revelations, while the Kaiser abdicated, literally and metaphorically. There were revolutionary events that paralleled those in St Petersburg a few months before. Sailors mutinied and collections of servicemen challenged individual town halls. In this tumult, what does your thinking architect want?

It is clear that a man such as Gropius was driven to pull the situation back together. He was an organiser, an architect unskilled in the private pleasures of drawing, so unsurprisingly committed to team effort. The everyday uncertainly bred a quasi-utopian aspiration. When everything looks as if it's falling apart, there is an equal and opposite urge to pull it back together. Meanwhile, in his own personal life Gropius has gone through the wringer; he was exhausted by the demands of the higher plane, of the esoteric. As a gentleman, he'd agreed to be caught with a prostitute to facilitate Alma's divorce. As a consequence, the Bauhaus in its Dessau incarnation looks like an interesting case of obsessive-compulsive disorder.

When Gropius handed over the reins in 1928, he did so to a hard-line communist, Hannes Meyer, a devout Functionalist who believed you could plan a house around the sex life of its inhabitants. The ethos was one of equality, especially with regard to class and wealth (or rather poverty). Famously there were plenty of female Bauhaus students, but we are still not sure if the gender politics was intrinsically radical. It was unfortunate that Gropius let slip that he thought women best at two-dimensional work (graphics/textiles) rather than three-; however, having completed the basic course, women could progress *towards* architecture.

But at first it was hardly an architectural school at all, just Gropius's and Adolf Meyer's office, yet from within its factory-like structure the notion of artistically led industrial production flourished, from chairs to chess sets. The school would make money as industry took up their patents, and it would become for modernity what Florence was to the Renaissance. However, just as the parties were notoriously long, its life was tragically short, for unsurprisingly the Bauhaus ethos irritated the burgeoning Nazis, busy fulfilling their destiny by building the ultimate war machine with a preindustrial mentality.

We miss out on the triumph of the Bauhaus if we forget that the pulling together of apparent idiosyncrasy might have been its point; that underneath, despite some misapprehensions, since we're all human, we

**108** European Modernism

share laws to our enjoyment; that good things are indeed good things. The Bauhaus colour wheels still work, but in a world of individualism their significance is merely decorative; you like what you like. Looking at a book of prints by Joseph Albers, we might enjoy the amazing luminosity of the images but tend to gloss over what seems the boring pseudoscientific reasoning. In this sense we can indeed see in Gropius's Bauhaus what we saw in Raphael's *School of Athens* – an attempt to pull everything together, this time under the egis of science and industrial production.

Adolf Loos, a Moravian resident in Vienna – whose set included Karl Kraus, Peter Altenberg and Ludwig Wittgenstein – also took against the esoteric claustrophobia of the Secession. They took against a great deal but, on the other hand, as almost pioneer Postmoderns, had great difficulty believing in anything either, especially a political alternative. Loos suggested that the communists wanted to make everybody proletarian, while he wanted to make everyone an aristocrat. Loos designed some fine houses, notably the Moller (1928) and Müller Houses (1930) and a department store in the centre of Vienna that so inflamed the chancellor he ordered his curtains shut against it. But he hardly had an office and not even a bank account. He couldn't bring himself to worry about such tawdry matters; he said an architect was just a bricklayer who spoke Latin.

He appreciated the practical. Having made a life-changing trip in 1893 to the United States – where he worked washing dishes – he was revolted by both Germany's drains and underwear, both of which he considered not up to hygienic standards. Instead he admired the hidden virtues of decent plumbing and understated British outfitters and considered (quite rightly) black wine glasses quite repugnant.

The sparse formality of Loos exteriors was in fact complemented by complex interiors, where rooms often shift in half levels that are fiendishly tricky to understand in plan. The arrangements – termed *Raumplan* – were intended for repose but could make you feel *literally* claustrophobic, since what is now termed 'the gaze' seems particularly active.

Much has been made of his voyeurism; his three wives were all very much younger than he was, and he was prosecuted for paedophilia twice. Altenberg was prosecuted, too. When we look at Loos's 'Elephant Trunk' side table, it's hard not to see eight young dancers' legs, and he had very much a thing for Josephine Baker, for whom he designed a house (never executed) that placed her, for want of a better expression, in a large fish tank. Loos found fish tanks calming, and he was very fond of dogs, no doubt preferring them to people. He ended his days in the '30s itinerant along the shores of the Côte d'Azur, like some character in Forster or Maugham, deaf from syphilis contracted from a youthful visit to a brothel with his godfather, bemoaning moths in his luggage, but his writing – complex,

European Modernism **109**

ironic, terse and funny – is the finest reflection of that 'man without qualities' for whom he seems to be Robert Musil's ideal model.

Meanwhile the Reds began, conceptually but not practically, with a political and aesthetic clean slate. The painter Kazimir Malevich provides precisely this: *Black Square* (1915) and *White on White* (1918). Both simultaneously stop and start the painting world.

There was the matter of civil war to address, and the complication of revolutionising a largely illiterate, immensely backward Russia (that's why so much so-called Russian Constructivist architecture sports so many radio aerials – to spread the message). But for the first time a whole series of bourgeois assumptions about life and how it should be lived were irrelevant. Women, for one, en masse, were finally first-class citizens. Women would no longer even cook for their families; this meant that in the famous Narkomfin block (Moisei Ginsberg 1932) there weren't even private kitchens. All cooking was to be done by professional cooks.

So, in fits and starts, each country soon exhibited strands of this radical, ruthless, white, sparse, sinuous architecture, making it all the more possible for spotters to note national and cultural difference. We can distinguish Functional Czech from Functional German, bourgeois French from bourgeois English, and Italian Futurist from Rationalist. We can even worry about a so-called organic strain and realise the importance of two separate incarnations with their origins in the USSR, both stemming from an interpretation of Marx's exhortation to exploit 'use value' (as opposed to 'exchange value') either technically or socially.

People call it the machine age, but really the previous chapter responds better to that title. Here (the USSR excepted) we are seeing a series of metaphorical interpretations of an idealised life with machines. The machines were not the problem, not even after the First World War. It was the people who were the problem, and give them enough fresh air, sunshine and exercise and not only would they be cured of crippling tuberculosis but they would be happy too. Architects stopped looking like gentleman mystics and started looking like engineers, taking proud photographs of their garages, while ladies of leisure appear to have explored alternative happiness via Christian Science, experimental theatre, militant feminism and lesbianism.

Drifting west, by the time the International Style reached England it was ready to be both supported and lampooned by Evelyn Waugh and Osbert Lancaster and pointedly adopted for housemasters at Eton. The English may have misunderstood Evelyn Waugh (the conservative philosopher Roger Scruton once claimed that Le Corbusier was so preposterous a figure as to be an invention of Waugh), since he reviewed the architect's *City of Tomorrow* in the positive for the *Observer* and was at pains to point

**110** European Modernism

out that *Decline and Fall* (1928) was *supposed* to be funny. It is clear from the opening pages of *Decline and Fall* that it is a satire on British society *in toto*, but it is also a form of resignation to the status quo. It features a modern architect, Prof Silenus, whose reputation rides on a rejected design for a chewing-gum factory published in a Hungarian quarterly and who sees beauty in the functionalities of digestion but in the end finds Greek goats lovelier than Greek temples.

Whatever, the progressives managed to gain ground in the English scene even if they did exude the whiff of toff, infused as they were with conventional, conservative social values. However, energised by a newly inspirational émigré or ten, even England managed to make its servant accommodation a little more inconspicuous, even if the sun decks looked rather superfluous.

And it is within this flux of all-too-visible ideology from Moscow and London, with Berlin at its most volatile in the middle, that modernity in the European theatre gained its power. Even the most timorous example cannot be dismissed as something that does not embody ideas. Even at its blandest, it appears packed full of content (something routinely dismissed by Postmodernists). Even in grotesque parody, within Nazism for instance, it communicates.

One of the more strenuous examples of European Modernism between the wars is the Open Air School by Jan Duiker (1930). The Dutch have never really given up the cause, and this school really demonstrates what this skin-and-bones architecture can do while appearing to be doing nothing at all. It is as if architecture had gone to the gym (both intellectually and physically) and then become a gym.

The building appears almost transparent, indeed reduced to Hennebique structure itself, and merely sheathed and painted white. There weren't even radiators but only heated ceiling panels. The core of the building is the proud pipes capped with water tanks running vertically and wrapped with a staircase. Meanwhile, the building from the southern aspect looks like a cube that has been eroded to create a stack of open terraces within. However, as we walk around, our perspective changes from 'cube eroded' to 'blocks established', and a geometric game becomes clearly evident. A look at the plan confirms the devious intent, as the staircase occupies a skewed 45-degree angle within the 45-degree skewed cube. Of course it is the absence of any extraneous architecture that allows us to appreciate the purity of this geometric game.

Others might make buildings look like ships, but Duiker fearlessly and elegantly straps his architecture to the mast of pure Functionalism while realising that Functionalism cannot exist by itself; in his case the articulation is mannered. Le Corbusier also realised this, utilising a synthesis of

European Modernism **111**

numerous impulses. The term 'machine for living in' is a misnomer, for it implies purely Functional criteria, and Le Corbusier never sanctioned that; he even said the German Functionalists, with their *Existenzminimum*, had got it all wrong. Meanwhile Mies van der Rohe relied on an essentially Classical root, extending Frank Lloyd Wright, but with the most luxurious of materials. Only poor Gropius got close to doing the one pure thing, with his prefabricated houses – but while they were 'interesting', as Mies said, they were not necessarily 'good'. Hence it seems you always need multiple reasons for completing even the apparently simplest of things.

Mies is sitting in the back of a Mercedes (it has to be a Mercedes). He has a glass of brandy in one hand and a cigar in the other. He can't get out of the car; he's too ill by now. It's 1968, and we are in Berlin. Mies is there to check that – as they lower the giant roof of the Berlin New National Gallery onto its eight supporting columns – he got the height right.

Mies has returned to Europe for his swansong, perhaps the ultimate modern building because it commands the right to be considered alongside the Parthenon. As an art gallery, it's useless; as a monument to the twentieth century (the will of an epoch made into space), it's genius. This is our horizontal cathedral. The roof is one big, thick, black, grid. Grids are representative of common measurement, like graph paper. You can't have an industrial age without standard measures. This one is so carefully engineered and so heavy that some flanges are secretly thicker and of higher grade than others so that the difference won't deflect to the naked eye. Mies has tried it plenty of times before, but it's not quite the same in Bermuda (the Bacardi Building) as it is here, right on the western side of the wall, back where *Kultur* was dead and buried and where it could now rise (or rather be lowered) again.

The New National Gallery has been compared to a car showroom, but is the only building I know to actually aid bodily functions, as you go into the toilet cubicle and stare at the tile grid, and see that it comes down to millimetres. The grid is everywhere, the grid is universal: you are very small.

Mies van der Rohe was the last director of the Bauhaus. He was appointed in 1930 because he was the only figure Gropius thought could deal with the Nazis. Both Le Corbusier and Mies van der Rohe understood that architecture was more than the politics that built it; both had (but hardly shared) visions that embraced a wider historical process than the contingency of the political here and now.

When the Nazis finally shut the Bauhaus, believing it an institution they would rather be without (not much more than that), Mies went to Nazi HQ each week in a businesslike fashion to argue technicalities.

**112** European Modernism

Finally meeting Alfred Rosenberg, he declared that Rosenberg's desk was so ugly he should throw it out of the window. That was the problem with the Nazis for Mies – no taste in desks. He had a point, of course; you can't blame the designer for the decrees signed on the desk.

The chief decree signer was Albert Speer. His tragedy started with a suitably agonised midnight walk around a forest, but once he joined up, he quickly rose through the ranks because he had a car and the fledgling Nazis needed a taxi service. He was soon awarding multiple building contracts on the Reich Chancellery simultaneously, meaning that hundreds of workers were competing with each other twenty-four hours a day to meet Hitler's version of boom and bust.

The Nazis overall were totally neurotic about technology. When Hitler built his country house, the papers announced 'no machine had been used', while the regime was dedicated to the most efficient of killing machinery. One look at the model of the railway sidings at Auschwitz in the Imperial War Museum in London chills us to the core: left or right, life or death.

For German architects caught up in the mess of what the Führer might or might not like, especially Rational Functionalists, life must have been unbearable. No wonder it pushed Mies to switch off his political radar altogether and led most famous architects to leave the country.

Ernst Sagebiel had worked for the Berlin Modernist Erich Mendelsohn – who had even built in the USSR – until 1932. Mendelsohn was a wealthy, cultivated Jew, who fled to England the next year. Sagebiel took his machine-age enthusiasms to the Luftwaffe and joined the SA. His drawings for Tempelhof Airport, featuring a tumult of aeroplanes gliding around under the terminal, are more indicative of Futurist enthusiasms (though they were fascists too) than Teutonic myth, hardly Nazi at all except in size (huge) and appliqué. The building even used prefabricated stripped Classicism, while the preposterous eagle over the entrance looks rather an afterthought. It's a building so good people still try not to think of it as Nazi at all. However, Sagebiel's other surviving contribution, his Air Ministry, reassures us of his doom-laden misery, and it was later used as the GDR's 'House of Ministries' – presumably all of them.

The other obvious surviving Nazi landmark is the Olympic Stadium (Werner March 1936), the location of which way east of the centre saved it from both bombing and the Battle for Berlin. It is a haunting structure, now home to Hertha Berlin football club, whose goalkeeper must struggle with the idea that up to fifty thousand synchronised, indoctrinated and gymnastic young Germans used to parade around the 'Mayfield' behind his net.

Sensibly, and clutching a Max Beckmann painting under his arm, Mies fled to the United States, where he would make his reputation and where his architecture would become the icon of American postwar prosperity. It's worth noting that plenty of architects made the decision to go east instead, but we tend not to hear about them.

'Less is more!' declared Mies, but don't think this 'less is more' stuff is easy. You have to remember the temperament of the engineer. One of the projects Mies would set his students was the 'wall problem'; he'd ask you to combine a picture and a shelf and an object on a wall. That was it, and he'd probably give you three weeks to draw it. Meanwhile, when he did his rounds to inspect your work, likely as not he would just stand behind you and not say a word. It was positively Jesuitical. Only later would you tell dirty jokes into the night as you demolished another bottle.

Another notorious demolisher of bottles was Alvar Aalto. So much so that the last ten years of his life seemed to disappear entirely. Aalto did not contemplate his adventures as if he were Odysseus (L–C) and was not as single-minded as Mies. He liked a good time, he visited porn cinemas, he and Aino were even, occasionally, given to swinging. And somewhat paradoxically, if there is a master of the Modern movement in architecture who was in any way reasonable, it was Aalto. He even went so far as to build himself an escape hatch from his office so that he could climb up a little ladder and out onto the roof and thereby avoid his clients.

Visit any Aalto building and you sense it immediately. Aalto is weak in one sense because he is not interested in the polemics that attach us to Le Corbusier or Mies van der Rohe, but he is stronger in another for simply being comfortable and supremely capable at making architecture that you actually like being in. He also had a successful creative relationship with his significant others Aino (and later) Elissa. With Le Corbusier we find the lonely Yvonne tippling the Ricard, and with Mies the idea is almost a contradiction in terms.

Aalto remained comfortable with Classicism while showing all the signs of that Modernist sensibility. His buildings are eclectic without looking like it and often try to tell a story (just like Schinkel's) rather than present a promenade. Look at Aalto's Villa Mairea (1939) and compare it with the Villa Savoye (L–C 1928). The latter suddenly appears somehow bereft of anything but the cinematographic, of moving without moving, as a place made for the movie camera to scan, while the former is a place to sit in, enjoy a vodka or two, and then go and have a sauna. Aalto was a master with materials, Le Corbusier was not, and the Villa Mairea tells a story in materials from front to back – the front modern, sophisticated, the back as rustic as the Finnish forests. Meanwhile it was soon apparent to the intellectuals who commissioned early L–C villas that they were rather poor showcases for their inherited furniture. The look was not unlike Biedermeier stacked in a warehouse

**114** European Modernism

if you didn't submit to the whole package and the help of Charlotte Perriand's furniture.

Compare that with the famous Aalto vase. How effortless – it is merely a pool of water caught on a table, raised into a glass container and filled with flowers once the water has been wiped away. That's poetic, isn't it? And it even works well as a vase. Therefore he appeals to modest but comfortable types, and, despite our relative lack of lakes and forests, his work has proved enduringly popular with the English. We even made our huge British Library a dead ringer for his tiny woodland council offices at Säynätsalo.

Which brings us to that last big fish, one Charles-Édouard Jeanneret, alias Le Corbusier: 'sculptor, catastrophic theorist, collagist, aphorist, total-itarian toady, collaborator, monk, socialite', as Jonathan Meades has him. He has already been mentioned here more than anybody else, and it's time to try to do him justice: a man who liked to dress up as a woman or as a prisoner when he was forced to go to parties.

Le Corbusier came from a watchmaking town, La Chaux-de-Fonds, on the Swiss-French borders, and he was born in 1887. He died – swimming out into his beloved Mediterranean until he could not return – in 1965. Le Corbusier saw himself as at least two things, both of which are endearing – first, as an Ancient Greek hero to be proved right in the end, and second, as a bumbling idiot knight tilting at windmills. His suicide was just to mark that it was all over, that he was done. He was the most famous architect in the world, yet he lived in a tiny *cabanon* – admittedly one usefully attached to a local restaurant – in which he designed perhaps his magnum opus (the capitol buildings at Chandigarh) while perched on a packing crate for a stool. Have we taken sufficient notice? Perhaps not, since the packing crate is now reproduced at absurd expense by Cassina.

So much for the machine age? Well, not quite. If you visit L–C's home in Paris – the top floors of 24 rue Nungesser et Coli – you will note that the seating arrangement is a bit odd. The main floor plan is arranged like an H: an area for cooking and dining and sleeping to the left, L–C's painting studio to the right, and, in the middle, squeezed by the lightwells and access, a sort of snug. There's a conspicuous box in this snug; it is the surround for the lift machinery that serves the lower floors but not this two-storey attic (which only has a service lift). Le Corbusier placed his easy chair right next to that box of lift machinery. So you can imagine him reading the paper, puffing his pipe, enjoying the periodic whirring and whining and clunking of the lift. This is not out of character; in *The City of Tomorrow*, he waxes lyrical about precisely the same thing on a grand scale, about the making of a dam high up in the Alps. And he may have hated what they had done to the skyscraper in New York, but he loved the energy: the air conditioning, the sound insulation, the jazz, the amplification the city moved to. And he loved aeroplanes not just for their technical virtuosity but because they gave you a new perspective on the ground; they were the modern equivalent of Brunelleschi's viewing apparatus.

So I'm sitting in an office with my favourite but scariest lecturer, Mark Wells, tutor for my undergraduate dissertation, titled 'Built Form and Setting in the Late Work of Le Corbusier'. I'm presently clueless, but I'm here to learn. It's nearly Christmas 1982. Nobody would say that Wells was easy; he was irascible and fairly furious with us most of the time. He was feared for his intelligence and admired for his wit, a man way beyond the accommodating pastors we find today. He demolished students on a very regular basis.

He simply picked up the phone, looked over his glasses, which sat over his huge nose, and said, 'You are free in the holidays aren't you . . . and . . . you have means? And then, speaking fluent French, he booked me a room at the monastery of La Tourette near Lyon. It is the most impressive piece of tutoring I've ever witnessed.

Now La Tourette (1959) is cold, loud and bare. For anybody, the first step into your monk's cell is bracing. Thirty years later I took Julie there, and she cried, and not for joy. We are not used to sitting in cells with nothing much to contemplate but an acorn or a flower. But over a few days – as you wander in and around the brooding hulk, perched up above its ridiculous slope – you are somehow loath to leave, perhaps because you have finally understood what architecture can be.

La Tourette is full of metaphor and magic as well as bare necessity. When the sun goes down and the light streams onto the undercroft of the church's flat concrete roof through a very carefully placed slot, it appears to take off. L–C called it a box of miracles, which it is, but also a lesson from the Pantheon. There are giant ears to listen to God; kidney-shaped pods that divide the pure souls from their visitors; an array of window types that includes some baffled against the view, compounding some notion of fortress, while others apportion rhythm. Stumbling around its undercroft, we find the underlying rationality occasionally propped with angled columns, just the way shipwrights prop boats on the shore. Of course, this is a building built from the top down, from humanity's datum, the deck of the roof, to the unruly slope of nature's ground.

Those boats again: the gymnasium on the roof of the Unité at Marseilles is the shape of an upturned keel on which Odysseus, at one crucial point, had to cling to carry on his journey. He clings on all right, and when Odysseus gets home, he gets to reap his revenge.

I weathered the rigours of just hitchhiking there (even down to Marseilles and back up to Ronchamp) that January. At the time my

**116** European Modernism

understanding was as foggy as the freezing weather, but I still treasure my sketchbook of notes interspersed with marker-pen pleas to passing motorists, and I never really stopped loving L-C from then on.

Jeanneret's early work in La Chaux-de-Fonds is relatively straightforward, a bit Arts and Crafts, classically conservative in planning, with the occasional gesture that would keep future academics busy for years. But it is not academicism that should be worrying any student of Le Corbusier. What should worry the student of Le Corbusier is that his buildings tend to be uninhabitable and brilliant at the same time, that each represents a mental exercise in the conjugation of rational, moral and empirical thinking with a flourish of art thrown in. Nobody who knows expects you to like the Villa Savoye (1928) the first time. You can't, for instance, make a decent living space of it; at least nobody has yet. Mme Savoye famously complained, and Le Corbusier, with considerable bravado, suggested she buy a golden visitors' book.

A painter school friend of mine once suggested to me that Le Corbusier was a far better painter than he was an architect and that he, with rather a shrug, would make a far better architect than he was a painter. He's now an architect. L-C habitually rose at 5.30 a.m. for calisthenics, painted in the mornings and did his architecture in the afternoon. His architectural career rather took off over lunch, when he discovered that his local restaurant in Paris – a double-height space with a mezzanine – was the ideal living space just like the ideal objects that made up his Purist paintings. Corbu's partner in Purism was Amédée Ozanfant. Together they decided their paintings were one step on from Cubism.

The Purist paintings depict what L-C termed '*objets types*', objects that have already reached their ultimate form, like guitars and wine bottles, in newly geometric arrangements. He wanted to find architectural *objets types* like his restaurant and put them together anew too. But that isn't the half of it; Le Corbusier is different, he's lyrical. If you put a marble on the floor just inside the entrance space of his Pavillon Suisse (1932) – his student accommodation at the Cité Universitaire – it rolls towards the reception desk. Michelangelo didn't think of that; he may have domed the floor of his Campidoglio but he didn't orientate the slope to a reception desk.

The basis for understanding Le Corbusier's early (pre-Second World War) work is to understand its form of construction and what you can do with it. In essence, we have the rediscovery of concrete, meaning we can build houses the way they look in Greece even now – slabs of horizontal concrete supported by columns. Nothing Arts and Crafts about this; it's light years away from wall and joist. We move from wall to platform (and we will move back again with Postmodernism). Meanwhile France was still a place where it was still okay to lay parquet flooring on bare earth. This infuriated Corbu; it was so stupid. So you rack it and stack it and improvise through the middle and you have something called the five points of a new architecture. You put pipes through the middle, not down the sides; you lift the floor off the ground and give yourself a roof terrace too. And what's more, what happens on one floor doesn't have to be what happens on the next, and windows don't have to be tall and thin but can be long and narrow.

Meanwhile, his compositions will always be based on that synthesis of sound moral, rational and empirical judgements, plus some puns that remind us of the origin of architecture in Ancient Greece, such as making the door to the church at La Tourette like that you might find in a submarine – watertight, clunk! All this is pulled together using his own proportioning system too – the Modulor which L–C was so proud of he showed it to Einstein.

Moral is the easiest: it is right to do this because we have an idea about it not just a desire for it. Rational isn't hard either. Imagine you are designing a prison; since the prison sentencing system is based on time spent in jail, it makes sense to make all the cells the same. Empiricism is a bit more tricky, since it implies lessons learnt from the past. and might appear a contradiction to the first two components, but no. For instance, when Le Corbusier completed the Unité d'Habitation in Marseilles in 1952, you could look at the 'trough' which seems to secure the building above the massive *pilotis* which clear the ground plane. Well, the trough is the equivalent of a grease trap you might find in any French kitchen, and the *pilotis* are reminiscent of giant ladies' thighs.

Is it easy for us to understand an architecture based on an enthusiasm for spark plugs and carburetors as well as acorns and sunshine? Of course it is, but we have ended up with St Albans and Iceland stores rather than Elysian fields. In the late '70s Charles Jencks published a volume called *Le Corbusier and the Tragic View of Architecture*; Mark said that it really should have been titled *Le Corbusier and the Tragic View of Mankind*, and he was absolutely right.

But if you want to marvel at the fiendishly complex (but somehow elemental) business of composition in *le style Corbu*, a tried and tested method is to attempt a model of the Villa Shodhan, a residence completed in Ahmedabad in 1956. For this all you need is some scale plans (spray-mounted to plain brown cardboard), a cutting board, a steel rule, a sharp scalpel, some wood glue, access to pictures of the building, some care and a good deal of patience. On completion, you will be delighted with both it and yourself.

So with that I'm going to leave European Modernism. What! you cry. So soon? If you want the encore, see Postmodernism. Instead I will offer an addendum.

## 118 European Modernism

Alison and Peter Smithson did a copycat Mies building commissioned in 1949, a school on the north Norfolk coast in Hunstanton. Alison and Peter were from what Jonathan Glancey entertainingly calls the 'I can piss higher up the wall than you can school of architecture'. Peter was known as Brutus, and they used to travel up to Hunstanton in a Willys Jeep (very chilly). They were both in their twenties and fresh out of the Architectural Association at the time.

Following a less rigorous Palladian logic than Palladio had (for his buildings very clearly relate to site), they boasted, in this rather severe location, that 'the bricks you see on the inside are the same bricks you see on the outside'. So went a certain damp chill down the collar of those unfortunate children and many more across Britain as the period rolled on. They also exposed all the pipework, in itself not a bad idea, and made the water tank into a symbolic *campanile*, which was utterly pretentious. But then again, they rode about in a Willys Jeep, a stupid form of transport except under wartime conditions firing guns, or maybe they thought they *were* in wartime conditions firing guns.

# 9

# AMERICAN MODERNISM

It was unlikely that the United States would trade in Jefferson's hand-me-down Classicism for long, even if it provided the grand, Haussmann-like boulevards for Washington and the White House itself. The frontier spirit, along with the wonder of the landscape (no longer exactly the mysterious home of the gods but surveyed by man), brought a particular affinity with nature, with God's country. Meanwhile, certain impulses distrustful of intellectualisation and committed to instinct, a raw can-do mentality, formed some kind of hegemony of communal understanding and empathy. Americans are individuals, but they are together in their individuality. Unity, in a sense, comes naturally, at least in theory.

So it is no surprise that in various incarnations, it is the word 'organic' that plagues American Modernism, even if there are plenty of downtowns without the whiff of anything organic about them at all – indeed, totally synthetic environments of the most peculiar kind (arrays of chilling tombstones, if you will). It is to the organic attachment to the land and people (and, for that matter, process) that the great moderns, Louis Sullivan and Frank Lloyd Wright, play. You will also find plenty of crystalline geometry in Louis Kahn, even when he is trying to bring Ancient Rome to modern Americans, while the folksiness of the American tradition will find itself manifest in Greene & Greene and the Shingle Style, and even the high style of the Case Study House Program could be thought of as pastoral, as machinery in the garden.

It is not until Robert Venturi in 1966 that you will find an American architect constituting a complex and contradictory language that is not in

**122** American Modernism

any way referent to the glories of nature. And even when he, Denise Scott Brown and Steven Izenour founded the new American vernacular in Las Vegas in 1968, there were still plenty of people who wanted to paint it brown. There were also plenty of people who thought it was fake; it took Dave Hickey to spell out that Las Vegas was actually a rather good lens through which to view modern America and that Las Vegas was certainly more real than Santa Fe.

Perhaps it was Walt Whitman's fault. Louis Sullivan read Whitman and tried to write like him and tried to build skyscrapers that would correspond. Amazingly, in buildings such as the Wainwright Building in St Louis (1891) and the Guaranty Building in Buffalo (1896), he succeeded. Indeed, he conjured the recipe for the aesthetically reconsidered tall building, built on a steel frame, home to Otis's lifts and Thomas Edison's electricity, strong and direct and smothered, if you look closely, with terracotta foliage. While clearly not organic in the slightest, these buildings were intensely redolent of the idea. What's more, they were fiercely practical. Sullivan had watched one of his early efforts – the Romanesque Chicago opera house – sink almost week by week under its own weight. The lighter steel frame was a godsend. Meanwhile, the office was based in Chicago, where Sullivan benefited not only from the rebuilding after the Great Fire of 1871 but from Chicagoans in general (as Kipling put it), 'the crudest, rawest and most savagely ambitious dreamers'.

In partnership with the engineer Dankmar Adler, Sullivan found the world seemingly at his feet, but his idealism, his volatile nature, his personal life, the appalling taste of his colleagues and the slings and arrows of the economy dogged him. It was one long fall until he died, pretty much destitute, in a rooming house, in 1924. It is tempting to think architects didn't do this sort of thing before Sullivan, that as secure professionals, they put two and two together just as they did their brickwork. But Sullivan illustrates perfectly the clash of the heroic Celtic demiurge with the realities of no-second-act capitalism. It proves heroism can go badly wrong. However, it was precisely this risk that was lionised by Ayn Rand in her fiercely anticommunist book (1943) and screenplay (1949) *The Fountainhead*, where the character of Cameron, the hero Howard Roark's mentor, is a dead ringer for Sullivan even if he dies thinking of plastics.

It was prophetic that Sullivan's most touching works were some of his last: a series of small banks out in the Midwest. Built for agricultural communities where payday came but once a year, these banks are closer to churches, sporting various exhortations to thrift and diligence. The bank vaults tend to occupy the space of the altarpiece, and Sullivan consciously

PHOTOGRAPH 9 In Berlin, when and where I decided to write this book.
*Credit*: Julie Cook

**124** American Modernism

overspecified them for effect. Meanwhile, the exteriors are sober blocks, with carefully hollowed openings fabulous with detail. Consider how discredited banking has become in the space of a century, and you can only feel for Sullivan's idealism.

Frank Lloyd Wright worked in Adler & Sullivan's office until he was fired for moonlighting. Luckily for him, Wright had been groomed for genius from the very start by his mother, and he was not going to be undone as Sullivan had been. Wright knew he had to capitalise on the subconscious identification of ordinary Americans with the natural, and he had to assume the mantle of greatness with it.

With half a career already behind him in 1909, Wright left Chicago, his wife and six children for his neighbour's wife and Europe. In Europe, where there was much talk of lords of art, he would be published and self-actualise his own artistic demiurge, don capes and flirt with dancers. His work would be published in Berlin and absorbed by many, including the young Mies van der Rohe.

The canonical Robie House was not yet complete, but he had a distinguished portfolio of houses in Oak Park behind him and was already worshipped by his staff. They even wore their hair in the same daring long style. Formally, he had mastered an architectural trick, to push and pull Palladian Classicism in plan, making the plans asymmetric, and to reorientate houses on their plots side-on, giving him more room to move.

So the root of FLW's architectural vocabulary was in fact the same as everybody else's – Palladianism – which above all he pulled, stretched and extended to exaggerated eccentricity and in doing so unwittingly gave us the cornerstone of modern, fluid, planning. Even at its most extreme, in the leftover stone outcrops that form the plan of Falling Water (1939), we can see a residual Classicism and the solid fireplace central to the composition. Fireplaces were of course essential concerns of the American vernacular, the architecture of the first settlers, short on labour and long on timber, for they were the only solid elements to a balloon-frame timber house. There was also a saying, 'it's time to move on when you see the smoke from your neighbour's chimney': chimneys were the honorific bastions of home life itself. Frank Lloyd Wright might move on, but his chimneys wouldn't.

Wright returned to the United States after a year to build Taliesen for his new family, but tragedy hit with an axe murderer, a fire and another marriage – to an aristocratic spiritualist morphine addict – that collapsed acrimoniously within six months. Then there was another fire and, finally, marriage to a ballet dancer from Macedonia. During this period Wright

American Modernism **125**

achieved a memorable piece of cross-fertilisation in his design for the Imperial Hotel Tokyo, which managed to fuse, in a most peculiar way, Eastern and Western site planning.

This was the kick-start for Wright's memorable 'textile block' Mayan-inspired houses in California and his complete assumption of genius: He demanded millionaire heiress Aline Barnsdall sleep on a futon and the Hannas share corridors no wider than Western Pacific coaches while living in a world of hexagons. He came complete with disciples and built Taliesin West in the Arizona desert to accommodate them in winter. On arrival, visitors were given a sheet and told to fashion their gown for supper. This sort of thing was not everybody's cup of tea. Even the disciples recognised the danger of being sucked in. John Lautner certainly thought twice and concentrated on constructional problems rather than join the design séance. Lautner went on to produce a series of sumptuous hideaways in Los Angeles that in the minds of Hollywood set designers doubled marvellously as the lairs of villains but fortunately represented rapturous peace and harmony to his clients.

With Wright, the catchphrase 'truth to materials' must be taken with a pinch of salt, even if it sounds reasonable enough, for here is another strategy (like 'form follows function') that cannot in itself create buildings, while being very handy as a soundbite and sobriquet for coffee-table picture books.

But it's not all tripe; the great buildings are obvious. The Johnson Wax Building (1939) seemed to reinvent everything in an inspirational workplace. Imagine, in the days of Edward Hopper, walking for the first time onto an office floor, into the clatter of typewriters and the murmur of business, that was suddenly cherished under an ethereal canopy of giant lily pads dappling the sky above Lake Michigan.

With Wright at the top of his game through this period, Taliesin West sits in the desert landscape as well as anything could, while Falling Water (also 1939) pushes this notion to an extreme, even if it cantilevers just a little too far, as did the Sturges House (1938). Later there are increasingly wacky moments, especially the Guggenheim Museum in New York (1959), a preposterous spiral that had to virtually bribe its way onto site and that inflamed the normally supplicant passions of exhibiting artists. Meanwhile, the Marin County complex in California, completed well after Wright's death, has more than a whiff of the Jetsons about it, and there are also some Unitarian churches that look like spaceships.

Wright's lionisation has been as much to do with the mythologies of the American psyche as with the considerable effort on his part, insomuch as the idea of organic unity is embedded in the constitution of the

**126** American Modernism

United States and tacit in the masterplan for America as laid down by Thomas Jefferson. The organic unity strived for by Sullivan was somehow domesticated by Wright, the lightning rod manifesting an ineffable new spirit wherever he went, even when it all became, towards the end of his life, plain peculiar. Wright's vision was primarily for himself, while Sullivan's had been for everyone else. His was sustainable where Sullivan's was not. And once the mantle of genius was bestowed, we would be progressively deprived of logic.

There is no doubt that the story of architecture needs figures as indefatigable as Bernini or Wright, but they are unlikable. The tragic air of Sullivan or Le Corbusier is perhaps more palatable. The lyrical Finn Alvar Aalto certainly saw through Wright's rhetoric; as he remarked robustly of Taliesen West, 'but it isn't built on rock, my research indicates that Taliesen is built on c**t'. Aalto being Aalto, he added this was a good idea.

There were curious hybrids that came out of the exchange between Europe and America in and around the First World War. Rudolph Schindler and Richard Neutra were both products of the Viennese Secession who were influenced by Wright and finally blossomed on the West Coast. Schindler had been a devotee of Otto Wagner, Neutra of Adolf Loos. Both worked for Wright, but Schindler had been left dealing with the frequent distress of Aline Barnsdall while Wright was away in Japan and Neutra had embarked on a pilgrimage to Wright's houses and found a raft of unimpressed, disgruntled inhabitants. The houses in Chicago's Oak Park had changed hands and been remodelled many times even by 1923, and the prairie setting had also disappeared.

Schindler, essentially an engineer, had made it to the States before the war and in his time off busied himself drawing rather peculiar Egon Schiele–style nudes of American girls. Neutra was drafted to serve in the Balkans and drew himself, amid total misery, as a scowling, self-loathing storm trooper. However, he recovered, marrying the accomplished cellist Dione Niedermann in Zurich, working for Mendelsohn in Berlin, and finally arriving in Chicago in 1923. Schindler had already gravitated west.

The two couples soon shared a house together in LA – a sort of jazz age commune – and are unique in sharing the same client for their respective best buildings: the neuropathic crank Dr Lovell. Lovell was new age before New Age, his 'Care of the Body' newspaper column making him a celebrity. If this all sounds very Californian, it is. Neutra's wife, Dione, complained that in Germany she had never heard so much talk of broken marriages and nervous breakdowns, while Schindler's wife, Pauline – who

American Modernism **127**

ran a kindergarten with Lovell's wife, Leah – wearing 'something resembling a toga', castigated her uptight attitudes and lack of free thinking. Neutra complained the Schindlers stayed up too late, 'sometimes to 2 a.m.', while he liked to go to bed at ten. Neutra was messianic about biorealism (his term), while Schindler soaked in the new bohemia.

Lovell commissioned three houses from Schindler, one of which, for an engineer, met the unfortunate fate of collapsing under snow load. The Lovell Beach House (1926) has become a modern icon, but Schindler's eccentricity – and his sexual chemistry with Leah – meant that the Lovell Health House commission went to Neutra in 1927 (and Pauline left Schindler the next year). In the end the Health House was a sensation: crystalline, cubic, confident, magnificent. On its completion, fifteen thousand amazed Angelenos poured through its doors, and its architect was famous. Neutra immediately sailed back to Europe to tell everybody.

But it was bad timing. Neutra returned to produce an incredibly consistent, if slightly sterile series of residences which you can hardly tell apart, at least from the perspective of the master photographer and purveyor of LA style Julius Shulman. He did so with a view to 'neutralising' what he saw as the unbearable state of the American psyche, waving an erasing shield. But in later life Neutra the idealist, like the Modernism he espoused, was eclipsed, and he felt it keenly, becoming almost pathologically depressed, often unbearable, until he died of a heart attack in 1970. Schindler had died in 1953.

When European Modernism reached the United States it would have to morph into something accommodated by American socioeconomics. Some took to this easily, like Mies, since he had little interest in the socioeconomic system in the first place. Miesian towers would become the language of downtown all over, with his disciples, Skidmore, Owings and Merrill, totally orthodox. Meanwhile, Walter Gropius, the great believer in teamwork for its own sake, while having a gratifying time at Harvard, ended up endorsing ceramic tiles and building the biggest prefabricated building at the time – the Pan Am Building – to little effect at all.

But even Mies didn't have it all his own way, especially when he reduced Edith Farnsworth's residence to a glass box. One could easily say this was another case of Mies creating something he couldn't resist; after all, he had a favourite phrase: 'never talk to your client about architecture'. In this case, Edith Farnsworth, a success in her own right, wasn't having it; the cost overruns and Mies's intransigence – coupled with an unreasonable dollop of emotional punishment – brought them to court. Mies won, but in the process the Farnsworth House (1951), and the International Style in

**128** American Modernism

general, was labelled 'anti-American'. Mies had been cruel; on a site visit to the building on completion, he asked Edith to give him a twirl on the terrace – she proudly did so – but he was just checking the height. He later said, 'she expected the architect to come with the house'.

But Mies could charm. A twenty-seven-year-old Phyllis Lambert demanded her father choose Mies for the Seagram Building, the Big Daddy corporate headquarters of them all. By 1958 it sat sleek as a big fat cat on Park Avenue. The conflict with Edith had been in all senses domestic; it wouldn't affect the embrace of Mies by the big shots downtown. Seagram was after all just a Canadian distiller with an image problem thanks to Prohibition; now it looked like just about the most respectable company on earth. The building was lush, extravagant, expensive, but it didn't look it; it looked sleek, distinguished and reserved. Meanwhile, Mies had his own architecture school, designed entirely by him – the Illinois Institute of Technology – at which, within a succession of glass temples, you learnt nothing but Mies. He cornered the market in good corners.

To practise, Mies went into partnership with Philip Johnson, the man who'd first scouted him out in Berlin. Johnson understood that architects were whores – he was even proud of it – and so was ideally placed. When there were just too many Miesian skyscrapers to maintain interest except among die-hards (Skidmore, Owings, and Merrill), Johnson would drop it and go postmodern (PoMo). Openly gay and independently wealthy, he was everything Louis Sullivan wasn't. A Svengali figure, he controlled the American architectural establishment from his corner table in Seagram's Four Seasons restaurant until his death, in 2005. To the annoyance of almost everyone except those who admired his power, it was clear Johnson believed in little but himself, and he could even take that on the chin. When a student wondered at the apparently facile nature of some of his later buildings, he replied, 'That's because I'm a bad architect'. Described as 'a charlatan, a mountebank and a juggler', he at least always got good press, in *Forbes*, *Fortune* and *Forum*.

But sooner or later someone was going to realise that architects were missing a bigger trick in such courtly self-indulgence. Why always work for clients anyway? Why not be the risk-taking entrepreneur instead? This figure would be John Portman.

In the early 1960s, Americans were evacuating their city centres in droves. It was the suburbs that had the appeal if you had the money, and the downtown areas were unsurprisingly run-down and criminalised. However, those downtown areas were also the obvious centres and the nexus of connectivity. Driving into Houston on an eighteen-lane freeway, you cannot but be impressed with the manmade mountain range of

## American Modernism 129

downtown looming in front of you and by the fact that you are travelling very fast towards it even if you don't want to.

Big hotels are therefore an especially safe bet in downtown areas, and land values were falling. John Portman's idea was to invert the exterior elevations onto a spectacular internal atrium. It didn't make much sense in terms of maid service, because you had single-loaded corridors rising thirty storeys up or so, but it made for a spectacular oasis for the travelling businessman.

Inadvertently, but proving the point, I've stayed in Portman's Hyatt Regency Houston, a particularly interesting example of a formula. I realised there was no real entrance on the street, just a taxi drop and slip-road to the underground car park, and the place looked like a fortress, clad in thirty-three storeys of brown brick. Inside, however, I was blown away, and as the glass lift to my room sped up the atrium I realised that this *was* the elevation, and it suddenly ran like a movie. You may remember the scene in *True Lies*, set in the Bonaventure in downtown LA, where 'Arnie' rides a horse in the lift; that's a Portman building too.

You could say this was a cynical urban planning move, but with hotel chains in his back pocket Portman was able to develop all over the United States, from downtown Atlanta to downtown Detroit, at least in all the sufficiently bad bits.

Fortresses of a different kind came naturally to Louis I. Kahn. He was brought up on an Estonian island that featured nothing much more than a dramatic castle, and the effect stayed with him. Kahn is widely acknowledged as a genius, so when Philip Johnson, of all people, calls him 'a phony, more of a phony than I am', we prick up our ears. After all, if anybody would know, Johnson would.

While Kahn talked easily as much baloney as Johnson, and both looked back to Rome – Kahn to the ruins of Hadrian and Johnson to Pope Julius III – Johnson's cattiness was probably a consequence of being unable to deny that Kahn's buildings were better, or at least more consistent, than his own. They rose from fierce and seemingly awkward geometric plans – nobody could put a staircase in a box like Kahn – into great cubes and circles in a manner totally at odds with the form-follows-function ethos, which Kahn reversed, preferring to imagine the spaces first and then their occupation.

So Kahn brought back a mystery to the process; he became a genius because he baffled everybody. Meanwhile, his buildings seemed jam-packed full of architecture, probably too much of it, so in general he built for patrons or universities with money, and when he didn't, for instance in Dhaka, Bangladesh, he went bust.

**130** American Modernism

The old universities always had money, but, by the 1950s, there was a new imperative to university building, both to bolster scientific research and as a bulwark against commercialisation. In 1958 the American economist J. K. Galbraith published *The Affluent Society*. This influential book warned that in a future world dominated by advertising there was effectively no difference between need and want, that desire would propel the consumer society. Such a view understandably horrified the British establishment to the point it encouraged massive university building and state subsidy of the arts, but the Americans were hardly immune, and Kahn's solidity was therefore deemed highly appropriate.

Kahn was also keenly aware of the problem of servicing, or pipes. He didn't like them, but as a consequence he put his considerable energies into dealing with them. In his Richards Memorial Laboratories for the University of Pennsylvania (1961) they were the building's defining characteristic, housed in a series of great monumental towers rising up the outside of the main envelope. In doing this he anticipated the 'High-Tech' architecture of Richard Rogers and Norman Foster, who encountered Kahn at Yale. It is easy to imagine them thinking that perhaps you could rip away the monumental brick towers and just leave the pipes, and that's exactly what they did.

Kahn was not easy to work with. He wilfully ignored both requirements and budgets, but he met his ideal client in the 'intuitive' scientist Dr Jonas Salk. Salk's research had found a cure for polio, but his methods were unorthodox and not unlike Kahn's approach to architecture. Salk would listen to Kahn the way nobody else could (Rem Koolhaas once crawled out of a Kahn lecture on his hands and knees, he found it so unbearable), and with the Salk Institute (1963), overlooking the Pacific at La Jolla, Kahn provided a masterpiece. It's a masterpiece for the view as much as anything, but it's a masterpiece.

He provided another with the Kimbell Art Museum in Fort Worth, but the essential Kahn would be found, obviously, in a place where there was both ubiquitous material and the cheapest labour. Kahn's monumental capitol at Dhaka exploited both of these. Incomplete and built during a civil war, the complex is apparently now cherished, but it does clock in at only 41 per cent net usable area, and, while looking the epitome of the naturally ventilated, it sucks up a large proportion of the city's electricity supply in air conditioning. It was also the building that did Kahn in, since Bangladesh also had difficulty paying bills. Kahn died in Penn Station in New York in 1974, essentially bankrupt.

But he was never good with money anyway. He was always scrambling around to pay off his girlfriends, rumoured to have included Ingrid

## American Modernism  **131**

Bergman. Anne Tyng published his letters, and it's clear there was also a problem with attribution; similarly, his engineer August Komendant made *Eighteen Years with Architect Louis I. Kahn* sound more like a prison sentence. Affectionately Vincent Scully called him 'an old rascal', but kept stumm over the complex personal life, which at one point meant being part of three families at the same time. One of his son's attempts to bring closure to their relationship is documented in the award-winning film *My Architect* (2003).

Another figure to supposedly wreck lives was the Californian 'architect' Craig Ellwood. Ellwood was born Jon Burke in Texas but soon changed his name on moving to Los Angeles, where he worked as a model. He got a regular job as a cost estimator in a construction firm and then doing PR for the Hollywood Bowl, both excellent grounding for when he reinvented himself as architecture's Cary Grant.

When you see a glass refrigerator full of cocktail glasses looking onto the living area of CSH16 (1953), you immediately know what this house is about. It is of course the birth of lifestyle, despite the perfectly genuine intentions of the Case Study House Program – the project of the progressive publisher John Entenza – to provide prototypes for popular housing. Exit Lucille Ball, enter Marilyn Monroe, Miles Davis and a Karmann Ghia amidst opaque (sliding, nonsliding, look as if they're sliding) glass walls, structure as 2 × 2-inch hollow steel sections with a chimney (fireplace and barbecue) like a relic, thrown to the extremity of the plan. Complete the scene with a pepper tree. This is California: image matters.

This being Hollywood, not many of these gems survive. Ellwood's CSH16 is a rarity – enjoyed by the original owner for life – but most were sold on and inevitably remodelled. The progressives, such as Esther McCoy, howled at the vandalism, but it was pure *genius loci*; according to John Chase, what could you expect? Other exceptions are the Stahl House (CSH22), by Pierre Koenig, earning its keep regularly from film shoots (*Galaxy Quest*) and advertising (Barclaycard, British Airways, Robbie Williams), and the Eames House (CSH8, 1949), a national treasure that anticipated an architecture assembled from IKEA and populated with ethnic knick-knacks.

All this might seem at odds with Ellwood's Miesian sympathies and his professed 'nonsensualism', but they qualify him as a kind of last gasp. A heady lifestyle that included four marriages (number three was to Miss Delaware), bitter employees, dangerous friends, a retreat from architecture into motor racing, sex addiction and abstract painting in Tuscany took its toll.

**132** American Modernism

So although Ellwood made it to Yale, where he shared an office (appropriately enough) with James Stirling, he wasn't exactly a natural academic. Robert Venturi was. Venturi wanted to find a substance to the architecture of the consumerist world. He greatly admired Kahn and went to work for him for a while but couldn't stand it. Instead (and encouraged by John Entenza), he took himself to Rome on a Graham Foundation grant and published the consequent book *Complexity and Contradiction in Architecture* in 1966, the year after L–C swam out to sea for the final time. This is widely held as a Postmodern text, but Venturi has never liked the label. However, it is the first orientated towards architecture in the age of consumerism. Venturi and Denise Scott Brown had a game, 'I can like something worse than you', so it's about choice and difficulty. It's also about pleasure.

To understand this 'gentle manifesto' further, we might go back to the difference between building and architecture as discussed in the introduction, comparing it with the difference between food and cuisine: that some process has to take that side of beef and turn it into cuisine, even if you are just shifting it into a finer restaurant. We can still call the most elemental of buildings 'architecture' if they have gone through some kind of mannered process. However, this is not always straightforward. Remember that L–C and Mies were not very appreciative of Gropius's prefabricated houses at the Weissenhof Siedlung in 1928 because they didn't seem to feature enough ingredients for their taste.

So what is the process going to be when you are confronted by endless choice? Hollywood shows us that if you want Louis XIV or Etruscan villas, you can have them. For Americans after the Second World War, within certain bounds, that was potentially everybody's choice.

Venturi's view was that in architecture worthy of the term, elements should be conjugated in a complex and contradictory way, just building an Etruscan villa wouldn't count but manipulating an Etruscan motif with a Palladian one might. It was this that marked out the masterpieces of the past. The cover of his book showed Michelangelo's Porta Pia, a grand gate featuring many such juxtapositions, and with a built-in joke. Unfortunately, *Complexity and Contradiction* wasn't straightforward but was quickly considered the most important thinking since *Towards a New Architecture*, just as *Catch-22* was the greatest American literature since Scott Fitzgerald.

Venturi's examples included Vanbrugh, Lutyens, Hawksmoor, Le Corbusier and Greene & Greene and ran across the whole history of essentially Classicist architecture. The book pointedly does not involve itself with the Gothic, but that's hardly a surprise. To illustrate it in practice, Venturi completed a house for his mother that we have all tried to

American Modernism **133**

like at one time or another. To understand the theory some more, you are advised to look carefully at the plan of the staircase as it canoodles around the chimney.

Further to that, Venturi was becoming interested in what architecture had to say in the age of mass media – what was its relationship to advertising? Probably architecture was becoming more wordy – he drew a big shed with a billboard above it saying 'I am a Monument' – and he wasn't shy of evoking comparison to the poetry of T. S. Eliot or pitting architecture's theories against those for poetic composition as set out by Cleanth Brookes. Meanwhile, was architecture suffering from a taste problem? Were the progressives dismissing those suburban tract homes too quickly? He quickly found the sociologist Herbert Gans supporting him there.

From here it was a short step to becoming interested not in the heroic, like Kahn – with whom Venturi was now utterly disillusioned – but in the everyday, the conventional, or 'the ugly and the ordinary'. It was clear that if you looked at anything long enough, these were just value judgements, both complacent and lazy in a period where Pop Art had superseded Abstract Expressionism. Venturi & Rauch's most apparently ugly and ordinary scheme, the Yale Mathematics Building (1969), featured a most ungainly core plan wriggling to get out. You just had to spot it.

So, in the quest for something real, Venturi, Scott Brown and Izenour took their Yale students to Las Vegas in 1968 and published *Learning from Las Vegas* in 1972. It is a fascinating book, first, because you won't learn much about Las Vegas from it and second, for the vitriol it metes out in its second half to those 'heroic and original' architects. This is its general subtext, that architects had got it wrong: they hadn't recognised the new Rome right in front of their noses or, as they put it, their own 'great proletarian cultural locomotive'. On the surface the victim of this calculated attack was Paul Rudolph, whose work Venturi fiercely contrasts with his own, while oedipally it was Kahn.

Las Vegas, the new city of signs – and signs 'the like of which the art world had never seen before', according to Tom Wolfe in his famous 1966 essay 'Las Vegas (Can't Hear You! Too Noisy)' – was an obvious venue for study, but Venturi *et al.* didn't go so far as to study its mechanics. It is not a book about how Vegas works or worked (that would have been a step too far), but one about the signs and symbols of a new ephemeral age. Like many fans of Las Vegas, Venturi and Scott Brown would lose their enthusiasm with time. Vegas had become mere scenography, a Disneyland, by the 1990s, whereas previously it had been less proscribed, more vernacular, authentic! Or rather: a fine (if extreme)

**134** American Modernism

representation of America being 'almost all right' just before the 1973 oil crisis if you were prepared to ignore the Vietnam War, the Cold War, and civil rights.

Tom Wolfe's first book, somewhat paradoxical for a man famous for wearing a white suit, was *The Electric Kool-Aid Acid Test*, the story of Ken Kesey's Merry Pranksters, who had taken to the road in a psychedelically painted school bus in 1964. We might be tempted to call them revolutionaries, but by now it is more apt to refer to the hippie movement and the preceding beatniks as the counterculture. You should read the nuance there: we don't have revolution any more; we have counterculture. Seeing hypocrisy and prejudice and going all out for spiritual enlightenment and emancipation, with money in their pockets, education and reliable cars, this generation saw the opportunity in a freshly nomadic nonconformity, the light touch of the electric gypsy. You wouldn't think this had much to do at all with architecture, which was all prim and proper, all suit and tie. However, Woodstock congregated 400,000 people in the same field for three days. It was a city facilitated by amplification and sustained on mung beans and pills, and critics such as Reyner Banham – raised on the technological imperative – weren't going to ignore it.

In England, encouraged by Banham and *AD* magazine, Archigram were the most consistent protagonists. It was clear that whatever Louis Kahn thought his rooms were going to do (or, for that matter, what *ideas* Robert Venturi had about his), Archigram were going to ask the question 'What is a room?' more blatantly. And they went to America to find out, tripping around Cape Canaveral and reading William Burroughs. Although they were charmingly English, Archigram's influences were American consumer products: the Sears Roebuck & Co catalogue, tape recorders, projectors and headphones, disposable bikinis! They drew instant cities and walking cities and singing tomatoes and *suitaloons* and all sorts and eventually gave conceptual answers to architectural questions in the manner of 'why bother at all?' Meanwhile, in Italy, a group called Superstudio panicked at the prospect of the military-industrial complex gone mad. They represented it all with a giant grid, an endless monument painted in the manner of Schinkel. Folks were perplexed – presented with a monument to what? To servicing? To conformity? To banality?

Many sniffed an air that wasn't so pleasant, and, if we remove the consumerist distractions, an oddball to end our discussion of American Modernism is the man who predicted its abject failure. Part soothsayer for the hippie generation, attempting to transcend chatter, was a strange man called Richard Buckminster Fuller.

American Modernism **135**

Fuller removed himself to think only on the basic principles of design for this planet, to devise an operating manual for spaceship earth, in around 1927. The reasons for his year of silence, his 'peeling off', were many and possibly self-mythologising, but Fuller convincingly began his thinking from scratch, or at least from the cosmos backwards. Words like 'sunrise' and 'sunset' were just plain outdated and should be replaced by 'sunsight' and 'suneclipse'; even 'up' and 'down' were contentious, since the earth was not a plane and vertical lines were not parallel.

Fuller was the first architect to suggest we were running the whole world backwards, that we needed a complete turnaround. He considered himself to think in 4D, and certainly in terms of circles rather than squares, and in scientific terms regarding the implementation of technology (which, he quite reasonably considered, once you abandon everything else that gets in the way, is what we do). So humans do technology: we discover things, and we do new things with the things we discover. Why we do this and under what motivation (disposable bikinis!?) was something Bucky wasn't too keen to answer, since all politicians and practitioners of such dark arts were stooges. Putting it simply, he appeared to believe humans might run earth like a skipper runs a yacht.

Since our technology inevitably evolves towards lighter, more efficient things, Buckminster Fuller's basic question for architects was 'How much does your building weigh?' If our cars get more miles per hour, then so should our buildings. On the back of all this, he nearly became the Henry Ford of the house-building business with his Dymaxion House (1947), but for a stream of mysterious reasons he blew it. He moved on to Black Mountain College – an American Bauhaus of sorts – where he developed the geodesic dome, which the hippies built in droves, sometimes using the strips from venetian blinds.

Going rather the opposite way, Bernard Rudofsky had published the enduring (obviously, given our Introduction) *Architecture without Architects* in 1964 and Paolo Soleri began the Arcosanti community in the desert outside Phoenix in 1970. This marriage of ecology and architecture, initially almost native Indian, became illustrative of a welter of paradox as it continues today, commercially funded by the sales of ethnic wind chimes and bells and clouded by images of the megalomania and intransigence of its visionary.

So young Americans, if born in 1947, came of age in 1968, a year that saw the Tet Offensive in Vietnam, the assassination of Martin Luther King, the assassination of Robert Kennedy, the shooting of a seventeen-year-old Black Panther by police, riots at the Democratic National

## 136 American Modernism

Convention in Chicago, the release of 'Street Fighting Man', and the strongest of demonstrations against Miss World. For those seeking an alternative life, communism may never have been an option, but communes were. Giving up the job at J. Walter Thompson to draw mandalas and talk to the trees was actually a possibility. Meanwhile, with the help of the former Nazi rocket scientist Werner von Braun, we were going to land on the moon.

# 10
## POSTMODERNISM

Usually I begin the Postmodern lecture with 'Dare' by Gorillaz, the cartoon band of Damon Albarn, with Shaun Ryder, in a haunted Modernist house. Whether all of rock music is Postmodern (therefore designating the modern as jazz, folk and blues) I'm not sure. Postmodernism has at its core a kind of recycling, and rock music certainly does that; if Led Zeppelin reconstituted the blues, then The Darkness reconstituted Led Zeppelin. Then again, Gothic cathedrals do that, too. However, The Darkness track 'Bald' is powerful, funny and ironic. It's about losing your hair – how un-rock 'n' roll is that? That seems very Postmodern. So does a cartoon rock band.

I can't remember irony being acceptable at all when I first went to architecture school to be educated by the likes of Mark Wells.

Architectural history books of this type published before the Second World War found a kind of triumphal, self-satisfied destination in Modernism. You cannot avoid sensing the smugness in the air – here it was at last, and jolly good! There's a picture of a bloke sitting down in his easy chair with his feet up reading a paper and smoking his pipe. It has to be said this smugness, in Britain at least, was largely middle class and perpetuated within a rather elite set of progressives, Fabians and the otherwise socially minded. Yes, the maid did mischievously spill ink on Winifred Roberts's Mondrian, but she was quickly forgiven because she did not understand. And Eton commissioned the Modern architect F.R.S. Yorke to build some masters' houses.

But something was wrong, as Sir John Summerson put it: 'By 1937 the Edwardians were finished. The modern was ready to take over which, in

**140** Postmodernism

1945, it did. It conquered the world and then fell into a dead faint, without, however, actually dying.' His chronology may be a little premature, but Modern architecture and Modern architects did steadily become that anathema to the postwar world: unpopular.

The question marks against the authority of Modernism were largely presented by the advent and eventual triumph of consumerism. The Second World War had simultaneously provided a tumult of technology and a great opportunity for rebuilding while demonstrating the power of the people especially that part of the community systematically ignored previously; women. I am minded of the British propaganda film *Millions Like Us* (1943) that presented the essential role of women as producers in the war economy. The consequences of J. K. Galbraith's *The Affluent Society* (1958) were at first useful to socially minded architects, with the new state support system – now called the 'nanny state' – providing masses of work building schools, hospitals, housing, new universities and arts complexes, but this was quaint in the long term, since all this would run contrary to market forces.

Of course, there was an alternative. The Soviet Union – once viewed as a paradise for architects in the late 1920s – was still there, a great lumbering opposition, but it was crippled by the cost of a Cold War it could ill afford and would eventually (see Introduction) trade everything down to numbers, just as we traded everything up to cash flow.

Meanwhile, it was no longer dirty machines that would save us from drudgery while the human situation improved. The new technology was electronic. This was tomorrow's world; the world at your fingertips. Our desires, historically repressed, would now be realised and exploited. From fashion to fast food, these desires were good for the economy. We were also suddenly in the realm of identity politics, of individualism, and our destiny as a society became unclear. Politics became pressure groups. British prime minister Margaret Thatcher went as far as to say society didn't exist, that 'society' was an old-fashioned, leftist notion (Thatcher was no Roman, although she may have acted like one). Eventually, folk are no longer quiet on the bus out of politeness, minding their own business; they are jabbering nonsensically into their new mobile phones.

We forgot about progress. Instead, history began to conveniently oscillate in circles. By 1992 Francis Fukuyama was prepared to say history had stopped altogether. Postmodernity as an adjunct of late capitalism was effectively pounced upon by cultural theorists (we now had such a thing) such as David Harvey (*The Condition of Post-Modernity*) and Fredric Jameson (*Postmodernism: Or, the Cultural Logic of Late Capitalism*) and opportunistically by magazines like *The Face*, since Postmodernism was all about you, and it was fun, and there were no more heroes any more.

With the lack of heroes, the horizon dimmed. *Blade Runner* (1982) is the film most quoted as a dystopian prequel, but Hollywood has done little

PHOTOGRAPH 10 Portraits of academics come a bit stereotypically serious. Karaoke, Bethnal Green Working Mens Club.
*Credit*: Sarah Ainslie

**142** Postmodernism

else but throw confetti and disaster at us ever since, to the point, perhaps, where we have been cynically numbed to both. Naomi Klein's books *No Logo* and *The Shock Doctrine* outline that process and its consequences.

As the Western masses started dancing to the music of time, there were still huge pits of misery in Africa and the rest of the world, but the Neoclassical perspective of TV still had us blind – until Bob Geldof. Meanwhile, we would develop ever-widening disparities in wealth and opportunity at home (see chapter 11). And while we were dancing to the music of cash tills, in terms of taste, the public would eventually just like what they liked. This was cynically facilitated by increased personal debt: Barclaycard was first introduced in 1966, Access in 1972. The fear within consumerism was obvious – environmental collapse – but doom-mongers were not going to be allowed to ruin the party (see chapter 11).

Meanwhile, architectural Modernism was considered dull (but probably even more dull in the GDR). That is, if you leaf through the pages of *The Architectural Review* from the 1960s, it looks very dull. The ethos of professionalism, including bow tie and membership in the masonic lodge, had hardly shifted; your architect was – until the more radically minded postwar generation matured in the new university system Galbraith recommended – almost exclusively middle class and almost exclusively male.

The weight of previous hope had seen idealism prone to scandal. As one politician, the one-time saviour of the north and 'mouth of the Tyne' T. Dan Smith, deftly put it: 'something happened on the road to utopia'. Smith was the Labour leader of Newcastle city council and was responsible for an unprecedented regeneration programme to make the city 'the Brasilia of the north'.

Smith was convicted of taking bribes from the architectural designer John Poulson, and the scandal was contagious, leading to the resignation of the Conservative home secretary, Reginald Maudling. Not actually an architect himself, Poulson pioneered design and build in the UK before we knew what design and build was and quickly built up a large practice. He saw himself as doing no wrong, but the litany of gifts and mutual back-scratching, along with the fact he was an active freemason, exposed a vivid and unfortunate picture of the upwardly aspirational mores of a deluded middle class. His own lawyer called him 'hypocritical, self-righteous, and something of a megalomaniac'. His world is uncannily reproduced, not in name but in tone, in the 1971 film *Get Carter* and effectively satirised in the 'Architects Sketch' from Monty Python, where architects are depicted as either slaves to the machine (designers of abattoirs) or rabid freemasons making funny handshakes (and silly walks). Poulson was jailed for five years, later increased to seven in 1974, with the judge describing him as 'incalculably evil'.

Postmodernism  **143**

Meanwhile, Europe was not about to say its postwar planning was 'almost all right'. The riots in Paris of May 1968 championed the beach beneath the paving slabs; development schemes that threatened existing communities were challenged. The revolutionary protestor Maurice Culot mounted a defence to save existing quarters from the faceless swathes of office blocks and urban motorway in Brussels, the new home of the EU. No matter that Colonel Seifert wanted to build contemporary monuments on the London skyline in the tradition of Wren; it was his financial chicanery that hit the news. Centre Point was a more profitable element of a property portfolio empty than occupied. Planners in the LCC, such as Brian Anson, preparing plans for the redevelopment of Covent Garden, suddenly found themselves swapping sides to attack their original proposals.

In the wake of this came the demand for effective participation. Lucien Kroll, another Belgian, went as far as to design systems which appeared to give users whatever they wanted, resulting in somewhat grandiose but undoubtedly jolly patchwork heaps.

There were practical disasters, too, such as the collapse of Ronan Point tower block in London's East End. Using the new prefabrication techniques, builders had cut corners. The pumps used to fill the joints clogged easily, and builders stuffed them with their daily copies of *The Sun*. Meanwhile, the new occupants were not always model citizens themselves, and for years the Ronan Point collapse was rumoured to have been caused not by a gas explosion but by one tenant's storage of dynamite for safe breaking. Then there were the much-vaunted social problems that plagued council estates through the '70s and '80s. And, of course, those original icons of the Modern Movement now looked terrible because they had been badly built, poorly maintained and politically abused.

The intentional dynamiting of the award-winning Pruitt Igoe housing project in St Louis in 1972 was the catalyst for a seismic shift to a new architectural style. It was the product not of a political economist like Marx or an anthropologist like Darwin or a founder of psychoanalysis like Freud or, for that matter, even the conscience of William Morris. It was not the dream of an engineer (Brunel), an artist (Le Corbusier) or an organiser (Gropius) but the enthusiasm of an American architectural wordsmith called Charles Jencks. This is the period when, to paraphrase Sigfried Giedion, journalism took command.

The failure of Bauhaus principles was illustrated perfectly in the fate of its building. Dessau saw some of the last furious fighting in World War II, and, as the city was gobbled up behind the Iron Curtain, any image of the building looked awful to Western eyes until reunification and refurbishment. Its architect faired little better; Gropius's Gropiusstadt mass housing

**144** Postmodernism

scheme in Berlin became the home of Vera Christiane Felscherinow. Her harrowing tale of her life as a teenage heroin addict became required reading for all teenagers in Germany's schools, and there was also a film, *Christiane F*, with a soundtrack (appropriately enough) by David Bowie. So if Gropius's reputation was not already sealed in the eyes of the public, it certainly was by 1981.

Jencks made his name with the book *Le Corbusier and the Tragic View of Architecture* (1974). While it may be a misleading title, it does reflect some notion that architecture might *not* be a tragic endeavour. Jencks was not particularly interested in political issues or social trends; he spotted failure and aesthetic dullness and unified them into the same thing. It would be correct to describe him as an apostle, for God was on his way back, too.

Jencks realised that architects needed to reinvent themselves with some fresh value added if they were going to compete. The old professional credo would fracture, and if architects weren't going to be literal doctors they could at least become faith healers crossed with brand managers. Meanwhile, there was a continual appetite for something new. That appetite was provided in an explosion of media opportunity and general quickening, even if this was put in the service, eventually, of ideas that were as good as preindustrial. Architectural Postmodernism in Britain would be closely allied to the fate of Jencks/St Martin's Press/Academy Editions under the charismatic wing of Andreas Papadakis, and the various editions of Jencks's *Language of Post-Modern Architecture* (1977) chart the movement's progress from slightly anarchic *ad hoc*-ism through to determined Neoclassicism within the space of a decade.

In America, Postmodernism was simply a logical extension of fashion. Die-hards (SOM) would continue to fight their corner as long as they could, Venturi Scott Brown would continue to champion difficulty, but the rehabilitation promised by Postmodernism – a rhetoric of architectural language that people would easily understand (whether it worked or not) – was hard to resist because it would improve profitability. Soon every mini-mall in the United States would sprout a vestigial pediment: split, holed or otherwise.

The most illuminating architect in the overtly Postmodern pantheon was the American Michael Graves. His Portland Building was a landmark exercise in Neoclassical high jinks for the 1980s, whereas today it is criticised (and threatened with demolition) for making Portlanders sad because the windows are too small. We will return to him. Others who epitomise the era are Also Rossi, in Italy, whose morbidity was endearing; O. M. Ungers, in Germany; and James Stirling in Britain. There were any

Postmodernism **145**

number of American fellow travellers, led by the Miesian defector Philip Johnson.

Aldo Rossi was a devotee of Adolf Loos, who had doubted architecture's ability to change anything even in the '20s. Rossi's buildings – especially the stunning Gallaratese apartment block in Milan (1974) – echo some lost city and have the sense of a de Chirico painting about them. Jim Stirling was an innovative Modernist who, with James Gowan, created some of the most vibrant, exciting and delightful modern architecture in postwar Britain until it fell apart. Philip Johnson was a social pariah of epic proportions who sustained himself with the belief that architects were whores.

Intellectually the groundwork for all this was rather inadvertently prepared by Colin Rowe, an Englishman who made his way to Cornell. He was a man for whom it is said James Stirling held the pencil, since he had been Stirling's influential tutor at Liverpool University. They certainly shared a taste for strong drink and antiques. Rowe would turn up to a lecture 'looking like an unmade bed', but he was an exceptionally gifted follower of Wittkower as a historian. He'd made his name with the essay 'The Mathematics of the Ideal Villa' in 1947, in which he daringly compared Le Corbusier's early villas to the work of Palladio, just as Wittkower had referred Palladio's to Alberti's.

This may mark the moment architects first, rather inadvertently, joined the dance. But the tempo increased considerably when, in 1961, Rowe reviewed La Tourette for *The Architectural Review*. Here it was clear that he had gone a step further and was not so much illuminating Le Corbusier's principles as embellishing his own, and the way was set for the triumph of language over L–C's 'plastic act in the service of poesie'.

The gradual ascendancy of the word correlates both with the all-pervasiveness of advertising and this proliferation of academic critique, and it was convenient that Le Corbusier was mouldering in the grave when the next lesson, *Complexity and Contradiction in Architecture,* was published, in 1966. As earlier stated, Venturi does not like to be thought of as a Postmodern architect, but he did much to define the condition. In his drawing of a shed with a billboard on top saying 'I am a Monument', he declares at once the ubiquity of the shed, the importance of advertising and the growing power of the word.

So the widespread postwar public housing boom had weathered its first twenty years continually compromised by corrupt local politics, flawed construction and defective social engineering, and it was time for architecture to take on a degree of circumspection as to its utopian aspirations on the one hand and a degree of pretension as to its purpose on the other. Local Authority architecture departments under the Galbraith model collapsed.

**146** Postmodernism

Meanwhile, the hierarchies of the traditional European city had been destroyed by bombing, panzers or Patton and were replaced by acres of generic retail and office space and lifeless piazzas. But on their holidays, clutching new Instamatic cameras and Super 8s, architects took advantage of newly affordable air travel and found themselves swooning at the ancient delights of, say, Palma, where they found charm, opportunity, even environmental sense in the cramped ancient layout, while they munched authentic peasant food and sipped satisfyingly rough local wine. Such an experience formed the basis for Rowe's second book, *Collage City*, written with Fred Koetter, a repudiation of modern town-planning principles, especially those espoused by Le Corbusier, in the light of better experiences of older things. *Collage City* seemed to reject the significance of the modern constructional column and the five points of architecture in favour of a return to the wall, the elemental act of building protection from prehistoric times. It also appeared to reverse the emphasis on the dwelling and drove us back to considerations regarding the space of our urban appearance. Reconstructing such ancient agoras and fora became something of an obsession. They would lack their original raison d'être, of course, and whether this mattered or not was a big question. Whatever, Leonardo Benevolo's *History of the City* became an atlas of urban possibility.

James Stirling was fifty by 1975 and had survived being parachuted out of a plane on D-Day. He never wanted to talk about it but set about his architectural career with bumptious enthusiasm. When the characteristic red tiling on James Stirling's university buildings began to fall off, when professors got fed up with the rain running down the inside of their windows and the students couldn't work for the noise of the fans and the stifling heat of the library – and, most important, when the university authorities had had enough – Big Jim unsurprisingly found himself without any work.

Sanguine, he joined the dance. With the help of a young Leon Krier, he republished his own work as *James Stirling: Buildings and Projects 1950–74* in exactly the same format as Le Corbusier's *Oeuvre Complète*. Krier's brother, Rob, was already working on *Urban Space,* a manual of traditional urban form. Listening hard, Stirling turned himself around into a witty master of architectural juxtaposition just as *Collage City* hit the bookshelves, winning plaudits galore in 1984 for his Neue Staatsgalerie in Stuttgart, a building memorably used to advertise Rover cars. This generation would find it easy to see the value in product tie-ins: if a culinary company invited you to put your signature to a pan cleaner or a kettle, you'd probably do it – it was a far more reliable way of making money than designing buildings.

Postmodernism **147**

The New York Five (Peter Eisenman, Charles Gwathmey, John Hejduk, Michael Graves and Richard Meier) became self-styled progenitors of energetic, picturesque, new white architecture that looked particularly beguiling in snow. Here the elements of modern architecture were dissected and mashed up again for their own sake. Successful versions by Richard Meier easily found themselves as lakeside retreats featured in coffee-table magazines, while intellectuals struggled to understand the interminable series of diagrams that went into the creation of any of Eisenman's houses. The scholasticism was all too clear, even if the intention wasn't.

Graves started out the 'cubist kitchen king', but within a decade Jencks had hailed him, like Hamlet, 'king of infinite space'. Initially jumbling up Le Corbusier's five villa types, projects such as the unbuilt Rockefeller House (1969) were picturesque but oddly appropriate. They were proposed in balloon frame, where wall and floor become essentially the same thing, and Alan Colquhoun noted these stage sets were almost logical, like something from *Gone with the Wind*. You certainly could not ignore the phenomenal relation – paper-cardboard-matchwood – especially when Graves's especially daring Snyderman House was burnt to the ground in a suspected arson attack by a property developer in 2002.

When Graves bought his own 'Tuscan' barn near the campus at Princeton, where he was chair of architecture, he underwent a somewhat Pauline conversion to the eternal battle with the keystone and solidity. After all, what you could do for Corbu you could do for Ledoux. There followed four volumes of citadel-like re-enactments of classical partis, with a roster of critical enthusiasm that it is difficult to muster against anybody else who has since managed to fall so quickly out of fashion: Colin Rowe, Kenneth Frampton, Alan Colquhoun, Peter Carl, Vincent Scully, Christian Norberg-Schulz, Charles Jencks, Robert Maxwell, Janet Abrams and Francisco Sanin all stuck their colours to this life raft. However, it is probably a building by Graves that none of those critics could bring themselves to enjoy that represents the epitome of the Postmodern architectural genre – his Team Disney headquarters in Burbank (1986). Even the name gives it away, but the elevation – a classical entablature supported by seven giant dwarfs – says it all. It's high concept, like *Top Gun*.

The difference between the greys (Venturi *et al.*) and the whites (Eisenman and Co.) was amusingly articulated in Tom Wolfe's volume *From Bauhaus to Our House* (1981) as centred around the issue of class. Venturi, supported by Herbert Gans's work, had far more faith in the developing popular culture (or proletarian cultural locomotive) than his rivals, who could hardly be prised away from their breakfast table shared with Philip Johnson.

**148** Postmodernism

Venturi's democratic faith did not go so far as to embrace high-concept architecture, but Graves rode the whirlwind, winning *GQ's* Man of the Year Award in 1999. Sadly, Graves didn't make any money from his famous kettle, only two cents per unit, but did supply this author's dishwasher brush and kitchen colour scheme. There are ups and there are downs, but overall the result is salad tongs with Classical tags.

Other career trajectories would take Richard Meier to become the apotheosis of smart modern white buildings with ramps and ships' railings, perfect for the broodingly sexy (yet psychotic) world of the film director Michael Mann, and led John Hejduk into a world of the fairies and spooky curiosities and Peter Eisenman to become the most heavyweight of meta-theorists and an intellectual bedfellow of Jacques Derrida.

Frank Gehry seized the opportunity from humble commercial beginnings. Swathing your house in Santa Monica with chicken wire had never been such an effective promotional tool. While others – like his rival Jon Jerde – built big from the start, Gehry settled for the artistic mid-market and various arty ploys, until graduating with his extraordinary Guggenheim art museum in Bilbao (1997), from which screwed-up paper style he never looked back, even at the age of eighty. Now known as the Bilbao effect, this success led regeneration committees lemming-like towards show-stopping (or rather show-starting) buildings as the salvation to blight and led young students fresh out of senior school to begin their architectural education thinking the best thing to do with paper was to screw it up rather than draw on it.

Europe was not immune to the high concept, either. Being a Catalan Marxist revolutionary certainly helped Ricardo Bofill as he built on the scale of Versailles for the overspill population of Paris at Marne-La-Vallée, near Disneyland Paris. These buildings manage to charm in their vulgarity (we joked he put the toilets inside the giant prefabricated concrete Classical columns), but the menacing aspect made them feature in the Terry Gilliam film *Brazil*.

Waving supportive letters from Jacques Derrida wouldn't get you very far if there weren't an appetite for it. To paraphrase a reflective Colin Rowe (quoting from Jarzombek), the theory-mongers searched for congratulatory applause from the cultural voyeurs fighting their quixotic struggles far from the site of any real battle, and the architectural schools became hotbeds of controversy. It didn't seem possible to teach Postmodernism; you just had to take a stand within it. In 1983 Stirling refused to pass any of Nigel Coates's 'NATO' unit as external examiner, accusing them of being nothing more than 'cartoons'. He made his point until he got bored

Postmodernism **149**

and went home, when the remaining tutors promptly passed everybody. Such emerging stars all benefited from an atmosphere of intellectual free-for-all sometimes known as 'Deconstruction'.

Students now brandished mountainous collections of philosophical texts in the demolition of Modernist principle, and there were developing sects. Still operating in the era immediately before the collapse of the Berlin Wall, in 1989, the Soviet regime had many defectors and detractors. Daniel Libeskind found his way out of Poland, as did the historian Joseph Rykwert and the phenomenologist Dalibor Vesely from Czechoslovakia. None was likely to champion Modernism; indeed, they had prostrated themselves against it. Resistance had been centred in the church crypts. These academics began to collect together at the Architectural Association and elsewhere under the umbrella of a powerful Heideggerian philosophy: phenomenology. It was comparable to a counterreformation. Suddenly humanity was alienated not just in terms of its production but also spiritually; there was 'a crisis in modern science'. Their Loyola was Dalibor.

So by the mid-'80s the roster of talent teaching in the Diploma in Architecture at the Polytechnic of Central London read Doug Clelland (healing the city), James Madge (chuckling at Otto Wagner), a dapper Demetri Porphyrios (reconstructing Ancient Greece as new urbanism) and a poetic David Greene (who said you could pick any style you liked except Future Systems, an anaesthetic derivative of his own Archigram group). There was also the unfortunate Laszlo Kiss, but the organic strain was by now largely relegated to the provinces.

I walked into that great concrete megastructure wearing my negative heel, pork-pie shoes one sunny autumn day in 1984. PCL had just hosted a Papadakis-organised conference on the big new American Postmodernists. It was on a high. On the occasion of my first crit Doug pounced: 'There you are with yer fookin' red scarf [actually it was a sort of peach-colour sweater from the Gap]. Who do you think you are? Fookin' Georgio fookin' Grassi?' Of course I didn't realise the full cultural context: that Clelland was a fully baptised phenomenologist, or the fact that Italian communists perpetually wear red scarves (Kath Shonfield was to assure me of this some years later), and I was certainly dim to the fact the two might be somehow antagonistic. But I did realise I was no way up to speed with the script.

I walked out again two years later feeling like Lloyd Cole while still looking alarmingly like Rick Astley. I found myself working for the die-hard Modernist Trevor Dannatt. I wasn't very good. I was in awe of Trevor's chief personal assistant, an icy Swiss girl whose drawings

## 150 Postmodernism

were so scarily accurate we would peep at them after hours. How did she do it?

All drawing was still done painstakingly by hand, but somehow our heads were already set on the ephemeral. In Dannatt's office I spent what seemed to me to be an inordinate time designing a single bathroom, then moved to a joinery schedule – where we still drew timber in pencil, for that mirrored the qualities of the material – but was more usefully put to work colouring in. One day I climbed the stairs to Trevor's eyrie and explained I was going to leave to 'design crap houses in Docklands'. He said I was making a grave error.

Actually I don't think I used the word 'crap', but I meant something at least zippier than what I was doing. I got a job with a small practice (Simon Smith and Michael Brooke) in Clapham running out of a shop. They had their record collection up on the wall, and that was good enough for me. Michael Brooke would design everything with his Montblanc fountain pen, and I distinctly remember him saying that he'd like to turn up for work wearing doublet and hose: ideal. It was fast, fluid, fun stuff. When they let me go several years later it wasn't the end of the world; it was going to teaching – sometimes Edinburgh, Leicester, Oxford and London schools in the same week.

So my next die-hard was Isi Metzstein, who with Andy MacMillan was the creative partnership behind Gillespie Kidd & Coia and the joint command post of Scottish architectural education. 'Flic' Good had got me a job with him at Edinburgh University. That didn't work out either: my consciousness of the word grated on Isi's Kahnian authority, and I think we nearly drove each other mad. Isi retired, and I experienced a hilarious interview for a job at the Mackintosh with MacMillan, where I tried to explain that architecture students should make pop videos. Eventually I got a full-time post in London and went to Las Vegas to find myself.

Those die-hards maintained a grip, providing a nagging conscience in this world of the word, but they were getting quite a beating. Nobody could think of Peter Ahrends (of Ahrends, Burton & Koralek) without 'carbuncles' attached. Even Prince Charles was a Papadakis acolyte. Meanwhile, the schools bristled with agitation. It wasn't just Postmodern confections of one kind or another; thanks to the hypnotic genius of Kevin Rhowbotham, there were even vaginas in boxes, on poles! Heaven forbid, some of us even wanted architecture to be fun.

Of course there were architects who simply refined their Modernism through the Postmodern period, hardly changing course. Some even assumed modesty thanks to Kenneth Frampton, whose critical regionalism fostered a Modernism with local flavour. However, a vast proportion

Postmodernism **151**

of these architects seemed to be Swiss. Powering on regardless was certainly the British High-Tech approach.

Richard Rogers, Baron Rogers of Riverside, Caesar-like, somehow always managed to convince us of his urban good intentions, while simultaneously presenting us with mountainous collections of prefabricated pods and gantries, the Lloyd's Building being a picturesque elevation of toilets in the manner of San Gimignano. It didn't/couldn't bother him that his career (and Renzo Piano's) was set with the Pompidou Centre, a consolation-prize art centre dealt out by Georges Pompidou in the wake of the riots of '68 and a building that positively shouted, 'Get on with your art!'

British High-Tech rather ignored the difficulties of Postmodernity. It was also a bit nerdy, and meanwhile it demanded teams of excessively hard-working employees. High-Tech was never popular in the architecture schools, where it was viewed as a bit of a cop-out. Paul Shepheard pointed out right at the beginning of his book *What Is Architecture?* that Rogers's premise was even fundamentally flawed, for if he wanted to express all the services on the outside of the building for ease of replacement, how was it that the escalators in the Lloyd's Building ran straight up the middle?

Norman Foster was rather more astringent, admitting his favourite building was the Boeing 747 and knowing how much it weighed. His buildings – starting out accommodating to the beanbag generation (such as the Willis Faber & Dumas insurance building in Ipswich) – soon became colder, bigger and more introverted to the point where nobody seemed to notice them very much except when the users ruined them with tat (Stansted Airport) – that is, until the event of the Gherkin in the City of London, a building whose shape produced a canny optical illusion that it was lower in height than the building next door but that, once the viewer was a mile or two away, towered way above everything else. Meanwhile, it was also clearly not a gherkin. However, the City of London appeared to boom, and each development was tagged – much to the distress of its architects – for easy recognition and marketing purposes: the Shard, the Walkie-Talkie, the Cheese Grater, the Rollercoaster and so on. The same thing was happening abroad, more precisely in Dubai, where collections of skyscrapers began to look, as Shumon Basar put it, 'depressing; like too many people smiling at a party'.

Towering away, the dramatic globalisation of the industry, the impact of global development and economics, and the influence of computing would all shift the business of architecture to, well, the business of doing architecture. Recognising this was the task of our last hero, Rem Koolhaas. If Le Corbusier was a martyr to the reform of the industrial landscape,

## 152 Postmodernism

Rem Koolhaas is a martyr to its processes, progression and perseverance. Quintessentially Postmodern, Rem produced not a manifesto but a *retroactive manifesto* on what we already had in his first book, *Delirious New York* (1978). Le Corbusier had hated New York – how could the Americans have all that equipment but put it together so stupidly? – but Koolhaas realised this was exactly the point.

Koolhaas's diagnostic approach, the doctor somehow enjoying his patients' maladies, inevitably led to buildings that compounded them – anxiety-ridden libraries, wonky media corporations and super-chic fashion emporia. These buildings proved extremely popular with students as somehow symptomatic. As far as 'healing the city' went, they were the opposite and, for those not quite up to speed with late capitalism's calamities, bang on.

*Delirious New York* was followed by a series of other tomes – notably *S/M/L/XL* – that chronicle a consumerist landscape of congestion and obsolescence: the 'Junkspace' of our dreams and desires. In many ways this was thoroughly and exhaustively depressing, and by the second decade of the twenty-first century Rem seemed so caught up in the whirligig of late capitalism that it became voguish to speculate on how he coped.

All of these competing avenues, even if I could have understood them, would been a bit hard to take when I began my architectural studies, one year before *The Face* first hit the newsstands, and one year after *Delirious New York*. Zaha had yet to produce her first space-age-looking sofa, let alone building, and I was a lad wearing a ridiculous pair of loon pants and wanting to save the world. I was interested in participation, in why architecture seemed to have little to do with the people who used it, and in why architects and architecture students seemed such a breed apart, with their architects' bars and curious cliques.

I remember attending an architects' winter school in Edinburgh when I was in my second year. I found myself deep in argument with another die-hard Modernist, Neave Brown, architect of what I now consider one of the best of social housing complexes in London, Alexandra Road. I remember he was upset with my vitriol, profoundly hurt. I think back on that encounter with regret. No surprise, then, that a couple of years ago I found myself supervising a dissertation on, well, the life and work of Neave Brown.

Perhaps worse, where once I chastised Berthold Lubetkin for giving it all up to become a pig farmer, I now gaze regularly up at Sivill House and its surrounding estate with admiration. Both are on my doorstep, and really good.

# 11
## THE FUTURE

To paraphrase A.J.P. Taylor, don't ask me to speculate on the future; I've already had a hard enough time reviewing the past. Historians, perhaps by nature, can be notoriously gloomy about it. Jacob Burckhardt, scholar of the Classical world and friend of Nietzsche, thought our prospects so awful he buried his head in his books. As we have seen, other writers from the first Industrial Revolution weren't exactly perky either.

Now we are in that second or postindustrial revolution, and I could feel gloomy about that too. Look at the pace of the previous chapter. You might be forgiven for thinking that I've written a whole book to inadvertently explain why Walter Gropius is the most significant figure for modern times, since such an idea is presently sadly incomprehensible, whilst a blink of the eye ago it was almost universal. But I suppose we might put that down to time of life as much as time of man.

Since I'm not a Classical historian, and I'm already beginning to scuff the surface of my own future past, and since at the end of every lecture course there's an obligation to round up, to consolidate, and provide a positive take home message, this feels like Achilles on the beach, decision time, except Achilles couldn't cut, paste, erase or otherwise rewrite his decision.

It's certainly taken a lot of thinking on this beach: evaluating the present condition. I've rewritten this chapter more than any other. That's why Achilles sits under his long black ships for so long. He had a choice: to fight and die or to return home in ignominy. Worse, if he so chose, he was going to have to fight for King Agamemnon, who'd run off with (as *Twitterature* charmingly puts it) his 'biscuit'.

**156** The future

But those steps into the unknown have to be taken. All the stories collected here were once futures: inspired, conceived, argued, commissioned, constructed, compromised, variously inhabited, even demolished, then picked over for significance so that we can distinguish (perhaps) some better ideas than others. Better ideas? Well, one of my students asked me today why exactly I thought people (she meant in general, not in particular) should live together if they had the money to live apart. It's a good question in this day and age, since a kind of financial apartheid has seeped into everyday life. I replied, cautiously: because we need each other. There, one step.

It's a battleground if we believe in progress, a tragic endeavour if we acknowledge the need for sock drawers (this will become clear). Historical sense conditions our understanding, and the longer the hindsight the better, while we recognise, of course, socks without friends will remain strewn across the floor forever.

In private and over a good lunch, my own professors of a certain age certainly fear it's all over. This is entirely understandable. They inherited the potential of Modernism and saw it dissipate. But an entirely negative view would still be a bit of a disservice, insufficiently robust. For what if it's not so much 'all over' as 'just beginning'? Or, as Winston Churchill put it, is this just 'the end of the beginning'? I guess it depends on you. But certainly I shouldn't lionise a previous generation too much just because I'm suddenly predisposed to nostalgia, especially when I've been iconoclastic enough over the years to work their destruction, as generations always do.

In this exercise we have at least re-established what seemed a decent enough trajectory. The road leading from Ancient Greek civilisation to today is undoubtedly a rough one, but it does represent a project of gradual enlightenment and, in its latter stages (at least in theory), an emancipation. To my knowledge the only people who think this is absolutely a bad idea are certain fundamentalists – Vivienne Westwood, fresh Goths, and my friend Scott, who's heading for Zen. However, we are nervous.

The Rights of Man, the rule of law, proved contagious; the imperial families retaliated with the Napoleonic wars and fought it out one last time in the First World War; but that brought the Russian Revolution. The rest of Europe was now highly agitated to the point where Le Corbusier would say it was either architecture or revolution. Without the drama of the time, it's hard to imagine such a phrase. Eventually, given the bungling at Versailles and the Depression, it was the people (be they Fascist *Volk* or Communist Reds or even industrious Americans) who were the essential combatants in the Second World War. As Stalin said with regard to the cost of his 20 million dead compatriots, the Russians

PHOTOGRAPH 11 Speeresque postmodernism comes to the adult industry; Penthouse strip club Las Vegas.

*Credit*: Julie Cook

brought blood, the Americans brought money and the English bought time. Today we are in the era of consumerism, and multinational corporations transcend national boundaries in a way that could have only been a glimmer in the eye of the Medicis, and students are likely to show greater allegiance to Apple than to England. Meanwhile, the great building sites are hardly in the West at all but in the Far East and at Mecca.

For thousands of years our architecture was a house for somebody we couldn't prove even existed. Then it became a palace for one single person presumed divine. Then, thank goodness, it became ordinary people's houses and then even the public space around them. Each phase of history

**158** The future

has found a rich varied architectural expression, and even subsequent to the death of God in 1882 – and prior to his resuscitation in 1989 – there has always been some kind of spiritual dimension, some belief system, to accompany even the strictest materialism.

A student showed me a plan of his family's kitchen.

'I'd have a nervous breakdown trying to cook in that kitchen,' I said.

'Well yes but the house has gone up in value,' he replied,

'But you are not an estate agent!' I said.

That's the point. In the modern era at least, you will find very few architects purely interested in the exchange value of things; you will find them still preoccupied with use, but it is use in the broadest of terms. They worry about the cost of doing what they want to do, not the sale price. Even John Portman, perhaps the most commercially minded of architects, built himself two extraordinary houses (Entelechy I and II) – one of which is reminiscent of the temple of Karnak – with the money, and he didn't build them to sell them.

Architects generally aren't bad. In our quick survey of two and a half thousand years, we have encountered only one case of 'incalculable evil', and he wasn't technically an architect. Charles Bronson plays an architect who turns vigilante in *Death Wish*, and there are vicious contemporary parodies in *Batman: Death by Design*, but the material rewards must be too few, the effort too large. Megalomaniac architects tend to be victims of events or their own vanity, and they tend not to make it through school. Only one architect in our story might be considered as thoroughly incomprehensible; that's when Ayn Rand gave Howard Roark the wrong end of the stick. We usually fight for the world, not against it.

So what is the overall spiritual dimension today? One of the things that crops up a good deal is the innate quality of materials, but it is surely impossible to appreciate such material without immediately thinking of the labour, or work, that goes into its fashioning, be it a pot from Cornwall or a football stadium in the Gulf States (we can argue the same with the concept of 'space', too). So if we return to the beginning and agree that architecture is a bit like cuisine, why are most of us now stuck in McDonald's?

In our case, resources are an issue in the first place, but even the most cursory economics lesson will demonstrate that the building industry needs to continually reduce costs. In the refurbishment of a housing block you will get a worse-quality kitchen built by less-skilled people by a bigger building company than if you farmed out the refurbishment of each single unit to a single skilled builder and a single architect who knew what they were doing. You would also get more variety and more joy, and it would probably cost about the same, but that is not how the industry works, and that's why your cupboard doors are falling off.

# The future  **159**

A most peculiar message is simple across the board: people are too expensive. To ameliorate this and to save money and time, prefabrication has been an enthusiasm since Paxton, in myriad different conceptions. Nikita Khrushchev enjoyed factory-based construction on the basis that (among other things) it kept the mass of Soviet workers warm but ended up feeding the technocratic numbers game. At the other end of the spectrum, High-Tech enthusiasts drove prefabrication almost bespoke. Robotics are presently voguish but niche, and the evidence so far seems to suggest that (for better or worse) hospitals still come more conspicuously hand-built than Hondas.

Meanwhile, as a consequence of this corporate superstructure, we've created celebrity chefs and signature architects (or 'starchitects'). While chefs don't seem to mind the term, architects get very sensitive about it. But it is a function of the business and media to create such entities, since that's how you create the value added to increase the exchange value of your commodity. Even a celebrity chef believes in authentic cooking, or craft, just as Peter Zumthor has faith in *many sheets of sandpaper* – but both have to tout their business from Lyon to Beijing. Meanwhile, by the time your celebrity chef or starchitect is doing all that, and supporting all those restaurant staff or all those CAD people and spending most of her time in aeroplanes and hotels – and all in the name of authenticity – she will get fed up, so what's the point? After all, you never wanted to be Amazon.com; you just weren't provided with an alternative business model.

So of course we have to be worried if our objective is better kitchens or bathrooms, because a better one in use will not be the same as a better one in image or even one that lurks, like some phantom, in the mind's eye.

In the 1960s Archigram propagated an optimistic view of a consumerist future that happened to correspond quite alarmingly with my experience of four days in downtown Houston on the occasion of my uncle's funeral.

The trip was arduous, but I was catered for; it was like being in a bubble. As I flew over the Atlantic in a 777 I settled down to watch the film *Gravity*. It was both appropriate and peculiar to be flying at 35,000 feet in a tin can of computing technology and watching the most outlandish of outer-space disaster movies, but the analogy did not stop when I landed, for the previous week a 777 had actually become a disaster movie: MH370 had disappeared over the South China Sea.

Once I had settled in another bubble, in that hotel room twenty-three floors up, I switched on the television to CNN, which was covering the crisis continuously. I wasn't to know, of course, just how continuous continuously would be, but it turned out to be 24/7 for the whole duration of my stay, to the expense of almost every other possible news item. Of

**160** The future

course the adage 'Houston, we have a problem' is engrained on the Houstonian psyche – you can buy T shirts with it emblazoned across the front at George Bush International – but it took me a while to realise the paranoia gripping the United States. When you rely on computers to do almost everything, that's the way it goes.

The audience were reduced to babies. The makers of CNN, the producers, the presenters, the pundits – all were thinking about the future; they were worried *their* planes would start disappearing. They were concerned, even hysterical, as to the extent of the problem and why other nations weren't doing more about it. In particular, I remember the particular complaint that information was not being shared.

When I landed back in England and returned to my third-floor flat in Bethnal Green, I turned on the television again, and this time it was the United States that wasn't sharing.

In July and August 1963, *Playboy* magazine ran a feature where science-fiction writers predicted what life would be like in 1984. We would all be wearing one-piece suits and smoking euphoria cigarettes while high-speed traffic whizzed past our windows. We would live forever in whatever induced-pleasure state we wanted. It's extraordinary how virulent this dream industry was at the time, but right from the off Raymond Chandler had been particularly scathing back in '53:

> Did you ever read what they call Science Fiction? It's a scream. It is written like this: 'I checked out with K19 on Aldabaran III, and stepped out through the crummalite hatch on my 22 Model Sirus Hardtop. I cocked the timejector in secondary and waded through the bright blue manda grass. My breath froze into pink pretzels. I flicked on the heat bars and the Brylls ran swiftly on five legs using their other two to send out crylon vibrations. The pressure was almost unbearable, but I caught the range on my wrist computer through the transparent cysicites. I pressed the trigger. The thin violet glow was icecold against the rust-colored mountains. The Brylls shrank to half an inch long and I worked fast stepping on them with the poltex. But it wasn't enough. The sudden brightness swung me around and the Fourth Moon had already risen. I had exactly four seconds to hot up the disintegrator and Google had told me it wasn't enough. He was right.'
>
> They pay brisk money for this crap?

When my Houstonian host actually took me on a ride to look at Highway 10, for the sake of looking at Highway 10 because it was 'awesome', I realised I was in this science-fiction dream. I also realised this was

The future  **161**

not a moment of revolutionary euphoria: if this was the architecture of the future, some people hadn't been thinking hard enough. A waiter asked me if he could photograph my steak as I made the first incision, to check it was perfectly cooked; the lady who ran the memorial service turned out to be an actor who was there to 'make it real'; and when I called down to room service for some toothpaste it arrived about a nanosecond later, and then the phone rang to check I was happy with it. It was toothpaste.

When I got home I had to take a walk to reassure myself that people on the street weren't about to kill me and cook to reassure myself that this was still an enjoyable thing to do. I rattled change in my pocket to check we still use it. I guess I must be old-fashioned.

While they did provide a critique of our need for architecture in the first place, Archigram's clairvoyance was matched by blindness both to the harsh realities of *Dreams Come True Inc* and to their apparent reading material (just as those sci-fi writers did not imagine women bosses or slave labour, just electronic armatures). You have to make allowances, of course. Many aspects of America are as irresistible as the gunning of a Harley, but, like a Neoclassical painting, their Arcadian view turns out an illusion (that's not at all bad; think of Nicolas Poussin). These days we realise it's *us* at the end of this technology's fingertips: issues of surveillance, climate change, the disparity between rich and poor, of energy and food supply, freedom of speech and even the nature of truth itself are at stake, and these will cause the wars of the second industrial revolution.

For Archigram, cities would pop up and then disappear, leaving no tangible evidence; everybody would get on gently and peacefully. Their politics (such as it was) was squarely directed against the status quo, against those old goats wearing bowler hats and the working mob wearing hobnail boots. It was about doing your own thing, and we are *not* doing our own thing; we have found ourselves doing somebody else's thing, so it turns out William Burroughs may be more pertinent than James Blish.

The estimation is that 70 per cent of us will live in our earthly cities by 2050 (we passed 50 per cent in 2010). These will be cities with big problems. We are not all going to live in Helsinki, an example of a beautiful city that works but where you constantly wonder where everybody has gone. Our new cities will be tough, congested places, and they will need to address principles in a way we haven't seen in the past fifty years. Surely they will need to be planned. The problem is that planning is now seen as something rather doctrinaire, something that gets in the way of our grand design.

The programmes of the digital age bring opportunities for pattern making and visualisation, but they don't seem to help in planning or making plans. In the realm of international starchitecture, with authenticity

**162** The future

suddenly unviable, even the idea of content is disavowed in favour of large, luminous but strangely mute shapes. Back home in London, a swathe of towers – the consequence of international money laundering – might indicate the content is just bad. These have sprung up so quickly we can barely consider them there at all, as if they might just disappear suddenly in a puff of smoke (which, of course, they just might). Overall, it looks as if just as perspective served humanism, the digital age serves the posthuman, and the posthuman doesn't look good; five screens are never enough.

So I sit in the pub with my friend Scott, and we imagine a new start, a curriculum starting with a one-room house, moving on to two, then four, projects where students might refurbish flats for real and dissertations as basic as 'The History of the Wardrobe' or 'Kitchens'. We get nostalgic for projects where the student ends with the calculation of the size of her water tanks as opposed to the resolution of her cosmological position vis-à-vis a pig farm on Venus. There seem so many real problems to address. Certainly if I were asking Scott to build a modest house looking over my beach, I would not be using computer software to design it; there are too many issues as to what something is rather than what it looks like that are better dealt with by hand (I said I was old-fashioned).

Meanwhile, they called Le Corbusier's Unité in Marseilles the 'madhouse' for years. Now it is the proud home of Jonathan Meades. Just the other day a student of mine confessed to finding no disadvantages in its conception whatsoever, and this must have been the first occurrence of such a thought in thirty years. Neave Brown's Alexandra Road was blighted by public enquiry during the Thatcher years but has stood the test of time. Estates such as the Barbican, once vilified, are now the enclave of the sophisticated well-to-do. Park Hill in Sheffield, once the biggest estate in Europe, designed by Ivor Smith and Jack Lynn when they were barely out of architecture school, is now rehabilitated as the most chichi of urban splashes. Even the really problematic Heygate Estate in south London – boasting some of the longest and most notorious housing blocks in the world – was defended against demolition by our own students, who were very quick to realise the cynical manipulation of the housing market that threw thousands of poor families out of central London.

And while we tend to associate utopia with the failed egalitarian left, utopia is actually the project of anybody who has sat down one day and tried to design a house: you really do imagine your partner might put his socks away in the drawer. As Oscar Wilde said, 'progress is the realisation of utopia', even when it comes to socks.

There are other utopias more sinisterly pursued. Technological utopia tends to stem from the political right, in tandem with that of the free market, and both tend to run roughshod over human vulnerability. It was no

The future **163**

wonder that in the worrisome but melodramatic opus *The Fountainhead* (1948), Ayn Rand chose an architect, because architects *do* have to demonstrate extraordinary qualities, just *not* those espoused by Howard Roark. Rand became the doyen of neoliberalism, of greed is good – Alan Greenspan erected a 6-foot-tall dollar sign over her grave – with thousands of Ayns and Randys running around Silicon Valley, but try reversing all her characters and you get some almost reasonable human beings.

Walt Disney was subtle by comparison. I introduce him here because he's pivotal, while not an architect in the strictest sense. Whereas Rand had escaped the tyranny of the USSR, Disney hailed from a poor Protestant farming family in the American Midwest. He drew his early cartoons with lumps of charcoal on toilet paper out in the fields, then became fascinated by cameras, staying up all night accompanied by a friendly field mouse. His first film staring Mickey Mouse was *Steamboat Willie*, in 1928. He went on to incorporate each emergent technology as it happened, musical accompaniment (*Silly Symphonies*) and colour (Technicolor), with a growing range of partners and assistants (animation being a labour-intensive business) and plenty of failure along the way. It's rags-to-riches stuff, and like anybody who goes from rags to riches, Disney believed everybody else had an obligation to do the same.

So from the '30s, Disney's cartoons mirrored the American experience. In the Depression it was three little pigs having their house repossessed by the big bad wolf. When the turnaround came it was heigh ho heigh ho and off to work we go. Walt represented Middle America and came up against not only the Jewish-owned Hollywood studios but also labour activists mischievous enough to make Mickey & Minnie porno movies. He became a federal agent in the McCarthy era.

He opened the gates of 'The Happiest Place on Earth' in Anaheim in 1955. Disneyland was intended as a set for and the real experience of TV: a virtual reality environment where you could be 'more of yourself'. In it Disney split his utopia three ways – Adventureland for nostalgia, Fantasyland for fantasy and Tomorrowland for the future – all accessed by an idealised Main Street USA (shopping) and enclosed by a giant isolating berm against the honky-tonk reality of Anaheim. Disneyland was so successful that the science-fiction writer Ray Bradbury quipped that maybe Disney could fix the whole of LA, but even he didn't realise Disneyland would become the virtual world's Jerusalem. Meanwhile, the world hadn't seen such stagecraft as urban theatre since Antoinette.

Disneyland California soon became Disney World in Florida, and just before Disney died, in 1966, he announced Epcot, an experimental community firmly seated in science-fiction territory (no retirees allowed). Epcot never quite got off the ground, but this didn't stop the Disney

**164** The future

Company in its attempt to foster communities of real people for longer than a day. Enter Celebration – planned with the most progressive education and health facilities but with the strongest whiff of paternalism – a town built from scratch that inspired *The Truman Show*. As somebody who has been thrown out of a Euro Disney nightclub for dancing while wearing a cap, I suspect, at least, that the nightlife in Celebration isn't up to much.

Disney's biggest problem *was* the future: Tomorrowland dated badly but featured necessary rides like 'Autopia' (sponsored by General Motors), where kids would experience how much fun it would be to be grown up. Team Disney took a wise commercial decision: the future, from now on, would be in the past. And as surely as Walt had pushed entertainment towards reality, reality now reversed into entertainment.

Thus the Marxist critic Mike Davis described CityWalk (1993) – a high-concept development linking multiple parking garages to the Universal Studios theme park in Los Angeles – as 'a degenerate utopia that should be burnt to the ground', while Rem Koolhaas, the master of Junkspace, decided it was the most important piece of architecture in the world today.

The logic behind CityWalk was partly a consequence of the relative invisibility of real Los Angeles. Driving around LA for the first time can be very disconcerting: although LA is the size of Northern Ireland, there is famously 'no there there'. CityWalk was designed using the same company that brought Disney to Las Vegas with Treasure Island (also 1993). Here architects as cartoonists had contrived an entire pirate village on the Strip with a big theatrical performance to match. The designers of City-Walk embraced the idea of a vivid collage of everything you *expected to see* in Los Angeles in one real place.

'So where were the porn stars?' I said to myself.

Soon, for the Spielbergs and Katzenbergs of the new Hollywood, it would be Cape Cod in Playa Vista and Urbino in Glendale and eventually for the rest of us almost anywhere anywhere: all in the name of placemaking. The craze was embraced in titanic proportions (and thank goodness with porn stars included) in Las Vegas, which already had Miami, Rome, the Sahara, the Barbary Coast, Rio, Imperial Japan and so on at least in name, with replicant and more or less interesting versions of Luxor, New York, Venice, Paris, Monte Carlo, Mandalay Bay and even a fully amped-up village of Bellagio.

It was reasonable to assume that architects, as people involved with the construction of the environment as a whole (as established by William Morris), wouldn't regress to being such dilettante set designers (although I hold nothing against dilettante set designers per se;

The future **165**

remember that Inigo Jones was one). However, before Grasshopper, Rhino, Python and so on, it looked like they might. I encouraged the phenomenon myself (after all, carbon atoms are carbon atoms and best reorganised for pleasure); even if the rule was that what you touched was real, the rest appearance, and when you picked up a menu in the Cheers bar in Las Vegas McCarran you realised it was a screenplay. Why not? It was fun.

But I realised older architects felt comfortable with all this stuff only when they thought they were doing something else. They were not dashing, comic-book-reading hipsters; they kept mentioning Frank Lloyd Wright. When one of the contributors to CityWalk was kind enough to give me an interview, he enthused about a book called *How Buildings Learn*. It was confusing. Meanwhile, the science of footfall and attraction was developed almost *as a science*, meaning plans for these individual attractions were remarkably similar, being based on the new language of 'space syntax' (shopping).

I'll admit the ideology did its job; it remained couched. For me at that time, Excalibur Las Vegas represented freedom, a sublime revelry, even if it was a bit crappy. Thus my students enthusiastically rendered 'Las Vegas Style Casinos in London' (or variations thereon) for years. They should be collectors' items by now, for that lightness and provocation surely dimmed. Globally things weren't turning out well, and locally our favourite places in Las Vegas were steadily being bulldozed (this happened to the Venturis too; perhaps we should have seen it coming). You can put it any way you like – 'all that is solid melts into air' (Karl Marx 1848) or 'they paved paradise and put up a parking lot' (Joni Mitchell 1966). Certainly you don't know what you've got till it's gone. I wrote a darkly comic novel – *Waking Up Is Hard to Do* – which still sits safely in the bedside cabinet.

Dave Hickey had been very good at delivering Vegas as the home of the American Dream, and even he quit for Albuquerque. Our last piece of work in Vegas was perhaps our best: Julie shot a series to become the book *Some Las Vegas Strip Clubs*. Here the architecture was absolutely in the service of the experience (content), even if you couldn't see it with the house lights down, and the experience was at once vicarious, simulated and real. Meanwhile those dancers were perfect aficionados of the late-capitalist environment, because they were their own means of production. They had succeeded in making themselves global commodities, and so to be heartily congratulated.

So it was hats off to the strippers. It was a case of shame we can't all do that, or perhaps, if you're reading this and you are successful at all, you already have (in one way or another).

**166** The future

But such a view, no matter how rigorously opined, was not going to wash. So I quit teaching studio and buried my head in a room full of books and lectured about how peculiar the world had become. It's good to be reminded of a few home truths.

So if we want better kitchens and bathrooms, what are we going to do again? Perhaps I'll get started on that house.

# FURTHER READING

## General reference

Benevelo, Leonardo, *The History of the City*, MIT Press, 1980.
Clark, Kenneth, *Civilisation*, BBC Books, 1969.
Collins, Matthew, *This Is Civilisation*, 21 Publishing, 2008.
Fletcher, Banister, *A History of Architecture on the Comparative Method,* Batsford, 1896.
Gombrich, E. H., *The Story of Art*, Phaidon, 1950.
Gombrich, E. H., *A Little History of the World*, Yale University Press, 2008.
Hughes, Robert, *The Shock of the New*, BBC Books, 1980.
Lancaster, Osbert, *Pillar to Post: The Pocket Lamp of Architecture*, John Murray, 1938.
Pevsner, Nicklaus, *An Outline of European Architecture*, Penguin, 1941.
Ruis, *Marx for Beginners*, Pantheon Books, 1979.
Stevens Curl, James, *Dictionary of Architecture*, Oxford University Press, 1999.

## The ancients

De La Ruffiniere du Prey, Pierre, *The Villas of Pliny from Antiquity to Posterity*, University of Chicago Press, 1994.
Hersey, George, *The Lost Meaning of Classical Architecture*, MIT Press, 1988.
Hughes, Robert, *Rome: A Cultural, Visual and Personal History*, Alfred A. Knopf, 2011.
Scully, Vincent, *The Earth the Temple and the Gods*, Yale University Press, 1962.

## The middle

Alberti, Leon Battista (trans Rykwert, J., Leach, N., & Tavenor, R.), *On the Art of Building in Ten Books*, MIT Press, 1988.
Bergdoll, Barry, *Karl Friedrich Schinkel: An Architecture for Prussia*, Rizzoli, 1994.

**168** Further reading

Chapman, J. M., & Chapman, Brian, *The Life and Times of Baron Haussmann*, Weidenfield & Nicolson, 1957.

Colquhoun, Kate, *A Thing in Disguise: The Visionary Life of Joseph Paxton*, Fourth Estate, 2003.

Girouard, Mark, *The Return to Camelot: Chivalry and The English Gentleman*, Yale University Press, 1981.

King, Ross, *Brunelleschi's Dome*, Pimlico, 2001.

Leapman, Michael, *The Troubled Life of Inigo Jones, Architect of the English Renaissance*, Review, 2003.

MacCarthy, Fiona, *William Morris*, Faber & Faber, 1994.

Marlow, Peter, *The English Cathedral*, Merrell, 2012.

Mordaunt Cook, J., *The Strange Genius of William Burgess*, National Gallery of Wales, 1981.

Pevsner, Nicklaus, *An Outline of European Architecture*, Penguin, 1941.

Rae, Isobel, *Charles Cameron Architect to the Court of Russia*, Elek Books, 1971.

Shepherd, J. C., & Jellicoe, G. A., *Italian Gardens of the Renaissance*, Alec Tiranti, 1953.

Smienk, G., & Niemeijer, M., *Palladio, the Villa and the Landscape*, Birkhauser, 2011.

Wittkower, Rudolf, *Architectural Principles in the Age of Humanism*, Alec Tiranti, 1952.

## The moderns

Beck-Loos, Claire, *Adolf Loos: A Private Portrait*, Doppelhouse Press, 2011.

Benevelo, Leonardo, *History of Modern Architecture Vols. 1&2*, Routledge & Kegan Paul, 1971.

Chase, John, *Glitter Stucco and Dumpster Diving*, Verso, 2000.

Cook, Peter [*et al.*] (ed.), *Archigram*, Studio Vista, 1972.

Dunster, David (ed.), *Michael Graves*, Academy Editions, 1979.

Eliot, Marc, *Walt Disney: Hollywood's Dark Prince*, Andre Deutsch, 1994.

Escher, Frank (ed.), *John Lautner Architect*, Artemis, 1994.

Fox Weber, Nicholas, *Le Corbusier [A life]*, Alfred A. Knopf, 2008.

Friedman, Alice T., *Women and the Making of the Modern House*, Harry N. Abrams, 1998.

Fuller, R. Buckminster, *Operating Manual for Spaceship Earth*, Lars Muller, 2008 (1969).

Giedion, S., *Walter Gropius*, Dover Publications, 1992.

Girouard, Mark, *Big Jim: The Life and Work of James Stirling*, Chatto & Windus, 1998.

Hess, Alan, *Viva Las Vegas: After Hours Architecture*, Chronicle Books, 1993.

Hickey, Dave, *Air Guitar: Essays on Art and Democracy*, Art Issues Press, 1997.

Hines, Thomas S., *Richard Neutra and the Search for Modern Architecture*, Oxford University Press, 1982.

Hochman, Elaine S., *Architects of Fortune: Mies van de Rohe and the Third Reich*, Weidenfield & Nicholson, 1989.

Jackson, Neil, *Craig Ellwood*, Lawrence King, 2002.

Jencks, Charles, *The Language of Post-Modern Architecture*, Academy Editions, 1977.

Meades, Jonathan, *Museum without Walls*, Unbound, 2012.

Melvin, Jeremy, *F.R.S. Yorke and the Evolution of English Modernism*, Wiley Academy, 2003.

# Further reading 169

Rowe, Colin, *Mathematics of the Ideal Villa and Other Essays*, MIT Press, 1976.

Schildt, Goran, *Alvar Aalto: His Life*, Alvar Aalto Museum, 2007.

Schulze, Franz, *Mies van der Rohe*, University of Chicago Press, 1985.

Scully, Vincent, *Frank Lloyd Wright*, George Braziller, 1960.

Sereny, Gitta, *Albert Speer: His Battle with the Truth*, Alfred A. Knopf, 1995.

Sudjic, Deyan, *New Architecture: Foster, Rogers, Stirling*, Royal Academy of Arts, 1986.

Von Moos, Stanislaus, *Le Corbusier: Elements of a Synthesis*, MIT Press, 1979.

Von Moos, Stanislaus, *Venturi Rauch & Scott Brown: Buildings and Projects*, Rizzoli, 1987.

Weingarden, Lauren S, *Louis H. Sullivan: The Banks*, MIT Press, 1987.

Whitford, Frank, *Bauhaus*, Thames & Hudson, 1984.

Wolfe, Tom, *From Bauhaus to Our House*, Jonathan Cape, 1982.

Wolfe, Tom, *The Kandy Kolored Tangerine Flake Streamline Baby*, Jonathan Cape, 1966.

Zaracor, Kimberley Elman, *Manufacturing a Socialist Modernity: Housing in Czechoslavakia 1945–1960*, University of Pittsburgh Press, 2011.

# INDEX

Aalto, Aino 113
Aalto, Alvar 126; Villa Mairea 113–14
Aalto, Elissa 113
Aalto vase 114
aborigines 4
Abrams, Janet 147
absolutism 9, 72–4
Abstract Expressionism 133
academicism 93
Academy Editions 144
Access card 142
Achilles 10–14, 155
Acropolis 10, 18
Adler, Dankmar 122
Adler & Sullivan 124
*AD* magazine 134
Adventureland 163
advertising 130–3
aeroplanes 115
*Affluent Society, The* (Galbraith) 130, 140
Afghanistan 33
Agamemnon 11, 14, 155
*Agony and the Ecstasy, The* 60
Ahrends, Peter 150
Air Ministry (Sagebiel) 112
aisles 41–2
Albarn, Damon 139
Albers, Joseph 108

Alberti, Leon Battista 145; *Ten Books on Architecture* 58
*Albert Speer: Architecture 1932–1942* (Krier) 20
Alexander the Great 25
Alexandra Road (Brown) 152, 162
alienation 94
Alma-Tadema, Lawrence 95
altarpieces/altars 15–16, 19–20, 41, 48, 122–4
Altenberg, Peter 108
Amalienburg 79
Amazon.com 159
Ambler, Eric 40
American Dream 165
American Modernism 121–36
American Revolution 76–7
Ammannati 61
Amsterdam 72
Anaheim 163
Ancient Egyptians 9–10
Ancient Greece 9–22, 25–6, 34, 39, 156
Ancient Rome 25–40, 47–8, 55, 77–8
ancient theatre 19
animal sacrifice 15–16
Anson, Brian 143
antiquity 104
Antoinette, Marie 75, 163
*Any Questions* 2

**172** Index

Apollo 12, 17
Apple Inc. 157
apses 41
aqueducts 28–30
Arcadia 35
Arcadianism 105–6
Arc-et-Senans (Ledoux) 81
arched roofs 36
arches 2, 30, 34, 50
Archigram 134, 149, 159, 161
Architects' Club 76
'Architects Sketch' (Monty Python) 142
Architectural Association 118, 149
architectural determinism 44
architectural language 16
*Architectural Review, The* 93, 142, 145
*architecture parlante* 81
*Architecture without Architects* (Rudofsky) 135
Arcosanti community 135
aristocracy 88
Aristotle 61
Arthur, King 47
'Artist and Individual Talent, The' (Eliot) 5
Art Nouveau 103–4
Arts and Crafts 100, 116
Ashley, Laura 43
*Asterix* 35–6
*Asterix and the Laurel Wreath* 28, 34
*Asterix and the Olympic Games* 28
Astley, Rick 149
atonal music 21
atriums 129
Attlee, Clement 99
Augustus 32
Auschwitz 88, 112
Austen, Jane 90
*Autobiography* (Cellini) 72
Autopia (ride) 164
axial plan 19

Bacardi Building (Mies van der Rohe) 111
bacchanalia 34–5
Bacon, Francis 61
Baker, Josephine 108
Baker Street 96
'Bald' (The Darkness) 139
Baldwin, Stanley 99

Ball, Lucille 131
balloon frame construction 77, 147
Banham, Reyner 134
banks 122–4
Banqueting House ( Jones) 66
barbarians 41, 44
Barbican 162
Barclaycard 142
Barnsdall, Aline 125–6
Baroque 63–4, 71
barrel roofs 36
Barthes, Roland: *The Face of Garbo* 13; 'The Romans in Films' 26
Basar, Shumon 151
Basildon 2
basilicas 41–2
bathing 49
*Baths of the Romans, The* (Cameron) 75
*Batman: Death by Design* 158
battens 50
Bauhaus 100–1, 104–8, 111–12, 143–4
Bauhaus colour wheels 108
Bazalgette, Joseph 98
beatniks 134
Beatty, Warren 63
Beaune, France 45
Beauvais Cathedral 46
Beaux-Arts 94, 104
Beckmann, Max 112
Bedford, Earl of 67
Belgium 101–4
bell towers 42
Benevolo, Leonardo: *The History of the City* 15, 146
*Ben Hur* 32
Berghaus Gothic 103
Bergman, Ingrid 130–1
Berlin 47–8, 81, 91, 112, 143–4
Berlin Academy of Science 75
Berlin Chancellery 75
Berlin Wall 149
Berman, Marshall 74
Bernini, Gian Lorenzo 65, 126; *Ecstasy of St Teresa* 63–4
Bible 62–3
Biedermeier 113–14
Bilbao effect 148
biorealism 127
Bismarck, Otto van 94
*Black Knight, The* 43

Black Metal 44
Black Mountain College 135
Black Panthers 135
Black Sabbath 44
*Black Square* (Malevich) 109
*Blade Runner* 140
Blish, James 161
blocks 72
blood and soil 20
Blumenthal, Heston 64
Boeing 747 151
Boeing 777 159
Bofill, Ricardo 148
Bonaventure (Portman) 129
Borromini 63–5; San Carlo alle Quattro
  Fontane 64
Botticelli 63
boulevards 71–2
Boullée, Étienne 80
bourgeois architecture 109
bourgeoisie 84, 95–7
Bournville 101
Bowie, David 144
Bradbury, Ray 163
Bramante, Donato: San Pietro in
  Montorio 58
Braun, Werner von 136
*Brazil* 148
Brenna 76
bridges 30
British Library 114
British manufacturing 87
British Museum (Smirke) 21–2
British Parliament 76–7
Bronson, Charles 158
Brooke, Michael 150
Brookes, Cleanth 133
Brosnan, Pierce 13
brothels 79–81
*Brothers Karamazov, The* (Dostoyevsky) 62
Brown, Denise Scott 122, 132; *Learning
  from Las Vegas* 133–4
Brown, Ford Maddox 95
Brown, Neave: Alexandra Road 152, 162
Bruges 55
Brunel 92–3
Brunelleschi, Filippo 56–8, 115; Duomo
  59; San Lorenzo 57–8; Santo Spirito
  57–8
Buchan, John 40

building industry 158
'Built Form and Setting in the Late
  Work of Le Corbusier' (Davies) 115
Burckhardt, Jacob 61, 155
Burges, William 46, 52
Burke, Jon *see* Ellwood, Craig
Burlington, Lord: Chiswick House 67
Burne-Jones, Edward 95, 99–100
Burroughs, William 134, 161
Bute, Earl of 46
buttresses 50–1
Byford, Biff 44
Byzantium 39–41

*cabanon* 114
CAD architecture 159
Caesar 26–7, 34
Caesars Palace 33–6
California Modern 35
Caligula 27, 32
*Camelot* 43
Cameron, Charles 66, 75–6; *The Baths of
  the Romans* 75
Cameron Gallery 76
Cameron, Walter 76
*campanile* 118
Campidoglio (Michelangelo) 116
*Campo Marzio* (Piranesi) 31–2
Cape Canaveral 134
capitalism 42, 87–8, 91, 94–5
Capitol 28
Captain Mainwaring (fictional
  character) 21
Cardiff Castle 46
'Care of the Body' (Lovell) 126
Carl, Peter 147
*Carry On Cleo* 15, 26–7
*Carry On Don't Lose Your Head* 72
*Carry On Henry* 72
caryatids 18
Casanova 59, 79, 96; *Story of My Life* 72
Case Study House Program 121, 131–2
Casino (Schinkel) 82–3
Cassina 114
castles 43–6, 51
*Catch 22* 132
cathedrals 42–3, 46–7, 50–1
Cathedral to the Wars of Liberation
  (Schinkel) 83
Catherine II 75–6

**174** Index

Catherine the Great 66
Catholic Church 62–4
cavalry 29
Ceausescu, Nicolae 65
Celebration 164
Cellini, Benvenuto 59, 71; *Autobiography* 72
Centaurs 22
Centre Point 143
*Centurion* 32–3
Chandigarh 114
Chandler, Raymond 160
charioteers 18
chariots 29–30
charity 45, 96
Charles I 67
Charles, Prince 150
Charlottenburg 47–8, 81
Chartres Cathedral 42–3, 47, 93
Chase, John 131
Chatsworth House 92
Cheers bar 165
Chicago opera house (Sullivan) 122
chimneys 124, 131
Chirico, Giorgio de 145
Chiswick House (Burlington) 67
chivalry 43
*Christiane F.* 144
Christian mosaics 40
Christians/Christianity 31–2, 41–2, 48, 74
Churchill, Winston 156
church roofs 49–51
Circus Maximus 28, 34–5
cities/city life 90–1, 161
citizenship 27
city blocks 72
city states 55
*City of Tomorrow* (Le Corbusier) 109–10,
    114–5
CityWalk 164–5
city walls 15
*Civilisation* (Clark) 42–3
civil rights 134
Clark, Alan 43, 46
Clark, Kenneth 45, 79; *Civilisation* 42–3
Clark, T. J. 68
Clark Kent (fictional character) 13
Classical architecture 16, 20, 42–4
Classical motifs 34, 80–2
Classicism 67–8, 103–4, 112–13, 121,
    124, 132; Scandinavian 20–1

Claudius 26–8, 59
Clelland, Doug 149
*Cleopatra* 34
Cleopatra's Barge 33
Clérisseau 76
cloak-and-dagger stories 40
cloisters 62
Close, Glen 80
CNN 68, 159–60
Coates, Nigel: NATO 148
Cold War 134, 140
Cole, Lloyd 149
Coliseum 34
*Collage City* (Rowe and Koetter) 146
Collings, Matthew: *This Is Civilisation* 45
Cologne Cathedral 50–1
colour wheels 108
Colquhoun, Alan 147
Columbus, Christopher 71
columns 16–18, 34, 41, 115
communes 136
*Complexity and Contradiction in
    Architecture* (Venturi) 132–3, 145
composition 34
computers 62, 157, 160
concrete 31, 36, 50, 116–17
*Condition of Post-Modernity, The* (Harvey)
    140
*Condition of the Working-Class in England,
    The* (Engels) 97–8
Constantine 32, 35, 40–1
consumerism 7, 130–4, 140–2, 152, 157–9
Cook, Julie 59, 77, 115; *Some Las Vegas
    Strip Clubs* 165
Córdoba 40
Corinthian style 16
Cornaro chapel 63–4
*Coronation Street* 12
corridors 129
cotton industry 88–92
counterculture 134
Counter-Reformation 62–3, 71
counterrevolution 78
courtly love 43
courtyards 82
Covent Garden 67, 143
craft 46
Cranach, Lucas 45
Crawley, England 2
creationism 32

## Index 175

Crete 18–19
critical regionalism 150
Crusades 46
Crystal Palace (Paxton) 92–4
CSH8 (Eames House; Eames) 131
CSH16 (Ellwood) 131
CSH22 (Stahl House; Koenig) 131
*CSI* 35
Cubism 116, 147
cuisine 4
Culot, Maurice 143
cultural theorists 140
Cure, The 44
curves 103
Cuvilliés 79
Czechoslovakia 1–4

damsels 43
dangerous knowledge 49
*Dangerous Liaisons* 72
Dannatt, Trevor 149–50
'Dare' (Gorillaz) 139
Dark Ages 36, 42
Darkness, The: 'Bald' 139
Darwin, Charles 103, 143
*Das Englische Haus* (Multhesius) 100
datum 16–17
David: *The Oath of the Horatii* 32, 77–8
Davies, Brian 87–8
Davies, Paul: 'Built Form and Setting in
    the Late Work of Le Corbusier' 115
*Da Vinci Code, The* 63
Davis, Bette 13
Davis, Mike 164
Davis, Miles 131
Davos 17
Death Metal 44
*Death Wish* 158
decadence 80
Declaration of Independence 77
*Decline and Fall* (Waugh) 110
*Decline and Fall of the Roman Empire*
    (Gibbon) 28
Deconstruction 149
Decorated Gothic architecture 51
decoration 103
*Delirious New York* (Koolhaas) 152
Delphi 17–18
Democratic National Convention
    135–6

Derrida, Jacques 148
Descartes 74
despotism 56, 78
Dessau 106–7, 143
Dhaka 129–30
Diana, Lady 16
Dickens, Charles 88, 92–5
Dickinson, Bruce 45
diesel engines 87
Dietrich, Marlene 13
digital age 161–2
Dion, Celine 34
Dionysus 12
Disney, Walt 163–4
Disneyland 133, 163
Disney World 163–4
domes 30, 36, 135
Donatello 56
Doric style 16
doss houses 45
Dostoyevsky, Fyodor: *The Brothers
    Karamazov* 62
drawing 30, 149–50
*Dreams Come True Inc* 161
drones 68
druids 48
Dubai 151
Duiker, Jan: Open Air School 110–11
Duke de Pommefrites (fictional
    character) 72
Duomo (Brunelleschi) 59
Durand 81, 94
Dymaxion House (Fuller) 135

Eames, Charles 131
Eames House (CSH8; Eames) 131
Early English Gothic architecture 51
*EastEnders* 12
Eco, Umberto: *The Name of the Rose* 49
*Ecstasy of St Teresa* (Bernini) 63–4
Edge, Alderley 97
Edict of Milan 32, 41
Edinburgh, Duke of 45–6
*Edinburgh Evening Courant* 76
Edinburgh University 150
Edison, Thomas 122
Edwardians 139
*Eighteen Years with Architect Louis I. Kahn*
    (Komendant) 131
Einstein, Albert 117

**176** Index

Eisenman, Peter 147–8
*Electric Kool-Aid Acid Test, The* (Wolfe) 134
elevations 129
Elgin, Lord 10
Eliot, T. S. 133; 'The Artist and Individual Talent' 5
Ellwood, Craig 131–2; CSH16 131
Ely Cathedral 51
*Emigrants, The* (Sebald) 98
empire states 71
Empiricism 117
encapsulation of space 29
Engels, Frederick 95; *The Condition of the Working-Class in England* 97–8
engineers 88–9
England 87–91
English imperialism 21
Enlightenment, The 29, 49, 56, 71–84
entablatures 21–2
Entenza, John 131
entitlement 45
entrepreneurship 88–9
environmental collapse 142
Epcot 163–4
epicureanism 80
Epidaurus 19
Erectheion 18
*esquisse* 94
eternal city 25
ethylene 17
*Et in Arcadia ego* (Poussin) 35
Eton 109, 139
Etruscan motifs 132
Etruscans 25
Euro Disney 164
European Modernism 103–18, 127
Euston Station 96
Excalibur Las Vegas 47, 165
exchange value 109, 158–9
*Existenzminimum* 111
exterior elevations 129

*Face, The* 140, 152
*Face of Garbo, The* (Barthes) 13
fairy tales 48
Falling Water (Wright) 124–5
Fantasyland 163

Farnsworth, Edith 127–8
Farnsworth House (Mies van der Rohe) 127–8
fascism 28, 34
*Faust* (Goethe) 91–2, 98
Felscherinow, Vera Christiane 144
*Finding of the Body of St Mark* (Tintoretto) 6
fireplaces 124
first-order logic 4
Fitzgerald, Scott 132
five points of a new architecture 117
Fleming, Ian 13; *Live and Let Die* 72
Fletcher, Banister: *History of Architecture* 49
Florence 55
flying buttresses 50–1
*Forbes* 128
Ford, Henry 135
forests 48
fortified houses 51
*Fortune* 128
*Forum* 128
Forum Shops 34
Foster, Norman 130; Gherkin 151; Stansted Airport 151; Willis Faber Dumas Building 151
*Fountainhead, The* (Rand) 122, 163
*Four Books of Architecture* (Palladio) 64
Fourier, Charles 104
Four Seasons Restaurant 128
Frampton, Kenneth 147, 150
France 5–7, 89–90
Frederick the Great 75
free market 94, 162–3
freemasonry 51, 142
Free Trade Hall 97
French chalet style 6
French Revolution 34, 75–80, 94–5
frescoes 19, 61
Freud, Sigmund 12, 104–6, 143; *The Interpretation of Dreams* 14
Friedrich Wilhelm III 81
friezes 20
*From Bauhaus to Our House* (Wolfe) 147
*From Lark Rise to Candleford* 90
*From Russia with Love* 40
Fukuyama, Francis 140
Fuller, Richard Buckminster 134–5; Dymaxion House 135

Functionalism 107–11
fundamentalism 156
Future Systems 149
Futurism 109, 112

*Galaxy Quest* 131
Galbraith, J. K. 142, 145; *The Affluent Society* 130, 140
Gallaratese apartment block (Rossi) 145
Gallis, Yvonne 113
Gans, Herbert 147
Garbo, Greta 13
Garden of Eden 62
Gardener's House (Schinkel) 81
*Gardeners' World* 3
Garnier, Charles 83
Garnier, Tony 104–6; *Une Cité Industrielle* 104–5
Gehry, Frank 7; Guggenheim Museum, Bilbao 148
Geldof, Bob 142
geodesic domes 135
George Bush International 160
Georgian London 72
Géricault, Théodore: *The Raft of the Medusa* 5
Germania 20, 33, 47–8
Germany 44–9
*Germinal* (Zola) 104
*Get Carter* 142
Gherkin (Foster) 151
giants 20
Gibbon, Edward 31–2, 74; *Decline and Fall of the Roman Empire* 28
Giedion, Sigfried 143
Gill, A. A. 97
Gillespie Kidd & Coia 150
Gilliam, Terry 148
Ginsberg, Moisei 109
Glancey, Jonathan 118
glass walls 131
Glienicke (Schinkel) 37
*Goddess of Victory, The* 18
God's country 121
gods/goddesses 10–18, 30–2, 49, 61, 91, 104, 158
Goethe, Johann Wolfgang von 88; *Faust* 91–2, 98
*GoldenEye* 13

Golden Palace 33
*Gone with the Wind* 147
Good, 'Flic' 150
Gorillaz: 'Dare' 139
Gothic, The 39–52, 82, 96, 132, 139
'Gothick' architecture 52
Gothic Revival 43–4
Goths 44, 47–8, 156
Gowan, James 145
Goya 61
*GQ* 148
Graeco-Roman Neoclassicism 35
Grand Central Station 91
*Grand Designs* 3
Grand Ducal School of Arts and Crafts 106
grand narrative 9
*Grand Projets* 84
Grand Tour 66–7
Grassi, Giorgio 149
Graves, Michael 147–8; Portland Building 144; Rockefeller House 147; Snyderman House 147; Team Disney headquarters 147
Graves, Robert: *I Claudius* 26
*Gravity* 159
Gray, Rose 82
Great Depression 156, 163
*Great Escape, The* 76
Great Exhibition 92
Great Fire of 1871 122
Greece *see* Ancient Greece
Greek mythology 20
Greene, David 149
Greene & Greene 121, 132
Greenspan, Alan 163
Gretchen 91
grids 15, 33, 77, 111, 134
Gropius, Walter 106–8, 111, 155; Gropiusstadt 143–4; Pan Am Building 127
Gropiusstadt (Gropius) 143–4
Guaranty Building (Sullivan) 122
Guarini 64
Guggenheim Museum, Bilbao (Gehry) 148
Guggenheim Museum (Wright) 125
guilds 76–9
Gutenberg, Johannes 62

**178** Index

Gwathmey, Charles 147
gymnasiums 29

Hadid, Zaha 152
Hadrian's Villa 36–7
Haggard, Rider 40
Hagia Sophia 40
half-gods 10–13
Hall of Mirrors 75
Hamilton, Christine 97
Hamilton, Neil 97
hammerbeams 50
Hanna House (Wright) 125
Hanseatic churches 44–5
Hapsburgs 71
Hardy, Thomas 90
Harlow, Jean 13
harmony 58
Harrison, Rex 60
*Harry Potter and the Order of the Phoenix* 3
Harvey, David: *The Condition of Post-Modernity* 140
Haussmann, Baron 83–4, 94, 121
Hawker Siddeley 87–8
Hawksmoor, Nicholas 75, 132
*Hawks and the Sparrows, The* (Pasolini) 43
heavy metal 44–6
Hector 11–13
Hejduk, John 147–8
Hellenistic art 25
Helsinki 161
Hennebique structure 110
Henry VIII 62
Hercules 12
Hermitage 65
heroes 12, 140
Herrera, Juan de: Plaza Mayor 71
Heston, Charlton 60
Heydrich, Reinhard 80
Heygate Estate 162
Heyworth, Rita 13
Hickey, Dave 122, 165
High-Tech 100, 130, 151, 159
hippies 17, 134–5
*History of Architecture* (Fletcher) 49
*History of the City, The* (Benevolo) 15, 146
Hitler, Adolf 20, 48, 75, 112
Hollywood 34, 77, 131, 164
Hollywood Bowl 131

Holy Bible 62–3
Holy Grail 45
Holy Roman Empire 32, 55–6
Homer: *Iliad* 10–16, 30; *Odyssey* 11–15
hookers 33
Hopper, Edward 125
Horta, Victor: Tassel House 103–4
Hôtel-Dieu 45
*House and Garden* 81
Houses of Parliament 43–4, 52
housing 1–3, 131, 152, 157, 162
Houston 77, 128–9, 159–61
Howard Roark (fictional character) 122, 158, 163
*How Buildings Learn* 165
Howerd, Frankie 32
Hughes, Robert 28, 33, 65; *The Shock of the New* 100
humanism 58
Humann, Karl 19
Hunt, William Holman 95
huts 14
Hyatt Regency Houston (Portman) 129

'I am a Monument' (Venturi) 133, 145
*I Claudius* (Graves) 26
identity politics 140
IKEA 131
Iktinos 25
*Iliad* (Homer) 10–16, 30
Illinois Institute of Technology (Mies van der Rohe) 128
Imperial Hotel Tokyo (Wright) 125
Imperial Rome *see* Ancient Rome
Imperial War Museum 112
Impressionist painting 94
*Indiana Jones and the Temple of Doom* 45
individualism 108, 140
indulgences 62
industrial architecture 82, 104
industrialised economy 36
Industrial Revolution 43, 72, 84, 87–101, 104
infrastructure 25, 96
Inquisition 48, 62–3, 74
*insulae* 28
internal atriums 129
International Style 109, 127–8
*Interpretation of Dreams, The* (Freud) 14
Inuit 4

Ionic style 16
iron 92
Ironbridge 92
Iron Curtain 143
Iron Maiden 45
Itten, Johannes 106
Izenour, Steven 122; *Learning from Las Vegas* 133–4

Jacobites 75
Jaguars 35
James, Sid 72
James Bond (fictional character) 13
Jameson, Fredric: *Postmodernism: Or, the Cultural Logic of Late Capitalism* 140
*James Stirling: Buildings and Projects 1950–74* (Stirling and Krier) 146
Jefferson, Thomas 77, 121, 126
Jencks, Charles 143–4, 147; *Language of Post-Modern Architecture* 144; *Le Corbusier and the Tragic View of Architecture* 117, 144
Jerde, Jon 148
Jerusalem 163
Jesuits 62–3
Jesus 40, 63
Jetsons 125
Jews/Judaism 20, 48
Johnson, Philip 59, 128, 145–7
Johnson Wax Building (Wright) 125
Jones, Inigo 66–7; Banqueting House 66; Queen's House 67
*Journey to the East* (Le Corbusier) 40
Jove 42
Judas 40
Julius II 60
Julius III 61
'Junkspace' (Koolhaas) 152, 164
*Just a Minute* 58–9
Juvenal 29

Kahn, Louis I. 4, 31, 121, 129–34; Kimbell Art Museum 130; Richards Memorial Laboratories 130; Salk Institute 130
Karmann Ghia 131
Katzenberg, Jeffrey 164
Kennedy, Robert 135
Kesey, Ken 134
Khrushchev, Nikita 159

Kimbell Art Museum (Kahn) 130
King, Martin Luther 135
king and queen posts 50
King's College Chapel 51
King's Cross Station 96
Kipling, Rudyard 122
Kiss, Laszlo 149
*Kiss, The* (Klimt) 106
kitchen tables 15–16
Klein, Naomi: *No Logo* 142; *The Shock Doctrine* 142
Klimt, Gustav: *The Kiss* 106
Klosterman, Chuck 40
knights 43
Knossos 19
Koenig, Pierre: Stahl House (CSH22) 131
Koetter, Fred: *Collage City* 146
Kokoschka, Oskar 106
Komendant, August: *Eighteen Years with Architect Louis I. Kahn* 131
Koolhaas, Rem 130, 152; *Delirious New York* 152; 'Junkspace' 152, 164; *S/M/L/XL* 152
Kraus, Karl 108
Krier, Leon 144; *Albert Speer: Architecture 1932–1942* 20; *James Stirling: Buildings and Projects 1950–74* 146
Krier, Rob: *Urban Space* 146
Kroll, Lucien 143

labour 89–90, 96, 158
La Chaux-de-Fonds 114
Lambert, Phyllis 128
Lancaster, Osbert 9–10, 109
Lance-a-Lotta Pasta 47
landscape architecture 37
*Landscape with a Man Killed by a Snake* (Poussin) 68, 98
*Language of Post-Modern Architecture* (Jencks) 144
Lapiths 22
La Pomme d'Or 5
Las Vegas 17, 33–6, 122, 133–4, 164–5
'Las Vegas (Can't Hear You! Too Noisy)' (Wolfe) 133
Las Vegas McCarran 165
late capitalism 140, 165
La Tourette (Le Corbusier) 115–17, 145
laurels 15
Laurentian Library (Michelangelo) 60–1

**180** Index

Lautner, John 125
leaded light windows 43
*Learning from Las Vegas* (Venturi, Brown, and Izenour) 133–4
Le Corbusier 6–7, 10, 36, 65, 75, 93, 111, 126, 156; *City of Tomorrow* 109–10, 114–5; *Journey to the East* 40; La Tourette 115–17, 145; *Oeuvre Complète* 146; Pavillon Suisse 116; Plan Voisin 12, 84; *The Radiant City* 58; Ronchamp Chapel 6–7; *Towards a New Architecture* 6, 58, 132; Unité d'Habitation 115–16, 162; Villa Savoye 113–16; Villa Shodhan 117
*Le Corbusier and the Tragic View of Architecture* ( Jencks) 117, 144
Ledoux, Claude Nicholas 79–81, 92; Arc-et-Senans 81
Led Zeppelin 139
*Led Zeppelin II* 91
legions 29, 48
Lego 61
Leipzig Goth Festival 44, 48–9
Lenin, Vladimir 78
Leonardo da Vinci 49
Les Acacias 5
Les Halles 84
*Les Liaisons Dangereuses* 80
liberal reformers 95
Liberty (department store) 100
Libeskind, Daniel 149
Lichfield Cathedral 51
lifestyle 131
Lime Street Station 96
*Live and Let Die* (Fleming) 72
Livy 28
Lloyd's Building (Rogers) 151
London Underground 96
Loos, Adolf 108–9, 126, 145; Moller House 108; Müller House 108
Los Angeles 164
Louis XIV 71–4, 132
Louis-Philippe 83
Louis XVI 78
Lovell Beach House (Schindler) 127
Lovell Health House (Neutra) 127
Lovell, Leah 127
Lovell, Philip 126–7; 'Care of the Body' 126
Loyola chapel 63

Loyola, Ignatius 62–3
LSD 17
Lubetkin, Berthold: Sivill House 152
Luther, Martin 62–3
Lutyens, Edwin 132
Lynn, Jack: Park Hill 162
lyres 21

Machiavelli, Niccoló *The Prince* 55–6
machine age 109, 114
MacMillan, Andy 150
Madge, James 149
Madonna 14
Madrid 71
Mahler, Alma 106–7
Mahler, Gustav 106
Main Street USA 163
Maison Carrée 30, 35
Malevich, Kazimir: *Black Square* 109; *White on White* 109
Malkovich, John 80
Manchester, England 88–90, 95–8
Manchester Ship Canal 97
Manchester Town Hall (Waterhouse) 43, 95
Mann, Michael 148
mannerism 60
Mansfield, Jayne 13
manufacturing 87
*Manufacturing a Socialist Modernity: Housing in Czechoslovakia 1945–60* 1
Mappa Mundi 51
maps 29, 51
March, Werner: Olympic Stadium 112
Marcos, Imelda 65
Marin County complex (Wright) 125
Marx, Karl 88, 94–5, 99, 103–4, 109, 143, 165
Marxism 43
Marxist buildings 3
masonic lodge 142
masons 50–1
masques 66
mass media 133
materialism 46, 158
'Mathematics of the Ideal Villa, The' (Rowe) 145
Maudling, Reginald 142
Maxwell, Robert 147
May 1968, riots of 84, 143, 151

Index **181**

Mayan gold 71
McCarthy era 163
McCloud, Kevin 3–4
McCoy, Esther 131
McDonald's 158
McLuhan, Marshall 29
Meades, Jonathan 114, 162
Mecca 157
Medicis 157
medievalism 32
megarons 18
Meier, Richard 147–8
memorials 16
Mendelsohn, Erich 112, 126
Mephistopheles 91
mercantile economy 55, 63
Merry Pranksters 134
Merthyr Rising 46
Metzstein, Isi 150
Meyer, Adolf 107
Meyer, Hannes 107
MH370 159–60
Michelangelo: Campidoglio 116;
    Laurentian Library 60–1; Piazza del
    Campidoglio 60–1; *Pietà* 60; Porta
    Pia 60, 132
Mickey Mouse 163
Mies van der Rohe, Ludwig 59, 91,
    111–13, 124; Bacardi Building 111;
    Farnsworth House 127–8; Illinois
    Institute of Technology 128; New
    National Gallery 111; Seagram
    Building 128
military-industrial complex 134
Millais, John Everett 95
Millions Like Us 140
mills 88–90
mining 92
Minoans 18–19
Minx 35
Miss World 136
Mitchell, Joni 165
Mitterrand, François 84
Modernism 20, 37, 139–43, 149;
    American 121–36; European 103–18,
    127
Modulor 117
Moller House (Loos) 108
monasteries 42, 49
monasticism 31

Mondrian, Piet 139
Monroe, Marilyn 13, 131
Montaigne, Michel de 56, 67, 80
Montesquieu 75
Montgolfier brothers 73
Monticello 77
Monty Python 47; 'Architects Sketch'
    142; 'Nobody Expects the Spanish
    Inquisition' 62
Morris & Co 99
Morris, Janey 99–100
Morris, William 98–100, 104, 143
mosaics 40
Mother Earth 16, 19
Mount Olympus 12
Müller House (Loos) 108
Multhesius, Hermann: *Das Englische
    Haus* 100
multinational corporations 157
music 21
Musil, Robert 109
*My Architect* 131
mythology 20, 42–3, 112

*Name of the Rose, The* (Eco) 49
*Nana* (Zola) 104
Napoleon III 72, 83, 94–5
Napoleonic wars 78, 156
Narkomfin block 109
Nash, John 92
National Geographic Channel 36
National Trust 72
NATO (Coates) 148
nature 4, 12, 19, 62, 121–2
naves 41–2, 49–50
navvies 96
Nazis/Nazism 20, 43–5, 80, 111–13, 136
Neoclassicism 20–1, 35, 68, 82, 96, 104,
    142
Neo-Gothic 95
neoliberalism 163
Nero 33
Neue Staatsgalerie (Stirling) 146
Neutra, Richard 126–7; Lovell Health
    House 127
New Labour 82
New National Gallery (Mies van der
    Rohe) 111
Newton, Isaac 74
New World 71

**182** Index

New York 77
New York Five 147–8
Niedermann, Dione 126–7
Nietzsche, Friedrich 14, 104
'Nobody Expects the Spanish
  Inquisition' (Monty Python) 62
*No Logo* (Klein) 142
nonsensualism 131
Norberg-Schulz, Christian 147
Norman Gothic architecture 51
*North and South* 90
nympheums 61–2

Oak Park (Wright) 124–6
*Oath of the Horatii, The* (David) 32,
  77–8
Obama, Barack 32
*objets types* 116
*Observer* 109
occult 45
October Revolution 78
oculi 30
*Odyssey* (Homer) 11–15
*Oeuvre Complète* (Le Corbusier) 146
oil crisis 134
Old George 98
Oliver, Jamie 82
Olympia 19, 22
Olympic Stadium (March) 112
*120 Days of Sodom* (Sade) 39
Open Air School (Duiker) 110–11
operating tables 16
optical illusions 21, 151
Opus Dei 63
oracles 17
order 36
organic 92–3, 121–2, 126
ormolu 64, 81
Ostrogoths 48
Otis lifts 122
Ozanfant, Amédée 116

packing crates 114
pagans 48
Page, Jimmy 43
Palace of Diocletian 37
palaces 72, 157
Palladianism 77, 124
Palladian motifs 132
Palladian villas 64, 67–8

Palladio, Andrea 66–8, 75, 118, 145; *Four
  Books of Architecture* 64; *Quattro Libri*
  67–8
Paltrow, Gwyneth 13–14
Pan 48
Pan Am Building (Gropius) 127
Pantheon 30–1, 56, 115
Papadakis, Andreas 144, 149–50
papyrus 29–31, 48
Paris 84, 94, 143, 151
Paris Commune 94
Park Hill (Smith and Lynn) 162
parquet flooring 117
Parthenon 10, 21–2, 25, 31, 93, 111
Pasolini, Pier Paolo: *The Hawks and the
  Sparrows* 43
patriotism 29, 44
Pavillon Suisse (Le Corbusier) 116
Paxton, Joseph 101, 159; Crystal Palace
  92–4
Paxton gutter 93
pediments 144
*Penthouse* 35
Pergamon Altar 19–20, 48
pergolas 82
Pericles 15
Perpendicular Gothic architecture 51
Perriand, Charlotte 114
perspective 56, 58
Peter the Great 66
Petit Hameau 75, 82
Petit Trianon 65, 75
Pevsner, Nicolaus 61
phenomenology 149
Phidias 15
Philip II 71
Piano, Renzo 7; Pompidou Centre 84,
  151
Piazza del Campidoglio (Michelangelo)
  60–1
*Pietà* (Michelangelo) 60
*pilotis* 117
pinnacles 50–1
pipes 130
Piranesi, Giovanni Battista: *Campo
  Marzio* 31–2
pirates/piracy 14, 25–6
Pius IV 60
placemaking 164
plans/planning 19, 41, 129, 146, 161–2

Index **183**

plantations 88
Plan Voisin (Le Corbusier) 12, 84
platforms 116
Plato 61; *Republic* 3
*Playboy* magazine 160
Plaza Mayor (Herrera) 71
plinths 17
Pliny's Villa 37
Pliny the Younger 36–7
poches 64
pockets 64
polis 15
Pollio 28
Polytechnic of Central London 149
Pompidou, George 151
Pompidou Centre (Piano) 84, 151
Pop Art 133
population growth 89–90, 161
porn stars 13, 164
Porphyrios, Demetri 149
Porta Pia (Michelangelo) 60, 132
Portland Building (Graves) 144
Portman, John 128–9, 158; Bonaventure 129; Hyatt Regency Houston 129
Port Sunlight 101
Poruba 1–4
post-and-beam structures 16
post-Hellenic culture 19
postindustrial revolution 155
post-Marxist buildings 3
Postmodernism 20, 37, 47, 108–10, 117, 128, 132, 139–52
*Postmodernism: Or, the Cultural Logic of Late Capitalism* ( Jameson) 140
posts 50
Poulson, John 142
Poussin, Nicolas: *Et in Arcadia ego* 35; *Landscape with a Man Killed by a Snake* 68, 98
Prague 80
prefabrication 93, 111, 143, 151, 159
Pre-Raphaelites 43–4, 95, 98–9
Price, Cedric 15
*Prince, The* (Machiavelli) 55–6
printing press 62
privies 46
processions 18
production engineering 87
product tie-ins 146
progress 140

progressives 110, 131–3
Prohibition 128
proletariat 95
proportional relationships 21
Protestant Church 96
Pruitt Igoe housing project 143
public schools 43
public spaces 157
Pugin, Augustus 46
*Punch* 93
punning 6, 16
Purism 116
purlins 50
Puvis de Chavannes, Pierre 105
pyramids 10
Pythagoras 21

Quakers 95
Quality Street chocolates 94
*Quattro Libri* (Palladio) 67–8
Queen's House ( Jones) 67

Ra 10
*Radiant City, The* (Le Corbusier) 58
rafters 50
*Raft of the Medusa, The* (Géricault) 5
railways 96
Rand, Ayn 158; *The Fountainhead* 122, 163
Raphael: *The School of Athens* 61, 108
Rastrelli 76
Rational Functionalists 112
Rationalism 109, 117
Rauch, Erik 133
*Raumplan* 108
ready-made 16
Realist literature 94, 104
reason 31, 74
Reformation 48, 62–3, 71
refurbishments 158
Reich Chancellery (Speer) 112
Rembrandt 74
Renaissance 28, 37, 49, 55–68
*Republic* (Plato) 3
revolutionaries/revolution 34, 74–80, 94–5, 134, 156–7
Rhowbotham, Kevin 150
Richards Memorial Laboratories (Kahn) 130
Richelieu, Cardinal 71

**184** Index

Rights of Man 78, 95, 156
River Café 82
Roberts, Winifred 139
Robie House (Wright) 124
robotics 159
Rockefeller House (Graves) 147
'Rockin' in the Free World' (Young) 87
Rococo 64, 74, 79–80
Rodney Ffing (fictional character) 72
Rogers, Richard 82, 130; Lloyd's
    Building 151
Rolin, Nicolas 45
Roman Empire *see* Ancient Rome
Romanesque 42
'Romans in Films, The' (Barthes) 26
Roman vaulting 6
Roman walls 31
Rome *see* Ancient Rome
*Rome's Greatest Battles* 36
Ronan Point 143
Ronchamp Chapel (Le Corbusier) 6–7
roofs 36, 42, 49–51
Rosenberg, Alfred 112
Rossetti, Gabriel 95, 99
Rossi, Aldo 144–5; Gallaratese apartment
    block 145
Rover cars 146
Rowe, Colin 147–8; *Collage City* 146; 'The
    Mathematics of the Ideal Villa' 145
Royal Societies 75
Rudofsky, Bernard: *Architecture without
    Architects* 135
Rudolph, Paul 133
Ruskin, John 52, 95, 106
Russian Constructivism 109
Russian Revolution 78, 156
Ruston & Hornsby 87
Ryder, Shaun 139
Rykwert, Joseph 149

sacred landscape 6
sacrifices 15–16
Sade, Marquis de: *120 Days of Sodom* 39
Sagebiel, Ernst: Air Ministry 112;
    Tempelhof Airport 112
Saint-Just, Louis 78
Saint-Simon, Henri de 104
Salford 90
Salisbury Cathedral 51
Salk, Jonas 130

Salk Institute (Kahn) 130
Saltaire 101
San Carlo alle Quattro Fontane
    (Borromini) 64
sanctuaries 15
San Gimignano 151
Sanin, Francisco 147
sanitation 94
San Lorenzo (Brunelleschi) 57–8
San Pietro in Montorio (Bramante) 58
Sanssouci 75, 81
Santa Fe 122
Santa Maria della Vittoria 63–4
Santo Spirito (Brunelleschi) 57–8
San Vitale 40
San Zeno Basilica 49
Savannah 13
Savonarola 63
Savoye, Madame 114
Saxon 44
Säynätsalo 114
Scamozzi 66
Scandinavian classicism 20–1
scenography 133–4
Schiele, Egon 126
Schindler, Pauline 127
Schindler, Rudolph 126–7; Lovell Beach
    House 127
Schinkel, Karl Friedrich 90, 134; Casino
    82–3; Cathedral to the Wars of
    Liberation 83; Gardener's House
    81–2; Glienicke 37; Schloss Glienicke
    82–3
Schloss Glienicke (Schinkel) 82–3
scholasticism 147
*School of Athens, The* (Raphael) 61, 108
schools 43
science fiction 160–1
Scott, Walter 43, 99
Scruton, Roger 109–10
Scully, Vincent 19, 131, 147
Seagram Building (Mies van der Rohe)
    128
Sears Roebuck & Co catalogues 134
Sebald, W. G.: *The Emigrants* 98
Secessionist Vienna 106–8, 126
sections 19
Segal, Walter 10
Seifert, Richard 143
Senate 26, 35

Index **185**

Sergeant Wilson (fictional character) 21
servicing 130
*Seven Ages of Woman, The* 45
sewerage systems 28–9, 98
Shaw, Norman 99
Shepheard, Paul: *What Is Architecture?*
    151
Shingle Style 121
shit carts 29
*Shock Doctrine, The* (Klein) 142
*Shock of the New, The* (Hughes) 100
Shonfield, Katherine 149
shrines 26
Shropshire 92
Shulman, Julius 127
Siege of Leningrad 65
signature architects 159
Silenus 110
Silicon Valley 88, 163
Simon Smith and Michael Brooke 150
single-loaded corridors 129
Sisters of Mercy 52
Sistine Chapel 60–1
Sivill House (Lubetkin) 152
Skidmore, Owings and Merrill 127–8
slavery 88–90
Smirke, Robert: British Museum 21–2
Smith, Ivor: Park Hill 162
Smith, Simon 150
Smith, T. Dan 142
Smithson, Alison 118
Smithson, Peter 118
*S/M/L/XL* (Koolhaas) 152
snobbery 97
Snyderman House (Graves) 147
social housing 152
social mobility 29
social provision 94
Social Realism 2
society 140
Society of Arts 93
socks 156, 162
Soleri, Paolo 135
*Some Las Vegas Strip Clubs* (Cook) 165
Soviet Union 1–2, 13, 140, 149, 159
space 29
spaceship earth 135
spaceships 125
'space syntax' 165
special effects 64

Speer, Albert 20, 144; Reich Chancellery
    112; 'Theory of Ruin Value' 32
Spielberg, Steven 164
spinning wheels 90
Spinoza 74
stability 16–17, 36
Stahl House (CSH22; Koenig) 131
stained glass 51
St Albans 1–2
Stalin, Joseph 156–7
Stalinism 78
Stansted Airport (Foster) 151
states 25, 32
statics 30
statuary 33
St Augustine 59
St Denis Cathedral 42
*Steamboat Willie* 163
steam engines 88
steel frames 122
St Francis 42–3
Stirling, James 132, 144–5, 148; *James
    Stirling: Buildings and Projects 1950–74*
    146; Neue Staatsgalerie 146
stirrups 29, 48
St Martin's Press 144
St Nicholas's Church 48–9
stoas 18, 41
stoicism 80
Stokesay Castle 51
Stonehenge 31
stonework 19, 96
storehouses 18
*Story of My Life* (Casanova) 72
Stourhead 35
St Pancras Station 43, 96
St Peter's Basilica 63, 93
St Petersburg 13, 65–6, 75–8
straight roads 29–30, 48
'Street Fighting Man' 136
Street, George 99
Strip, The 164
strippers/strip clubs 34–6, 165
Sturges House (Wright) 125
suburbs 128–9, 133
Suger, Abbé 42
*suitaloons* 134
Sullivan, Louis 121–8; Chicago opera
    house 122; Guaranty Building 122;
    Wainwright Building 122

**186** Index

Summerson, John 139–40
*Sun, The* 143
sundials 30
*Sunset Boulevard* 13
superheroes 12–13
Superman 13
superstition 26
Superstudio 134
supporting walls 50
surrealism 103
Swanson, Gloria 13

taboos 21
Tacitus 20
Taliesen (Wright) 124–6
Taliesin West (Wright) 125–6
Tassel House (Horta) 103–4
Taylor, A. J. P. 155
Taylor, Elizabeth 13, 34
Team Disney headquarters (Graves) 147
Telford 92
Tempelhof Airport (Sagebiel) 112
Temple of Apollo 17
temples 16–19, 22, 42
Temple of Zeus 19, 22
*Ten Books on Architecture* (Alberti) 58
*Ten Books of Architecture* (Vitruvius) 25, 30
terraces 72
terror 14
Terror, The 34
Tessenow, Heinrich 100
Tet Offensive 135
Teutonic myth 112
textile block houses 125
Thames 96
Thatcher, Margaret 43, 140, 162
theatre 19
'Theory of Ruin Value' (Speer) 32
Third Reich 20, 28
Thirty Years War 71
*This Is Civilisation* (Collings) 45
tholos 17
Thomas Cook 101
'thousand bomber' raids 51
*Three Musketeers, The* 72
Tiberius 59
Tiepelo 64,
tiles 50

timber 77
timepieces 30, 56
Tintoretto 67; *Finding of the Body of St Mark* 61
Titans 20
Titian 67
Tomorrowland 163–4
tonal music 21
*Top Gun* 147
tourists/tourism 7, 10, 17, 28
*Towards a New Architecture* (Le Corbusier) 6, 58, 132
tower houses 82
town halls 21
town planning 146
trabeation 16
tract homes 133
tradition 5
tragedy 21
Trajan's Column 34
Treasure Island 164
tribes 14, 20–2, 25–6, 44, 47–8
trigonometry 56
triumphal arches 2, 34
triumvirates 25
Trojan War 14
troping 16
troughs 117
Troy 11–15
*True Lies* 129
*Truman Show, The* 164
trusses 50
Tsarskoe Selo 76
Turin 64
Twitter 13
Tyng, Anne 131

undercrofts 96, 115
*Une Cité Industrielle* (Garnier) 104–5
Ungers, O. M. 144
Unité d'Habitation (Le Corbusier) 115–16, 162
United States 32, 77; *see also* American Modernism
Universal Studios 164
university building 130
University of Pennsylvania 130
*Up Pompeii!* 32
urbanity 36

Index **187**

urban planning 129
*Urban Space* (Krier) 146
use value 109, 158
usury 63
utopian thought 104, 162–3

Vanbrugh, John 132
Vasari 61
Vatican 66
vaulting 6, 50
Velázquez 61
Velde, Henry van de 104
Venturi, Robert 121–2, 147–8;
   *Complexity and Contradiction in
   Architecture* 132–3, 145; 'I am a
   Monument' 133, 145; *Learning from
   Las Vegas* 133–4
Venturi & Rauch: Yale Mathematics
   Building 133
Venturi Scott Brown 144
Vermeer 74
Versailles 65, 71, 75, 156
Vesely, Dalibor 149
Vicenza 64
Victorian architecture 43–4, 95–101
Vietnam War 134, 135
Vignola 61–2; Villa Lante 62, 82
Viking longboats 42
Villa Giulia 37, 61–2
Villa Lante (Vignola) 62, 82
Villa Mairea (Aalto) 113–14
Villa Savoye (Le Corbusier) 113–16
Villa Shodhan (Le Corbusier) 117
virtual world 163
virtue 78–80
Visigoths 48
visual acoustics 6
Vitruvius 56–8, 67; *Ten Books of
   Architecture* 25, 30
Voltaire 74–5, 79
Vuitton, Louis 7

Wagner, Otto 126, 149
Wainwright Building (Sullivan) 122
wall and joist 116
walls 116, 146; city 15; glass 131; Roman
   31; supporting 50
Wapping 96
Ware, Isaac 75

Warhol, Andy 33
Waterhouse, Alfred: Manchester Town
   Hall 43, 95
Waterhouse, John William 52, 95
Waugh, Evelyn 109–10; *Decline and Fall*
   110
wedding cake 2
Weimar Academy of Fine Art 106
Weissenhof Siedlung 132
Wells, Mark 115, 139
Welwyn Garden City 100
Werkbund 104
Westminster, Duke of 67
Westminster Abbey 46, 67
Westwood, Vivienne 156
*What Is Architecture?* (Shepheard)
   151
Wheatley, Dennis 44
White House 121
*White on White* (Malevich) 109
Whitman, Walt 122
Whitsun 44
Wikipedia 1
Wilde, Oscar 162
Williams, Kenneth 15, 26–7
Willis Faber Dumas Building (Foster)
   151
Wilmslow 43
wine cellars 77
Winnie the Pooh 100
Winter Palace 78
Wittgenstein, Ludwig 108
Wittkower, Rudolf 145
Wolfe, Tom: *From Bauhaus to Our House*
   147; *The Electric Kool-Aid Acid Test*
   134; 'Las Vegas (Can't Hear You! Too
   Noisy)' 133
Woodstock 134
*World at War, The* 20
World War I 107–9, 126, 156
World War II 132, 139–40, 156–7
Wotton, Henry 67
Wren, Christopher 74–5, 143
Wright, Frank Lloyd 111, 121, 165;
   Falling Water 124–5; Guggenheim
   Museum 125; Hanna House 125;
   Imperial Hotel Tokyo 125; Johnson
   Wax Building 125; Marin County
   complex 125; Oak Park 124–6;

## 188 Index

Robie House 124; Sturges House 125; Taliesen 124–6; Taliesin West 125

Yale 131–2
Yale Mathematics Building (Venturi & Rauch) 133
Yorke, F.R.S. 139
Yosemite Sam 100

Young, Neil 88; 'Rockin' in the Free World' 87

Zen 21
Zeus 12
Zola, Émile: *Germinal* 104; *Nana* 104
Zumthor, Peter 100, 159